INTERNATIONAL BARTENDER'S GUIDE

S

Edited by
JOSEPH W. SORA

**RANDOM HOUSE
REFERENCE**

International Bartender's Guide

Copyright © 2002, 1997, 1984 by Random House, Inc.

All inquiries should be addressed to Random House Reference, Random House, Inc., New York, NY. Published in the United States by Random House, Inc., New York and simultaneously in Canada by Random House of Canada, Ltd. This is a revised and completely retypeset edition of the *New International Bartender's Guide*, originally published in 1984 by Random House, Inc.

Library of Congress Cataloging-in-Publication Data.
International bartender's guide.—Rev. ed.
   p. cm.
  ISBN 0-375-42575-6 (alk. paper)
  1. Bartending. 2. Cocktails.
  TX951 .I58 2002
  591.5—dc21   2002069741
Typeset and printed in the United States of America.

Cover Design: Mark Weaver
Interior Book Design: Caron Harris

Random House Reference Web site: www.randomwords.com

Revised Edition 10 9 8 7 6 5 4 3 2 1

October 2002

ISBN 0-375-42575-6

New York Toronto London Sydney Auckland

CONTENTS

EQUIPPING THE BAR

BASIC EQUIPMENT

There are numerous items on the market that fall into the category of bar equipment. Some are functional, and some are simply attractive gadgets. Listed below is the *basic* equipment that should be a part of the home bar. Following the list of basic equipment is a list of *desirable* items that would make attractive and often useful additions but are not essential.

- bottle and can opener (including beer-can opener)
- corkscrew
- double-ended measure with half and quarter ounces clearly marked; a jigger (1½–2 oz) on one end, a pony (1 oz) on the other
- measuring cup and set of spoons
- long-handled bar spoon (10 inches); some have a muddler on the end of the handle (see *muddling,* p. xiii)
- juice squeezer
- cutting board and sharp paring knife
- ice bucket and tongs
- 2-piece mixing glass and shaker set; glass and metal
- strainer, preferably coil-rimmed
- bottle sealers and a champagne stopper
- cocktail napkins and coasters
- swizzle sticks, straws (including short straws for sipping frappés), and cocktail picks
- towels
- glassware (see p. ix)
- electric blender (a must for any *frozen* drink)

DESIRABLE EQUIPMENT

- ice crusher (manual or electric)
- wooden muddler
- ice chipper or pick
- twist cutter or vegetable peeler for fruit peels
- funnel
- ice scoop
- grater
- bowls of sugar and salt (for coating rim of glasses)

STOCKING THE BAR

BASIC LIQUORS, WINES, AND LIQUEURS

Below is a list of liquors, mixes, etc., to permit the host to make the drinks that are most often requested (Martini, Manhattan, Bloody Mary, etc.). As tastes are variable, no bartender can anticipate every request, and even the most professional bar may be unable to meet every demand (a specific brand of whiskey or gin, an exotic liqueur, etc.). So be content with the basic provisions, perhaps adding to them from time to time, and meanwhile learning to combine these basics with as much skill, precision, and ingenuity as befits an experienced host.

The number of bottles to be stocked will, of course, depend on the number of guests expected, their anticipated requirements, and the amount of time to be devoted to drinking (a drink or two before dinner, a three-hour cocktail party, etc.). *Bottle Sizes and Contents*, below, will help you estimate your requirements. In general, the well-stocked bar should have at least the following:

- gin (London dry)
- vodka
- Canadian whiskey
- bourbon
- Scotch whiskey
- rum (light)
- vermouth, dry and sweet
- tequila
- white wine (dry)
- red wine (dry)
- beer
- cognac or other brandy

LIQUEURS

- Dubonnet
- Lillet
- amaretto
- Chambord
- Triple Sec
- Grand Marnier
- Kahlúa
- Sambuca

BOTTLE SIZES AND CONTENTS

	U.S. Measures	Metric Measure	Yield*
split (champagne)	6.3 oz	187 milliliters	2 glasses
fifth	25.3 oz	750 milliliters	13–17 drinks
wine bottle	25.3 oz	750 milliliters	6 glasses
champagne bottle	25.3 oz	750 milliliters	6–12 glasses
quart	32 oz	0.9464 liter	16–21 drinks
liter	33.8 oz	1000 milliliters	17–22 drinks
magnum (wine)	50.7 oz	1.5 liters	12 glasses

| half gallon | 64 oz | 1.75 liters | 32–42 drinks |
| gallon (liquor or wine) | 128 oz | 3.5 liters | 64–85 drinks or 32 glasses |

*Based on a jigger of 1½–2 oz and a wine glass filled approximately half full (4 oz)

BASIC MIXERS, FLAVORINGS, GARNISHES, ETC.

- club soda
- tonic water
- ginger ale
- 7-Up
- cola
- sours mix
- heavy cream
- maraschino liqueur
- Tabasco sauce
- salt and pepper
- tomato juice
- orange juice
- pineapple juice
- cranberry juice
- grapefruit juice
- milk
- bitters (Angostura)
- grenadine
- Worcestershire sauce
- sugar

SYRUPS

- cassis (kä sēs′)—a black-currant-flavored nonalcoholic syrup
- fraise (frez)—a nonalcoholic strawberry syrup
- framboise (främ bwäz′), a nonalcoholic raspberry syrup
- orgeat (or zhä′), an almond-flavored, nonalcoholic syrup
- grenadine—a sweet, nonalcoholic red syrup flavored with pomegranate juice

GARNISHES

These are used to enhance both the flavor and appearance of a drink. Among the most popular are cocktail onions, olives, maraschino cherries, and fresh fruits. When garnishing with a slice of fresh fruit (lemon, lime, orange) cut a ¼- to ½-inch wedge or slice. In order to fix the slice to the rim of the glass, make a slit toward the center so the slice can straddle the rim. Garnishes of onions or cherries can be dropped into the drink or skewered on a cocktail pick that also serves as a swizzle stick.

- maraschino cherries
- cocktail onions
- green olives (small)
- lemons, limes, and oranges

GLASSWARE

No host could be expected to have the precisely correct glass for serving every drink. To do so would require that one own several hundred items of glassware. These glasses are the absolute musts for the average home bar:

- old-fashioned (4–5 oz)
- highball (up to 13 oz)
- wineglasses (especially for red wine)

The most common types of glasses are the following:

- all-purpose wine (8–10 oz)
- cocktail or martini (3–4 oz)
- collins (8–13 oz)
- balloon wine, red wine, white wine, German wine

- champagne: flute or tulip; the saucer and hollow-stem glasses should be avoided
- brandy snifter (6 oz)
- cordial (1 oz)
- sherry (2½ oz)
- shot, or jigger (1½–2 oz)

With a half dozen or so of each of these, a host can easily serve almost any kind of drink. If one is likely to serve punches, a punch bowl with at least a 4-qt capacity and 10 to 12 handled cups is necessary. The other glasses described above are often desirable, however, and should be added when feasible. An adequate supply of the proper glassware is as much a complement to the bartender's art as a well-stocked bar.

MEASUREMENTS AND MEASURING

When making a drink for the first time it is best to be precise when measuring out the ingredients called for in a recipe. Freehand pouring can quickly ruin a drink by making it too weak, too strong, or unbalanced with the dominating flavor of a particular ingredient. Be creative on your own if you wish, but try to refrain from experimenting on your guests. These are the standard measurements used in the recipes:

- drop
- dash—2 or 3 drops
- teaspoon—⅙ oz
- tablespoon—½ oz (3 teaspoons)
- ounce—2 tablespoons
- pony—1 oz (2 tablespoons)
- jigger—1½–2 oz (3–4 tablespoons)
- cup—8 oz

- pound—16 oz (2 cups)
- pint—16 oz (2 cups)
- quart—32 oz (4 cups)
- gallon—128 oz (4 quarts)

TIPS AND TECHNIQUES

CHILLING AND FROSTING GLASSWARE

Glasses can be chilled by storing them in the refrigerator for an hour or in a freezer for 5–10 minutes. If there is not adequate space in the refrigerator or freezer, glasses should be chilled by filling them with ice *and water* and letting them sit while you are mixing the drinks. Some drink recipes call for a *frosted* glass instead of a chilled one, particularly for a mint julep or planter's punch. Glasses are frosted by dipping them in water and placing them in the freezer for half an hour. Mugs with handles are convenient to hold and are attractive for serving such tall cold drinks as Pimm's cup and moscow mule. Silver or other metal mugs will frost better than glass ones.

COATING THE RIM OF A GLASS

To sugar-rim a glass, simply rub the rim of a chilled glass with a piece of citrus fruit (or dip the rim into citrus juice), then dip the glass into a bowl of superfine sugar. Gently shake off any excess. Some recipes call for dipping the rim of the glass into a liqueur before dipping it into sugar. Some glasses, as for a margarita cocktail, are dipped (lightly) into salt instead of sugar.

MIXING

When filling a cocktail shaker, always put the ice in first and the liquor last. There are no hard and fast rules about the order of ingredients added between the ice and the liquor (fruit juices, bitters, etc.). By putting the ice in the shaker or mixing container first, all the ingredients to follow will be chilled as they pass over the ice. The liquor is added last so that there will be less dilution.

STIRRING VS SHAKING

A cocktail that is stirred rather than shaken will retain its clarity, and recipes using clear liquors (martinis, manhattans, etc.) are usually mixed in this manner, regardless of what James Bond would have you believe. A stirred drink will also remain free of ice chips. A cocktail must be stirred enough to mix the ingredients but not so much that the ice begins to dilute the liquor; 12 to 15 stirs are usually sufficient for proper mixing. If a carbonated beverage is used in a recipe, stir *gently and briefly* to retain the sparkle. Recipes using fruit juices, eggs, cream, or other hard-to-mix ingredients should be shaken *vigorously* to ensure that they are mixed thoroughly. For extra frothiness, use a blender.

FLOATING

Floating a liqueur on top of a drink is most easily done by allowing the liqueur to trickle slowly over the back of a demitasse spoon held over or placed in the glass. The purpose of floating is to keep each ingredient—liqueur, cream, brandy, etc.—in its own separate layer, so that it does not mix with the other ingredients. The pousse-café is a good example of a drink in which several ingredients are floating.

MUDDLING

Muddling is the mixing (or crushing) of ingredients, such as the sugar cube, bitters, and water in an old-fashioned, or the mint leaves, sugar, and water in a mint julep. The muddling can be done with a special *muddler* or with the back of a long-handled bar spoon.

POURING

Regardless of the shape of glass used, *never fill a glass to the brim.* A fairly full champagne glass is fine, but when serving wine, never fill the glass more than half full, to allow the bouquet to collect in the top of the glass. When making an "on the rocks" drink, always pour the liquor into the glass *over* the ice. When pouring beer, pour it first down the side of the glass (to avoid an excess of foam) and then into the middle to aerate the beer and release the flavor.

FRUIT JUICES

Fresh citrus juice may of course be used whenever "fruit juice" is called for in a recipe. However, some connoisseurs insist that liquor tends to overpower fresh orange juice, for example, and prefer the frozen concentrated variety. Your own taste reactions will have to decide the issue. When using fresh fruit, soak the fruit in hot water or roll it on a cutting board before squeezing to allow the juice to flow more freely. Rose's lime juice is sweetened; you can't use fresh lime juice to replace it unless you add sugar.

FRUIT PEELS

When a recipe calls for a twist of peel from a fruit, use only the colored peel of the fruit, not the white pith, which is bitter. There are special *twist cutters* on the market, but a sharp paring knife or a vegetable peeler will also do the job. Cut a section of peel about 1 inch by ½ inch, twist the peel over the drink to release a drop or so of the oil, then drop the peel into the drink. If desired, rub the rim of the glass with the peel before twisting.

CREAM

Heavy cream should be used in all recipes calling for "cream" unless otherwise specified. In recipes calling for lemon juice and cream, mix the drink as close to serving time as possible. Cream tends to thicken when mixed with lemon juice, especially if it is allowed to stand for more than a few minutes. Always be certain that the cream to be used is absolutely fresh.

SUGAR SYRUP

Sugar syrup, also called gomme syrup, can be substituted for loose sugar in a drink recipe. In fact, some recipes call specifically for sugar syrup because it does not take excessive stirring or shaking to dissolve. To make the syrup, add 1 cup sugar to 1 cup boiling water and let it simmer for two or three minutes until all the sugar is dissolved and the mixture is clear. Bottle the mixture after it has cooled and store it in a cool place.

ABBREVIATIONS

tsp	teaspoon
tbsp	tablespoon
oz	ounce
pt	pint
qt	quart
lb	pound
gal	gallon

METRIC EQUIVALENTS

1 tsp	(⅙ oz)	0.4929 centiliter
1 tbsp	(½ oz)	1.4786 centiliters
1 oz		2.9573 centiliters
1 jigger	(1½ oz)	4.4360 centiliters
1 cup	(8 oz)	23.6584 centiliters
1 pt	(16 oz)	0.4732 liter
1 qt	(32 oz)	0.9464 liter
1 gal	(128 oz)	3.7854 liters

CLASSIC COCKTAILS

Unless otherwise specified, all recipes given are for one drink.

A

Abbey Cocktail

1½ oz (3 tbsp) gin
1 oz (2 tbsp) orange juice
1 dash orange bitters
maraschino cherry

Shake liquid ingredients with ice and strain into a chilled cocktail glass. Garnish with the cherry.

Absinthe Cocktail

1¾ oz (3½ tbsp) Pernod or other
absinthe substitute
1 oz (2 tbsp) water
1 tsp anisette
1–2 dashes orange bitters

Shake ingredients with ice and strain into a chilled cocktail glass.

Absinthe Suissesse

A more elegant Absinthe Cocktail, named in honor of a "Swiss girl."

1½ oz (3 tbsp) Pernod or other
absinthe substitute

1 dash anisette
½ oz (1 tbsp) white crème de menthe

Shake ingredients vigorously with ice and strain into a chilled cocktail glass.

———— Acapulco ————

(serves 2)

2 oz (4 tbsp) light rum
1 oz (2 tbsp) Cointreau or Triple Sec
1 oz (2 tbsp) lime juice
2 tsp sugar
fresh mint leaves

Shake first 4 ingredients with ice and strain into chilled cocktail glasses over ice cubes. Garnish with mint.

Variations: can be served in highball glasses and topped off with chilled club soda. Pineapple or grapefruit juice can be substituted for the lime. Garnish with fresh pineapple.

Tequila Acapulco: Substitute tequila for Cointreau.

———— Adonis Cocktail ————

2 oz (4 tbsp) dry sherry
1 oz (2 tbsp) sweet vermouth
2 dashes Angostura bitters

Stir ingredients with ice and strain into a chilled cocktail glass.

Variation: Substitute orange bitters for Angostura and garnish with an orange peel.

———— Affinity Cocktail ————

1 oz (2 tbsp) Scotch
1 oz (2 tbsp) dry vermouth
1 oz (2 tbsp) sweet vermouth
2 dashes Angostura bitters
twist of lemon peel
maraschino cherry (optional)

Stir liquid ingredients with ice and strain into a chilled cocktail glass. Garnish with the lemon peel and cherry.

Variation: Substitute orange bitters for Angostura.

———— Afterglow ————

1½ oz (3 tbsp) blended whiskey
1 oz (2 tbsp) Southern Comfort
½ oz (1 tbsp) banana liqueur
1 tsp grenadine
1 tsp lemon juice
1–2 dashes orange bitters
pineapple stick (optional)

Place first 6 ingredients in shaker with 5 or 6 ice cubes, cover, and shake vigorously several times. Strain into large old-fashioned glass half-filled with cracked ice. Garnish with pineapple stick, if desired.

———— Alabama Fizz ————

1½ oz (3 tbsp) gin
juice of ½ lemon
1 tsp sugar
chilled club soda
sprig of fresh mint

(continued)

Shake first 3 ingredients with ice and strain into a chilled collins glass over ice cubes. Top with soda and garnish with mint.

——— Alabama Slammer ———

1½ oz (3 tbsp) amaretto
1 oz (2 tbsp) Southern Comfort
1 oz (2 tbsp) sloe gin
½ oz (1 tbsp) lemon juice

Place all ingredients in shaker with ice and shake vigorously to combine. Strain into an ice-filled old-fashioned glass or into several shot glasses and serve.

——— Alaska Cocktail ———

2 oz (4 tbsp) gin
½ oz (1 tbsp) yellow Chartreuse
2 dashes orange bitters

Stir ingredients with ice and strain into a chilled cocktail glass.

Variation: Add ½ oz (1 tbsp) dry sherry. Substitute a twist of lemon peel for the bitters.

——— Alexander Cocktail ———

1 oz (2 tbsp) gin
1 oz (2 tbsp) white crème de cacao
1 oz (2 tbsp) cream
nutmeg

Shake liquid ingredients vigorously with ice and strain into a chilled cocktail glass. Sprinkle with nutmeg.

Variations: Substitute vodka for gin. Substitute coffee liqueur or prunelle for crème de cacao. If using prunelle, sprinkle with cinnamon instead of nutmeg.

Alexander's Sister Cocktail: Substitute crème de menthe for crème de cacao.

Brandy Alexander: Substitute 2 oz (4 tbsp) brandy for the gin.

——— **Alfonso Cocktail** ———

1 oz (2 tbsp) Dubonnet
1 lump sugar
2 dashes Angostura bitters
chilled champagne
twist of lemon peel

Put sugar lump into a chilled highball or wine glass and shake bitters over it. Add ice and Dubonnet. Stir and top off with champagne. Garnish with lemon twist.

——— **Alfonso Special** ———

1½ oz (3 tbsp) Grand Marnier
¾ oz gin
¾ oz dry vermouth
4 dashes sweet vermouth
1 dash Angostura bitters

Stir or shake ingredients with ice and strain into a chilled cocktail glass.

Variation: Use equal parts (1 oz [2 tbsp] each) of Grand Marnier, gin, and dry vermouth

Algonquin

This drink originated at the famous Algonquin Hotel in New York City.

2 oz (4 tbsp) rye whiskey
1 oz (2 tbsp) dry vermouth
1 oz (2 tbsp) pineapple juice

Shake ingredients with ice and strain into a chilled cocktail glass or into an old-fashioned glass over ice cubes.

All-American Fizz

1 1/4 oz (2 1/2 tbsp) gin
1 oz (2 tbsp) brandy
juice of 1/2 lemon
2 dashes grenadine
chilled club soda

Shake gin, brandy, lemon, and grenadine with ice and strain into a chilled collins or highball glass over ice cubes. Fill with soda and stir.

Allegheny

1 oz (2 tbsp) bourbon
1 oz (2 tbsp) dry vermouth
1/4 oz (1/2 tbsp) blackberry brandy
1/4 oz (1/2 tbsp) lemon juice
1 dash Angostura bitters
twist of lemon peel

Shake liquid ingredients with ice and strain into a chilled cocktail glass. Garnish with lemon twist.

Allen Cocktail

1½ oz (3 tbsp) gin
½ oz (1 tbsp) maraschino liqueur
1½ tsp lemon juice

Stir or shake ingredients with ice and strain into a chilled cocktail glass.

Variation: For a sweeter drink, increase maraschino to ¾ oz (1½ tbsp).

Allies Cocktail

1 oz (2 tbsp) gin
1 oz (2 tbsp) dry vermouth
2 dashes kümmel

Stir ingredients with ice and strain into a chilled cocktail glass.

All-White Frappé

¾ oz (1½ tbsp) white crème de menthe
¾ oz (1½ tbsp) anisette
¾ oz (1½ tbsp) peppermint schnapps
¾ oz (1½ tbsp) lemon juice

Shake ingredients with ice. Strain into a large chilled cocktail glass over crushed ice.

Variation: Substitute white crème de cacao for the peppermint schnapps.

Amaretto Cream

1½ oz (3 tbsp) amaretto
1½ oz (3 tbsp) cream

(continued)

Shake ingredients with ice and strain into a chilled cocktail glass.

Amaretto Sour

1½ oz (3 tbsp) amaretto
½ oz (2 tbsp) lemon juice
maraschino cherry

Shake amaretto and lemon juice with ice and pour into a chilled old-fashioned glass. Garnish with a cherry.

Variation: Substitute sours mix for lemon juice.

Ambrosia Cocktail

Said to have originated in New Orleans, quite possibly at Arnaud's restaurant, about the time Prohibition ended.

juice of 1 lemon
1 oz (2 tbsp) applejack
1 oz (2 tbsp) brandy
½ oz (1 tbsp) Cointreau
cold champagne

Shake together the lemon juice, applejack, brandy, and Cointreau. Pour into a chilled hollow-stemmed champagne glass and top with champagne.

Americana

1 oz (2 tbsp) bourbon
½ tsp sugar
1 dash Angostura bitters
chilled champagne
slice of fresh peach

Stir bourbon, sugar, and bitters in a chilled champagne glass. Fill with champagne and garnish with peach.

——————— **American Beauty Cocktail** ———————

1 oz (2 tbsp) brandy
1 oz (2 tbsp) dry vermouth
1 oz (2 tbsp) orange juice
1 dash grenadine
1 dash white crème de menthe
½ oz (1 tbsp) port

Shake all ingredients, except the port, with ice. Strain into a large chilled cocktail glass or old-fashioned glass. Float the port on top.

——————— **Americano** ———————

2 oz (4 tbsp) sweet vermouth
2 oz (4 tbsp) Campari
chilled club soda
twist of lemon or orange peel

Pour vermouth and Campari over ice cubes in a high-ball or large wine glass. Fill with soda and garnish with fruit peel.

——————— **Amer Picon Cocktail** ———————

1 oz (2 tbsp) Amer Picon
1 oz (2 tbsp) sweet vermouth

Shake ingredients with ice and strain into a chilled cocktail glass.

Variation: Increase Amer Picon to 1½ oz (3 tbsp) and substitute juice of 1 lime and 1 tsp grenadine for the vermouth.

——— **Andalusia** ———

1½ oz (3 tbsp) dry sherry
½ oz (1 tbsp) brandy or cognac
½ oz (1 tbsp) light rum
1 dash Angostura bitters (optional)

Stir ingredients with ice and strain into a chilled cocktail glass.

——— **Angel Face** ———

1 oz (2 tbsp) gin
1 oz (2 tbsp) apricot brandy
1 oz (2 tbsp) apple brandy or calvados

Shake ingredients with ice and strain into a chilled cocktail glass.

——— **Angel's Delight** ———

½ oz (1 tbsp) grenadine
½ oz (1 tbsp) Triple Sec
½ oz (1 tbsp) sloe gin
½ oz (1 tbsp) cream

Pour ingredients, in order given, into a pousse-café glass, being careful that the ingredients remain in layers and do not mix.

——— **Angel's Dream** ———

1½ oz (3 tbsp) dark crème de cacao
½ tsp cream

Pour crème de cacao into a 2-oz liqueur glass. Float cream on top.

Angel's Kiss

½ oz (1 tbsp) white or dark crème de cacao
½ oz (1 tbsp) sloe gin
½ oz (1 tbsp) brandy
½ oz (1 tbsp) cream

Pour ingredients, in order given, into a pousse-café glass, being careful that the ingredients remain in layers and do not mix.

Angel's Tip

1 oz (2 tbsp) white crème de cacao
⅓ oz (2 tsp) cream
maraschino cherry (optional)

Pour crème de cacao into a cordial glass. Slowly float cream on top so the two will be in layers and not mix. Insert a toothpick into the cherry and place on top.

Angel's Wing

⅓ oz (2 tsp) white crème de cacao
⅓ oz (2 tsp) brandy
⅓ oz (2 tsp) cream

Pour ingredients, in order given, into a pousse-café glass, being careful that the ingredients remain in layers and do not mix.

Apple Fizz

2 oz (4 tbsp) apple brandy
1 tsp lemon juice
1 tsp sugar
chilled club soda

(continued)

Shake ingredients with ice and strain into a chilled highball glass over several ice cubes. Top with soda.

———— Apple Brandy Cocktail ————

1½ oz (3 tbsp) apple brandy
1 tsp lemon juice
1 tsp grenadine

Shake ingredients with ice and strain into a chilled cocktail glass.

Variation: Omit lemon juice and grenadine and add ¾ oz (1½ tbsp) brandy, ¾ oz (1½ tbsp) gin, and 1½ oz (3 tbsp) sweet cider. Stir with ice and strain into a large chilled cocktail or wine glass.

———— Applejack Collins ————

See *Tom Collins.*

———— Applejack Cooler ————

1½ oz (3 tbsp) applejack
juice of ½ lemon
1 tsp sugar
chilled club soda

Shake ingredients, except soda, with ice and strain into a chilled collins or highball glass over ice cubes. Top with soda and stir gently.

Variation: Add ½ tsp brandy.

——— **Applejack Punch** ———

(serves 10–12)

2 qts apple brandy
6 oz grenadine
1 pt lemon juice
1 pt orange juice
2 qts chilled ginger ale
1 apple, sliced

Stir all ingredients, except ginger ale, in a punch bowl with a large block of ice. Add ginger ale just before serving.

——— **Applejack Rabbit** ———

1½ oz (3 tbsp) apple brandy
½ oz (1 tbsp) lemon juice
½ oz (1 tbsp) orange (or lime) juice
½ tsp maple syrup

Shake ingredients vigorously with ice. Strain into a chilled cocktail glass or into an old-fashioned glass over ice cubes.

Variation: Sugar-rim the glass by dipping into maple syrup and then into sugar.

——— **Applejack Sour** ———

See *Whiskey Sour.*

——— **Apple Martini** ———

See *Martini.*

─────── **Apple Pie Cocktail** ───────

1 oz (2 tbsp) light rum
1 oz (2 tbsp) sweet vermouth
1 tsp apple brandy
½ tsp grenadine
1 tsp lemon juice

Shake ingredients with ice and strain into a chilled cocktail glass.

─────── **Apricot Anise Collins** ───────

1½ oz (3 tbsp) gin
½ oz (1 tbsp) apricot brandy
½ oz (1 tbsp) anisette
½ oz (1 tbsp) lemon juice
chilled club soda
slice of apricot or lemon

Shake gin, brandy, anisette, and lemon juice with ice. Strain into a chilled collins glass over ice cubes. Top with soda and garnish with apricot or lemon.

─────── **Apricot Cocktail** ───────

1½ oz (3 tbsp) apricot brandy
1 tsp gin
⅔ oz (1¼ tbsp) orange juice
⅔ oz (1¼ tbsp) lemon juice

Shake ingredients with ice and strain into a chilled cocktail glass.

─────── **Apricot Cooler** ───────

2 oz (4 tbsp) apricot brandy
½ tsp sugar

juice of ½ lemon
juice of ½ lime
1 dash grenadine (optional)
chilled club soda
twist of lemon peel

Shake liquid ingredients, except soda, with ice. Strain into a chilled highball glass over ice cubes. Top with soda and garnish with lemon peel.

Apricot Fizz

2 oz (4 tbsp) apricot brandy
juice of ¾ lime
½ tsp sugar
chilled club soda

Shake brandy, lime juice, and sugar with ice and strain into a chilled collins or highball glass. Fill with soda and stir gently.

Apricot Lady

(serves 2)

2 oz (4 tbsp) light rum
2 oz (4 tbsp) apricot brandy
½ oz (1 tbsp) Cointreau or Triple Sec
1 oz (2 tbsp) lime juice
2 slices of orange

Shake liquid ingredients vigorously with ice. Strain into chilled old-fashioned glasses over ice cubes and garnish with orange slices.

——— Apricot Sour ———

1 oz (2 tbsp) lemon juice
1 tsp sugar syrup
2 oz (4 tbsp) apricot brandy
orange slice and maraschino cherry

Pour juice and syrup into shaker and stir to combine thoroughly. Add brandy and 5 or 6 ice cubes. Cover and shake vigorously several times. Strain into a chilled sour or cocktail glass and garnish.

——— Aqueduct ———

1½ oz (3 tbsp) vodka
¼ oz (½ tbsp) curaçao
¼ oz (½ tbsp) apricot brandy
½ oz (1 tbsp) lime juice
twist of orange peel

Shake liquid ingredients with ice and strain into a chilled cocktail glass. Garnish with orange peel.

——— Archbishop ———

2 oz (4 tbsp) gin
1 oz (2 tbsp) ginger wine
½ oz (1 tbsp) B & B
thin slice lime

Fill an old-fashioned glass halfway with cracked ice. Add liquors and stir gently to combine. Float lime slice on top.

———— **Artillery Punch** ————

(serves 12–16)

1 qt bourbon
8 oz Jamaican rum
6 oz apricot brandy
1 qt strong black tea
1 qt orange juice
8 oz lemon juice
¼ cup sugar

Blend ingredients and refrigerate for an hour. Pour into a punch bowl over a block of ice.

B

———— **B & B** ————

This liqueur is commercially available as a ready-mix. For those who prefer to mix their own, the proportions are equal.

1 oz (2 tbsp) Benedictine
1 oz (2 tbsp) brandy or cognac

Mix and serve in a cordial glass with or without crushed ice.

Variation: Pour slowly into the glass so the drink will be in layers.

———— **Babbie's Special Cocktail** ————

2 oz (4 tbsp) apricot brandy
1 oz (2 tbsp) cream
½ tsp gin

(continued)

Shake ingredients with ice and strain into a chilled cocktail glass.

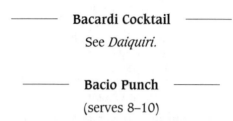

Bacardi Cocktail

See *Daiquiri.*

Bacio Punch

(serves 8–10)

"Bacio" (pronounced bah´ cho) is the Italian word for "kiss." Many think the drink is aptly named.

8 oz gin
3 oz (6 tbsp) anisette
8 oz grapefruit juice
slices of oranges and lemons
1 qt chilled club soda
1 split chilled champagne

Pour gin, anisette, and grapefruit juice over a block of ice in a punch bowl and add fruit slices. Before serving add soda and champagne. Serve in chilled punch cups.

Back Bay

2 oz (4 tbsp) Jamaican rum
1 oz (2 tbsp) brandy
½ oz (1 tbsp) peach brandy
1 tsp lime juice

Shake all ingredients with ice and strain into old-fashioned glass half-filled with cracked ice.

─────── **Ballerina I** ───────

2 oz (4 tbsp) white rum
½ oz (1 tbsp) chocolate-orange liqueur
½ oz (1 tbsp) curaçao
2 tsp champagne cognac

Place ingredients in shaker with ½ cup cracked ice. Cover and shake vigorously several times. Strain into a chilled wineglass.

─────── **Ballerina II** ───────

4 oz (8 tbsp) dry white wine chilled
½ oz (1 tbsp) amaretto
orange zest

Pour wine into a chilled wineglass. Add amaretto and stir gently. Twist zest over glass to release oils and drop it in.

─────── **Baltimore Eggnog** ───────

See *Eggnog I.*

─────── **Bamboo Cocktail** ───────

1 oz (2 tbsp) dry sherry
1 oz (2 tbsp) dry vermouth
1 dash orange bitters
twist of lemon peel (optional)

Shake liquid ingredients with ice and strain into a chilled cocktail glass. Garnish with lemon peel.

Variation: Substitute Angostura bitters for orange bitters.

——— Banana Bliss ———

1 oz (2 tbsp) light rum
1 oz (2 tbsp) banana liqueur
1/2 oz (1 tbsp) orange juice
1 dash Angostura bitters
1 oz (2 tbsp) cream
dash of grenadine
banana slices

Shake all ingredients, except grenadine and banana slices, vigorously with ice. Strain into a chilled old-fashioned glass. Garnish with a few drops of grenadine and the banana.

Variation: A simplified version is to mix 1 oz (2 tbsp) rum (or brandy) with 1 oz (2 tbsp) banana liqueur and serve in a cordial glass.

——— Banana Colada ———

See *Piña Colada.*

——— Banana Daiquiri ———

See *Daiquiri.*

——— Banana Rum Cream ———

2 oz (4 tbsp) golden rum
1/2 oz (1 tbsp) banana liqueur
1 oz (2 tbsp) light cream

Place ingredients in shaker with 4 or 5 ice cubes. Cover and shake briskly several times. Strain into a chilled wineglass.

--------- ### Banana Rum Frappé ---------

1 oz (2 tbsp) white rum
1/2 oz (1 tbsp) banana liqueur
1 oz (2 tbsp) orange juice

Combine all ingredients in blender with 4 or 5 ice cubes. Cover and blend at high speed until ice cubes are just frappéed. Pour into a chilled wineglass.

--------- ### Barbados Rum Swizzle ---------

2 oz (4 tbsp) Barbados rum
juice and rind of 1/2 lime
1–2 dashes Angostura bitters
1/2 tsp sugar

Squeeze lime into a chilled collins or highball glass and drop in the rind. Fill the glass nearly full with shaved ice and add bitters, rum, and sugar. Stir and serve with a swizzle stick.

--------- ### Barbary Coast Cocktail ---------

3/4 oz (1 1/2 tbsp) gin
3/4 oz (1 1/2 tbsp) Scotch
3/4 oz (1 1/2 tbsp) crème de cacao
3/4 oz (1 1/2 tbsp) cream

Shake ingredients vigorously with ice and strain into a chilled cocktail glass.

Variation: Add 3/4 oz (1 1/2 tbsp) light rum.

--------- ### Barton Special ---------

1 oz (2 tbsp) apple brandy
1/2 oz (1 tbsp) Scotch

(continued)

½ oz (1 tbsp) gin
twist of lemon peel

Shake liquid ingredients with ice and strain into a chilled cocktail glass or into an old-fashioned glass over ice cubes. Garnish with lemon peel.

——— Baybreeze ———

2 oz (4 tbsp) vodka
2 oz (4 tbsp) orange juice
2 oz (4 tbsp) pineapple juice
orange slice

Shake all liquid ingredients with ice. Pour into a chilled highball glass. Garnish with orange slice.

——— Beachcomber ———

1½ oz (3 tbsp) light rum
½ oz (1 tbsp) Cointreau or Triple Sec
½ oz (1 tbsp) lime juice
1 dash of maraschino liqueur

Sugar-rim a chilled cocktail glass by rubbing with lime and dipping into sugar. Shake ingredients with ice and strain into the glass.

——— Beef-A-Mato Cocktail ———

4 oz (8 tbsp) tomato juice
2 oz (4 tbsp) full-strength beef bouillon
1–2 dashes Worcestershire sauce
1½ oz (3 tbsp) vodka
lemon zest

Place 3 or 4 ice cubes in highball glass and add liquid ingredients. Stir gently to combine. Twist zest over glass and add to drink.

─────── **Beer Buster** ───────

1½ oz (3 tbsp) chilled vodka
chilled beer or ale
2 dashes Tabasco sauce

Put vodka and Tabasco into a chilled highball glass or beer mug, fill with beer, and stir lightly.

─────── **Bee's Knees** ───────

2 oz (4 tbsp) white rum
½ oz (1 tbsp) Cointreau or Triple Sec
2 tsp fresh lemon juice
1 tsp sugar
orange slice (optional)

Shake first 4 ingredients with ice cubes and strain into an old-fashioned glass filled with cracked ice. Garnish, if desired, with half orange slice on rim.

─────── **Bel Air Cocktail** ───────

2 oz (4 tbsp) gin
1 oz (2 tbsp) apricot brandy
1 tsp grenadine
1 egg white

Shake together vigorously with ice cubes and strain into a chilled wineglass.

——— Bellini ———

2 oz (4 tbsp) peach juice
4 oz (8 tbsp) chilled champagne
1 dash grenadine (optional)
slice of fresh peach

Pour peach juice over crushed ice in a large wine-glass. Top with champagne, add grenadine, and garnish with peach slice.

——— Bellini Punch ———

(serves 16–18)

2 ripe peaches, seeded and peeled
½ oz (1 tbsp) fresh lemon juice
⅓ cup sugar
3 (or more) bottles of champagne
block of ice

In blender purée peaches, lemon juice, and sugar. Cover and refrigerate overnight if possible (do not freeze). When ready to serve, put block of ice in large punch bowl and spread purée on bottom of bowl around block. Pour 3 or 4 bottles of champagne over ice and ladle into punch cups.

——— Belmont Cocktail ———

2 oz (4 tbsp) gin
1 tsp grenadine
¾ oz (1½ tbsp) cream

Shake ingredients vigorously with ice and strain into a chilled cocktail glass.

Variation: Substitute raspberry syrup for grenadine.

—————— **Belvedere Cocktail** ——————

A belvedere is a summerhouse, a quiet retreat. And here's the perfect refreshment.

1½ oz (3 tbsp) gin
½ oz (1 tbsp) Galliano
½ oz (1 tbsp) banana liqueur
½ oz (1 tbsp) grapefruit juice

Place all ingredients in shaker with cracked ice. Cover and shake vigorously several times. Strain into a chilled cocktail glass.

—————— **Bennett Cocktail** ——————

1½ oz (3 tbsp) gin
½ oz (1 tbsp) lime juice
½ tsp sugar
2 dashes Angostura bitters

Shake ingredients with ice and strain into a chilled cocktail glass.

Variation: Substitute orange bitters for Angostura. Increase sugar to 1 tsp.

—————— **Bentley** ——————

1½ oz (3 tbsp) apple brandy or calvados
1½ oz (3 tbsp) Dubonnet
twist of lemon peel

Stir liquid ingredients with ice and strain into a chilled cocktail glass. Garnish with lemon peel.

———— Bermuda Highball ————

¾ oz (1½ tbsp) gin
¾ oz (1½ tbsp) dry vermouth
¾ oz (1½ tbsp) brandy
chilled ginger ale or club soda
twist of lemon peel

Pour gin, vermouth, and brandy into a chilled high-ball glass over ice cubes. Top with ginger ale or soda and garnish with lemon peel.

———— Bermuda Rose Cocktail ————

1¼ oz (2½ tbsp) gin
1½ tsp apricot brandy
1½ tsp lime juice
1 dash grenadine

Shake ingredients with ice and strain into a chilled cocktail glass.

Variation: Substitute lemon juice for lime.

———— Berritini ————

See *Martini.*

———— Betsy Ross Cocktail ————

1½ oz (3 tbsp) brandy
1½ oz (3 tbsp) port
1 dash Cointreau or Triple Sec
1 dash Angostura bitters (optional)

Stir ingredients with ice and strain into a chilled cock-tail glass.

——— **Between-the-Sheets Cocktail** ———

1 oz (2 tbsp) brandy
1 oz (2 tbsp) light rum
1 oz (2 tbsp) Cointreau or Triple Sec
1 oz (2 tbsp) lemon juice
twist of lemon peel

Shake liquid ingredients with ice and strain into a large chilled cocktail glass. Garnish with lemon peel.

Variation: Substitute lime juice for lemon and garnish with a twist of lime peel.

——— **Bijou Cocktail** ———

1 oz (2 tbsp) gin
1 oz (2 tbsp) green Chartreuse
1 oz (2 tbsp) sweet vermouth
1 dash orange bitters
maraschino cherry (optional)
twist of lemon peel (optional)

Stir liquid ingredients with ice and strain into a chilled cocktail glass. Garnish with cherry or lemon.

——— **Bird of Paradise I** ———

1½ oz (3 tbsp) tequila
½ oz (1 tbsp) white crème de cacao
½ oz (1 tbsp) Galliano
1 oz (2 tbsp) orange juice
½ oz (1 tbsp) heavy cream

Put ingredients in blender with ½ cup cracked ice and blend about 10 seconds, or just until ice is puréed. Pour into chilled hollow-stemmed champagne glass.

——— **Bird of Paradise II** ———

1 oz (2 tbsp) chocolate liqueur
$\frac{1}{2}$ oz (1 tbsp) peppermint schnapps
2 oz (4 tbsp) heavy cream
sprig of mint (optional)

Place first three ingredients into blender with $\frac{1}{2}$ cup cracked ice and blend at high speed 10–15 seconds or until ice is just puréed. Pour into a chilled wineglass and garnish, if desired, with mint sprig.

——— **Bishop** ———

Burgundy wine
juice of $\frac{1}{4}$ lemon
juice of $\frac{1}{4}$ orange
1 tsp sugar
3 dashes light rum or brandy (optional)
slices of orange and lemon

Mix sugar, lemon, and orange juice in a highball glass. Add ice cubes and fill with Burgundy. Add rum or brandy if desired and garnish with fruit.

Variations: To serve hot, mix ingredients and heat in a pan to just below boiling. Serve in a heated mug.

The Cardinal: Substitute Bordeaux wine for Burgundy.

The Pope: Substitute champagne for Burgundy.

——— **Bittersweet** ———

$1\frac{1}{2}$ oz (3 tbsp) sweet vermouth
$1\frac{1}{2}$ oz (3 tbsp) dry vermouth
1 dash orange bitters
1 dash Angostura bitters
twist of orange peel

Shake liquid ingredients with ice and strain into a chilled cocktail glass. Garnish with orange peel.

Variation: Substitute 2 oz (4 tbsp) whiskey and 1 oz (2 tbsp) orange juice for the sweet and dry vermouths.

――――― **Black Devil** ―――――

2 oz (4 tbsp) light rum
½ oz (1 tbsp) dry vermouth
black olive

Shake liquid ingredients with ice and strain into a chilled cocktail glass. Garnish with the olive.

――――― **Black Hawk Cocktail** ―――――

1½ oz (3 tbsp) bourbon
1½ oz (3 tbsp) sloe gin
maraschino cherry

Stir liquid ingredients with ice and strain into a chilled cocktail glass. Garnish with the cherry.

Variation: Add ½ oz (1 tbsp) lemon juice and shake instead of stirring.

――――― **Blackjack** ―――――

1 oz (2 tbsp) brandy
½ oz (1 tbsp) kirsch
1 oz (2 tbsp) cold black coffee
twist of lemon peel

(continued)

Stir liquid ingredients with ice and strain into a chilled cocktail glass or into an old-fashioned glass over ice cubes. Garnish with lemon peel.

Variation: Substitute gin for brandy.

——— Blackout ———

2 oz (4 tbsp) dark Jamaican rum
1 oz (2 tbsp) Kahlúa or other coffee liqueur
1 tsp fresh lemon juice

Place ingredients in shaker with 4 or 5 ice cubes, cover, and shake vigorously several times. Strain into an old-fashioned glass filled with cracked ice.

——— Black Russian ———

2 oz (4 tbsp) vodka
1 oz (2 tbsp) Kahlúa, Tia Maria,
or coffee brandy

Pour ingredients into a chilled old-fashioned glass over ice cubes.

Variation: Stir ingredients with ice and strain into a chilled cocktail glass. Add a few drops of lemon juice.

——— Blackthorn ———

1½ oz (3 tbsp) sloe gin
1 oz (2 tbsp) sweet vermouth
2 dashes orange bitters (optional)
twist of lemon peel

Stir liquid ingredients with ice and strain into a chilled cocktail glass. Garnish with lemon peel.

See also *Irish Blackthorn.*

─────── **Black Velvet** ───────

6 oz chilled stout
6 oz chilled dry champagne

Pour ingredients simultaneously into a chilled highball glass.

Variation: Pour carefully, in the order given above,
into a chilled glass. Do not stir.

─────── **Blanche** ───────

1 oz (2 tbsp) white curaçao
1 oz (2 tbsp) anisette
1 oz (2 tbsp) Cointreau or Triple Sec

Shake ingredients with ice and strain into a chilled
cocktail glass.

─────── **Blarney Stone** ───────

2 oz (4 tbsp) Irish whiskey
2 tsp Pernod
2 tsp white curaçao
1 tsp clear maraschino liqueur
dash bitters
1 strip orange peel

Shake first 5 ingredients with ice cubes and strain
into a chilled cocktail glass. Twist peel to release oils
and drop into drink.

─────── **Blended Comfort** ───────

2 oz (4 tbsp) bourbon
1 oz (2 tbsp) Southern Comfort
½ oz (1 tbsp) dry vermouth

(continued)

1 oz (2 tbsp) lemon juice
¼ cup skinned peach slices
1 tsp sugar
1 oz (2 tbsp) orange juice (optional)
½ cup crushed ice
slice of peach and orange for garnish

Put ingredients, except for fruit slices, in a blender and blend at low speed until smooth. Pour into a chilled collins or highball glass and add ice cubes. Garnish with peach and orange slices.

————— Blood & Sand Cocktail —————

1 oz (2 tbsp) Scotch
1 oz (2 tbsp) cherry brandy
1 oz (2 tbsp) sweet vermouth
½ oz (1 tbsp) orange juice

Shake ingredients with ice and strain into a chilled cocktail glass.

————— Bloodhound Cocktail —————

1 oz (2 tbsp) gin
½ oz (1 tbsp) dry vermouth
½ oz (1 tbsp) sweet vermouth
½ oz (1 tbsp) strawberry liqueur
2 fresh strawberries

Shake liquid ingredients with ice and strain into a chilled cocktail glass. Garnish with strawberries.

————— Bloody Caesar —————

See *Bloody Mary.*

——— **Bloody Maria** ———

See *Bloody Mary.*

——— **Bloody Mary** ———

Perhaps named for Queen Mary I of England, whose relentless pursuit of the Protestants earned her the nickname "Bloody Mary," the drink is thought to have made its debut in the United States in the mid-1930s. The Bloody Mary is a popular brunch drink (or a morning-after hangover cure). Some individuals prefer a mild version, others are heavy-handed with the Tabasco and Worcestershire sauces.

2 oz (4 tbsp) vodka
4 oz (8 tbsp) tomato juice
2 dashes lemon juice
2 dashes Worcestershire sauce
2–3 drops Tabasco sauce
½ tsp sugar (optional)
1 dash celery salt
salt and pepper to taste
celery stalk for garnish (optional)

Shake ingredients with ice and strain into a large chilled wineglass. Sprinkle with salt, celery salt, and pepper. Garnish with celery stalk.

Variations: Serve "on the rocks" by straining into a chilled highball glass or beer goblet over ice cubes.

Substitute 2 tbsp of pepper vodka for regular vodka.

Bloody Caesar: Substitute Clamato juice for tomato juice.

Bloody Maria: Substitute 1½ oz (3 tbsp) tequila for the vodka, use only 3 oz (6 tbsp) tomato juice, 1

(continued)

dash lemon juice, 1 dash Tabasco sauce, and 1 dash Worcestershire sauce. Omit sugar, salt, and pepper. Garnish with slice of lemon.

——— Blue Angel ———

½ oz (1 tbsp) blue curaçao
½ oz (1 tbsp) brandy
½ oz (1 tbsp) parfait d'amour
½ oz (1 tbsp) cream
1 dash lemon juice

Shake ingredients with ice and strain into a chilled cocktail glass.

——— Blue Blazer ———

3 oz (6 tbsp) warmed whiskey
3 oz (6 tbsp) boiling water
1½ tsp sugar or honey
twist of lemon peel

Using 2 metal mugs, pour whiskey into one mug and dissolve sugar or honey in boiling water in the second mug. Ignite whiskey and while it blazes mix ingredients by pouring back and forth several times from one mug to the other. Serve in a heated wineglass or mug. Garnish with lemon peel.

Variation: Substitute Irish whiskey or Scotch for the whiskey.

——— Blue Devil ———

1½ oz (3 tbsp) gin
¾ tsp blue curaçao
¾ oz lemon or lime juice
½ oz (1 tbsp) maraschino liqueur

Shake ingredients with ice and strain into a chilled cocktail glass.

———— Bluegrass Cocktail ————

2 oz (4 tbsp) bourbon
½ oz (1 tbsp) apricot brandy
1 tsp lemon juice
1 tsp sugar syrup
chilled club soda
stemmed maraschino cherry

Place first 4 ingredients in highball glass filled with ice cubes. Top with chilled soda and stir gently. Garnish with cherry.

———— Blue Hawaiian ————

2 oz (4 tbsp) light rum
½ oz (1 tbsp) blue curaçao
½ oz (1 tbsp) Cointreau or Triple Sec
¾ oz (1½ tbsp) cream
1 tsp coconut cream

Shake ingredients with ice and strain into a chilled cocktail glass.

Variation: Substitute ½ oz (1 tbsp) pineapple juice for the Cointreau.

———— Blue Lady ————

(serves 2)

3 oz (6 tbsp) blue curaçao
1½ oz (3 tbsp) light rum
1½ oz (3 tbsp) lemon juice

(continued)

Shake ingredients vigorously with ice and strain into chilled cocktail glasses.

Variation: Substitute gin for the rum.

——————— **Blue Lagoon** ———————

1½ oz (3 tbsp) vodka
½ oz (1 tbsp) blue curaçao
4 oz (8 tbsp) white grape juice
orange slice

Place 3 or 4 ice cubes in highball glass. Add liquid ingredients in order given and stir to combine. Garnish with half slice of orange on rim.

——————— **Blue Monday** ———————

Nothing sad about this one, and it's refreshing anytime.

2 oz (4 tbsp) vodka
½ oz (1 tbsp) Cointreau
½ oz (1 tbsp) blue curaçao
zest of lemon

Add liquors to shaker with half a cup of cracked ice. Cover and shake vigorously several times and strain into chilled cocktail glass. Twist lemon zest over glass to release oils and add to drink.

——————— **Blue Moon Cocktail** ———————

1½ oz (3 tbsp) gin
¾ oz blue curaçao
twist of lemon

Shake liquid ingredients with ice and strain into a chilled cocktail glass. Garnish with lemon peel.

Variation: Substitute 1 egg white and ½ oz (1 tbsp) maraschino liqueur for the curaçao and eliminate the lemon twist.

─────── **Blush Wine Cooler** ───────

4 oz (8 tbsp) white zinfandel
1 tsp lime juice
1 tsp grenadine
chilled club soda
thin slice lime

In mixing glass stir to combine first 3 ingredients. Pour into a highball glass half filled with cracked ice. Top with a little soda and stir. Garnish with lime slice.

─────── **Bobby Burns Cocktail** ───────

1½ oz (3 tbsp) Scotch
1½ oz (3 tbsp) sweet vermouth
2 dashes Benedictine
twist of lemon peel

Stir liquid ingredients with ice and strain into a chilled cocktail glass. Garnish with lemon peel.

Variation: Reduce sweet vermouth to 1 oz (2 tbsp) and add 1 oz (2 tbsp) dry vermouth.

─────── **Boilermaker** ───────

Serve 2 oz (4 tbsp) whiskey in a shot glass or cordial glass with a glass of beer on the side as a chaser.

————— **Bolero Cocktail** —————

1½ oz (3 tbsp) light rum
¾ oz (1½ tbsp) apple brandy
2 dashes sweet vermouth

Stir ingredients with ice and strain into a chilled cocktail glass.

Variation: Substitute cognac for apple brandy.

————— **Bolo** —————

3 oz (6 tbsp) light rum
1 tsp sugar
juice of ½ orange
juice of ½ lemon or lime

Shake ingredients with ice and strain into a chilled cocktail glass.

See also *English Bolo.*

————— **Bolshoi** —————

2 oz (4 tbsp) vodka
1 oz (2 tbsp) Campari
lemon zest

Pour vodka and Campari into an old-fashioned glass with 3 or 4 ice cubes. Stir to blend. Twist peel over glass to release oil and add to drink.

————— **Bombardier** —————

4 oz (8 tbsp) beef bouillon
1½ oz (3 tbsp) bourbon
fresh lemon juice

Add first 2 ingredients to a highball glass half-filled with cracked ice. Top with a few drops lemon juice and stir gently.

─────── **Bombay Cocktail** ───────

1½ oz (3 tbsp) brandy
¾ oz (1½ tbsp) sweet vermouth
¾ oz (1½ tbsp) dry vermouth
1 dash Pernod
2 dashes orange curaçao

Stir ingredients with ice and strain into a chilled cocktail glass.

Variation: Substitute Cointreau or Triple Sec for the curaçao.

─────── **Bombay Punch** ───────

(serves 16–20)

1 qt dry sherry
1 qt brandy
½ cup maraschino liqueur
½ cup Cointreau or Triple Sec
2 qts chilled club soda
4 bottles chilled champagne
juice of 12 lemons
1 oz (2 tbsp) sugar

Mix sugar and lemon juice. Pour the mixture over a block of ice in a large punch bowl. Add sherry, brandy, maraschino, and Cointreau and stir well. Just before serving add soda and champagne.

Variation: Add 2 packages frozen peaches, half-thawed, or other fruit in season.

——— Bonanza Cocktail ———

1½ oz (3 tbsp) rye whiskey
1 tsp fresh lime juice
½ oz (1 tbsp) Triple Sec
dash of bitters
maraschino cherry

Place first 4 ingredients in shaker with 4 or 5 ice cubes. Cover and shake vigorously. Strain into a chilled cocktail glass and add cherry.

——— Boomerang ———

1½ oz (3 tbsp) dry vermouth
1 dash Angostura bitters
twist of lemon peel

Stir liquid ingredients with ice and strain into a chilled cocktail glass.

——— Borinquen ———

1½ oz (3 tbsp) light rum
½ oz (1 tbsp) passionfruit syrup
¾ oz (1½ tbsp) lime juice
¾ oz (1½ tbsp) orange juice
1 tsp 151-proof rum
½ cup crushed ice

Put ingredients in a blender and blend at low speed for 10–15 seconds. Pour into a chilled old-fashioned glass.

——— Bosom Caresser ———

2 oz (4 tbsp) brandy
1 oz (2 tbsp) Madeira

1 oz (2 tbsp) curaçao
1 tsp grenadine
1 egg yolk

Shake ingredients with ice and strain into a chilled wineglass.

Variations: Eliminate grenadine and egg yolk; stir brandy, Madeira, and curaçao with ice and strain into a chilled cocktail glass. Cointreau or Triple Sec can be substituted for curaçao.

Bossa Nova

1 oz (2 tbsp) dark rum
1 oz (2 tbsp) Galliano
½ oz (1 tbsp) apricot brandy
3 oz (6 tbsp) passionfruit juice

Put ingredients in a blender with 4 ice cubes. Blend for 15 seconds and pour into a chilled highball or wineglass.

Variation: Substitute pineapple juice for passionfruit juice.

Boston Bullet

See *Martini.*

Boston Cocktail

1½ oz (3 tbsp) gin
1½ oz (3 tbsp) apricot brandy
2 dashes grenadine
1 tsp lemon juice
twist of lemon peel

(continued)

Shake liquid ingredients with ice and strain into a chilled cocktail glass. Garnish with lemon peel.

Boston Cooler

2 oz (4 tbsp) light rum
juice of ⅓ lemon
½–1 tsp sugar
chilled club soda or ginger ale
twist of lemon peel

Shake rum, lemon, and sugar with ice and strain into a chilled collins or highball glass over ice cubes. Top with soda, stir gently, and garnish with lemon peel.

Variation: Substitute cognac for rum and add a dash of rum over the top of the drink.

Boston Sidecar

See *Sidecar.*

Boston Sour

2 oz (4 tbsp) bourbon
juice of ½ lemon
1 tsp sugar
slice of lemon
maraschino cherry

Shake ingredients, except lemon slice and cherry, vigorously with ice and strain into a chilled cocktail or sour glass. Garnish with lemon slice and cherry.

Variation: Strain into a chilled collins glass over ice cubes and top with chilled club soda.

BOURBON

An American whiskey (produced largely in Kentucky), bourbon is distilled from a fermented mash of grain that must contain at least 51 percent corn. Aged in charred white oak barrels for at least two and up to four years, it is distinguished from rye whiskey by its high proportion of corn. Straight bourbon is generally fuller in flavor and body than blended bourbon, which is bourbon that has been blended with other whiskey or a neutral spirit.

———— Bourbon Cobbler ————

½ oz (1 tbsp) lemon juice
2 tsp sugar syrup
2 oz (4 tbsp) bourbon
club soda
lemon slice or mint sprig (optional)

In highball glass thoroughly blend lemon juice and sugar syrup. Add 4 or 5 ice cubes, then pour in bourbon. Top with club soda and stir gently. Garnish, if desired, with lemon slice or mint.

———— Bourbon Cocktail ————

2 oz (4 tbsp) bourbon
⅓ oz curaçao
⅓ oz Benedictine
⅓ oz lemon juice
1 dash Angostura bitters
twist of lemon peel

Shake liquid ingredients with ice and strain into a chilled cocktail or old-fashioned glass over ice cubes. Garnish with lemon peel.

———— Bourbon Daisy ————

There are other versions, but we like this one.

1½ oz (3 tbsp) bourbon
½ oz (1 tbsp) lemon juice
½ oz (1 tbsp) grenadine
½ oz (1 tbsp) Southern Comfort
orange slice and maraschino cherry (optional)

Place liquors and juices into shaker with 5 or 6 ice cubes. Cover and shake vigorously several times. Strain into an old-fashioned glass filled two-thirds with cracked ice. Garnish, if desired, with orange slice and cherry.

———— Bourbon Eggnog ————

(serves 8)

A Christmastime favorite. Makes one quart, but can easily be doubled or tripled.

6 eggs, separated
½ cup sugar
½ cup bourbon (or rye) whiskey
½ cup brandy
3 cups heavy cream
grated nutmeg

Beat egg yolks with sugar until light yellow. Add bourbon and brandy and blend well. Refrigerate several hours or overnight. Whip cream until slightly thickened and fold into yolk mixture. Beat egg whites until peaks form and fold into mixture. Chill until ready to serve. Serve in punch cups with a few gratings of nutmeg. Makes eight 4-oz servings.

——— **Bourbon and Ginger Ale** ———

3 oz (6 tbsp) bourbon
6 oz ginger ale
$\frac{1}{2}$ oz (1 tbsp) lemon juice
slice of lemon

Fill a highball or collins glass with ice. Pour all ingredients in except lemon slice. Place shaker over glass; shake to mix and garnish with lemon slice.

——— **Bourbon Mist** ———

See *Scotch Mist.*

BRANDY

Brandy is a distillation of the fermented juice of grapes or other fruits. When a fruit other than grapes is used, the type of fruit is used in the name of the brandy (apple brandy, cherry brandy, etc.). The best-known types of brandy are cognac and Armagnac, which are typically consumed straight. Cheaper substitutes can be used in the drinks below.

——— **Brandied Cranberry Punch** ———

(serves 20–24)

A great favorite at Christmastime.

1 qt cranberry juice
1 bottle dry white wine
1 cup brandy
1 lemon thinly sliced
$\frac{1}{4}$–$\frac{1}{2}$ cup sugar, to taste

(continued)

1 or 2 bottles club soda, to taste
block of ice

In large crock combine cranberry juice, wine, brandy, lemon slices, and 1/4 cup of the sugar. Stir to combine well and taste for tartness. Add more sugar if needed. Cover and refrigerate overnight. When ready to serve, place block of ice in large punch bowl and pour in cranberry mix. Pour one bottle soda over ice. Stir and taste. If a lighter punch is desired, add second bottle. Ladle into punch cups.

Brandied Ginger

1 1/2 oz (3 tbsp) brandy
1/2 oz (1 tbsp) ginger brandy
1 tsp lime juice
1 tsp orange juice
1 piece preserved ginger

Shake liquid ingredients with ice and strain into a chilled cocktail glass. Garnish with piece of ginger.

Variation: Sprinkle with grated chocolate.

Brandied Madeira

1 oz (2 tbsp) Madeira
1 oz (2 tbsp) brandy
1/2 oz (1 tbsp) dry vermouth
twist of lemon peel

Stir liquid ingredients with ice and strain into a chilled cocktail glass or into an old-fashioned glass over ice cubes. Garnish with lemon-peel.

—————   **Brandied Port**   —————

1 oz (2 tbsp) brandy
1 oz (2 tbsp) tawny port
½ oz (1 tbsp) lemon juice
1 tsp maraschino liqueur
slice of orange

Shake liquid ingredients with ice and strain into an old-fashioned glass over ice cubes. Garnish with orange slice.

—————   **Brandy Alexander**   —————

See *Alexander Cocktail.*

—————   **Brandy Blazer**   —————

3 oz (6 tbsp) warmed brandy
1 lump sugar
1 strip lemon peel
1 strip orange peel

Muddle sugar, lemon and orange peels, and brandy in an old-fashioned glass. Ignite brandy and serve.

—————   **Brandy Cassis**   —————

1¾ oz (3½ tbsp) brandy
1 oz (2 tbsp) lemon juice
2–3 dashes crème de cassis
twist of lemon peel

Shake ingredients with ice and strain into a chilled cocktail glass. Garnish with lemon peel.

———— **Brandy Cobbler** ————

2 oz (4 tbsp) brandy
1 tsp sugar
2 oz (4 tbsp) chilled club soda
fruits in season

In a highball glass dissolve sugar in soda. Fill glass ³⁄₄ full of cracked ice and add brandy. Stir and garnish with fruits in season.

Variation: Add 1 tsp curaçao.

———— **Brandy Cocktail** ————

3 oz (6 tbsp) brandy
¹⁄₂ tsp sugar
2 dashes orange bitters
twist of lemon peel

Stir liquid ingredients to dissolve sugar. Shake with ice and strain into a chilled cocktail glass. Garnish with lemon peel.

Variation: Substitute Angostura bitters for orange bitters and add ³⁄₄ oz sweet vermouth or ³⁄₄ oz curaçao. Garnish with a maraschino cherry.

———— **Brandy Collins** ————

See *Tom Collins.*

———— **Brandy Crusta Cocktail** ————

2 oz (4 tbsp) brandy
¹⁄₂ oz (1 tbsp) Triple Sec
1 tsp lemon juice
1 tsp maraschino liqueur

1 dash Angostura bitters
peel of ½ lemon (cut in a continuous spiral)

Sugar-rim a chilled cocktail glass by rubbing with lemon and dipping into sugar. Put lemon peel in the glass. Shake liquid ingredients with ice and strain into the glass.

————— **Brandy Daisy** —————

2 oz (4 tbsp) brandy
juice of ½ lemon
1 tsp grenadine or raspberry syrup
chilled club soda
fresh fruit for garnish

Shake brandy, lemon, and grenadine. Strain into a highball or large wineglass that has been filled with ice cubes. Top with soda and garnish with fruit.

Variation: Eliminate club soda.

————— **Brandy Eggnog** —————

See *Eggnog I.*

————— **Brandy Fix** —————

2½ oz (5 tbsp) brandy
1 tsp sugar
1 tsp water
juice of ½ lemon
slice of lemon

Mix sugar, water, and lemon juice in a highball glass. Fill glass with shaved ice, add brandy, and mix. Garnish with lemon slice.

(continued)

Variation: Reduce brandy to 1½ oz (3 tbsp) and add 1 oz (2 tbsp) cherry brandy.

——————— **Brandy Fizz** ———————

2 oz (4 tbsp) brandy
1 tsp sugar
juice of ½ lemon
chilled club soda

Shake brandy, sugar, and lemon with ice. Strain into a chilled highball glass over ice cubes and top with soda.

——————— **Brandy Flip** ———————

2 oz (4 tbsp) brandy
1 tsp sugar
2 tsp cream
nutmeg

Shake first 3 ingredients vigorously with ice. Strain into a chilled cocktail glass and sprinkle with nutmeg.

——————— **Brandy Float** ———————

Widely favored as a mild after-dinner drink.

1½ oz (3 tbsp) white crème de menthe
½ oz (1 tbsp) brandy

Fill a small brandy snifter or old-fashioned glass halfway with crushed ice. Pour crème de menthe over the ice, followed by the brandy poured very slowly so the liquors stay in two separate layers. Serve with a short straw.

——— **Brandy Gump Cocktail** ———

2 oz (4 tbsp) brandy
juice of ½ lemon
2 dashes grenadine

Shake ingredients with ice and strain into a chilled cocktail glass.

——— **Brandy Highball** ———

See *Whiskey Highball.*

——— **Brandy Milk Punch** ———

3 oz (6 tbsp) brandy
6 oz chilled milk
1 tsp sugar
nutmeg

Shake first 3 ingredients vigorously with ice. Strain into a chilled highball glass and sprinkle with nutmeg.

——— **Brandy Puff** ———

2 oz (4 tbsp) brandy
2 oz (4 tbsp) milk
2 ice cubes
club soda

Place ice cubes in a small tumbler and add brandy and milk. Fill with soda, stir lightly, and serve.

Variations: Substitute rum, whiskey, or gin for the brandy.

——— Brandy Punch ———

(serves 12–16)

juice of 4 oranges
juice of 12 lemons
3 tsp sugar
1 qt chilled club soda
1 cup grenadine
2 qts brandy
1 cup Cointreau or Triple Sec
fresh fruit in season

Mix first 5 ingredients and pour into a punch bowl over a block of ice. Add brandy and Cointreau and stir well. Garnish with fruit.

Variation: Add 2 cups strong black tea when adding the brandy and Cointreau.

——— Brandy Sangaree ———

See *Sangaree.*

——— Brandy Shrub ———

(serves 12–16)

2 qts brandy
juice of 6 lemons
peel of 3 lemons
1 lb sugar
8 oz sherry (optional)

Mix the lemon juice, lemon peel, and brandy and store in a covered container for 3 days. Add the sugar and sherry, strain the mixture, and bottle it. Store in a cool place for at least a week. (Longer storage will improve the flavor.) Serve as a punch, over a block of ice, or as an individual drink, either straight or diluted with water, in a brandy snifter.

─────── **Brandy Sling** ───────

2 oz (4 tbsp) brandy
1 tsp sugar
1 tsp water
juice of ½ lemon
twist of lemon peel

Dissolve sugar in water and lemon juice in a chilled old-fashioned glass. Add ice cubes and brandy and garnish with lemon peel.

Variation: Add 1 dash Angostura bitters, serve in a chilled highball glass, and top with plain chilled water.

─────── **Brandy Smash** ───────

A smash is a small-size julep, usually served in an old-fashioned glass.

2 oz (4 tbsp) brandy
1 lump sugar
1 oz (2 tbsp) chilled club soda
4 sprigs fresh mint
mint for garnish

Muddle sugar, soda, and mint sprigs in a chilled old-fashioned glass. Add ice cubes and brandy. Garnish with additional mint.

Variation: Gin, whiskey, or other liquor may be substituted for the brandy, and the smash is then named for the liquor used (Gin Smash, etc.).

——————   **Brandy Sour**   ——————

See *Whiskey Sour.*

——————   **Brandy Vermouth Cocktail**   ——————

3 oz (6 tbsp) brandy
3/4 oz (1 1/2 tbsp) sweet vermouth
1 dash Angostura bitters

Stir ingredients with ice and strain into a chilled cocktail glass.

——————   **Brave Bull**   ——————

1 1/2 oz (3 tbsp) tequila
1 1/2 oz (3 tbsp) Kahlúa or Tia Maria
twist of lemon peel

Stir liquid ingredients with ice and strain into a chilled old-dashioned glass over ice cubes. Garnish with lemon peel.

——————   **Brazil Cocktail**   ——————

1 1/2 oz (3 tbsp) dry sherry
1 1/2 oz (3 tbsp) dry vermouth
1 dash Pernod
1 dash Angostura bitters
twist of lemon peel

Stir liquid ingredients with ice and strain into a chilled cocktail glass. Garnish with lemon peel.

——————   **Breakfast Eggnog**   ——————

See *Eggnog I.*

---------- **Brewster Special** ----------

2 oz (4 tbsp) vodka
sweet cider
strip of orange peel
orange slice (optional)

Place 2 or 3 ice cubes in a collins glass, add orange peel, and pour vodka over it. Top with cider and garnish with orange slice if desired.

Variation: Float ½ oz (1 tbsp) Galliano on top.

---------- **Brighton Punch** ----------

1 oz (2 tbsp) bourbon
1 oz (2 tbsp) brandy
1 oz (2 tbsp) Benedictine
juice of ½ orange
juice of ½ lemon
chilled club soda
slices of orange and lemon

Shake first 5 ingredients with ice. Strain into a chilled highball glass over ice cubes and top with soda. Stir gently and garnish with orange and lemon.

Variation: Eliminate Benedictine, reduce bourbon to ½ oz (1 tbsp), and substitute ¾ oz (1½ tbsp) peach brandy and ¾ oz (1½ tbsp) apricot brandy for the 1 oz (2 tbsp) brandy.

---------- **Broken Spur Cocktail** ----------

1½ oz (3 tbsp) white port
¾ oz (1½ tbsp) sweet vermouth
¼ oz (½ tbsp) Cointreau or Triple Sec

(continued)

Stir ingredients with ice and strain into a chilled cock-tail glass.

Variation: Substitute ¾ oz (1½ tbsp) gin for the Cointreau and add 1 egg yolk. Shake with ice and strain.

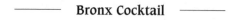

Bronx Cocktail

A classic cocktail, the Bronx is named after the New York borough and was invented around 1919 when gin was substituted for whiskey in a Manhattan.

1½ oz (3 tbsp) gin
½ oz (1 tbsp) dry vermouth
½ oz (1 tbsp) sweet vermouth
juice of ¼ orange
slice of orange

Shake liquid ingredients with ice and strain into a chilled cocktail glass or into an old-fashioned glass over ice cubes. Garnish with orange slices.

Bronx Golden Cocktail: Add 1 egg yolk, shake vigorously, and strain.

Dry Bronx Cocktail: Eliminate the sweet vermouth.

See also *Bronx Silver Cocktail.*

Bronx River

2 oz (4 tbsp) gin
¾ oz (1½ tbsp) sweet vermouth
½ tsp sugar
juice of ½ lemon

Stir ingredients with ice and strain into a chilled cock-tail glass.

--------- **Bronx Silver Cocktail** ---------

1 oz (2 tbsp) gin
1/2 oz (1 tbsp) dry vermouth
juice of 1/2 orange

Shake ingredients vigorously with ice and strain into a chilled cocktail glass.

--------- **Bronx Terrace Cocktail** ---------

1 1/2 oz (3 tbsp) gin
1/2 oz (1 tbsp) dry vermouth
juice of 1/2 lime
maraschino cherry

Shake liquid ingredients with ice and strain into a chilled cocktail glass. Garnish with cherry.

--------- **Brooklyn** ---------

2 oz (4 tbsp) rye whiskey
1 oz (2 tbsp) dry vermouth
1 dash Angostura bitters
1 dash maraschino liqueur

Stir ingredients with ice and strain into a chilled cocktail glass.

Variations: Substitute sweet vermouth for the dry. Add 1 dash Amer Picon. Eliminate bitters.

--------- **Buck's Fizz** ---------

2 oz (4 tbsp) chilled orange juice
chilled champagne

Put 2–3 ice cubes in a chilled collins or large wine glass. Add orange juice and top with champagne.

(continued)

Variation: Add a dash of grenadine and stir very gently.

———— Bulldog Cocktail I ————

2 oz (4 tbsp) gin
juice of 1 orange
chilled ginger ale

Pour gin and orange juice into a chilled highball glass over ice cubes. Top with ginger ale and stir gently.

———— Bulldog Cocktail II ————

1½ oz (3 tbsp) cherry brandy
½ oz (1 tbsp) light rum
juice of ½ lime

Shake ingredients with ice and strain into a chilled cocktail glass.

Variation: Substitute gin for rum.

———— Bullfrog ————

2 oz (4 tbsp) vodka
2 tsp Cointreau
4 oz (8 tbsp) lemonade
lemon slice

Place 3 or 4 ice cubes in a highball glass. Add liquid ingredients in order given and stir to combine well. Float lemon slice.

———— Bullshot ————

Often regarded as a good "hair-of-the-dog" morning-after hangover cure, the Bullshot is a fairly recent drink. It is an offshoot of the Bloody Mary, but the exact origin is unknown.

2½ oz (5 tbsp) vodka
5 oz strong chilled beef bouillon
1 dash Worcestershire sauce
salt and pepper to taste

Shake ingredients with ice and strain into a large chilled wineglass. Sprinkle with salt and pepper.

Variation: Add a dash of Tabasco sauce, 2 dashes lemon juice, and a dash of celery salt. Can also be served over ice cubes.

———— **Burgundy Bishop** ————

See *Bishop.*

———— **Bushranger** ————

1 oz (2 tbsp) light rum
1 oz (2 tbsp) Dubonnet
1 dash Angostura bitters
twist of lemon peel

Shake liquid ingredients with ice and strain into a chilled cocktail glass. Garnish with lemon peel.

———— **B.V.D.** ————

Originally, equal parts of brandy, vermouth, and Dubonnet, hence the initials.

¾ oz (1½ tbsp) light rum
¾ oz (1½ tbsp) dry vermouth
¾ oz (1½ tbsp) gin

(continued)

Stir ingredients with ice and strain into a chilled cocktail glass.

Variation: Substitute ¾ oz (1½ tbsp) Dubonnet for the gin.

-------- **Byrrh Cassis** --------

1½ oz (3 tbsp) Byrrh
1 oz (2 tbsp) crème de cassis
chilled club soda

Mix Byrrh and crème de cassis in a large chilled wineglass. Add ice cubes and top with soda.

-------- **Byrrh Cocktail** --------

1 oz (2 tbsp) Byrrh
1 oz (2 tbsp) rye whiskey
1 oz (2 tbsp) dry vermouth

Stir ingredients with ice and strain into a chilled cocktail glass.

C

-------- **Cabana Café** --------

1 oz (2 tbsp) coffee liqueur
3 oz (6 tbsp) club soda
½ tsp lime juice
lime wedge

Pour first 3 ingredients into collins glass with ice and stir. Garnish with lime wedge.

——— **Cabaret Cocktail** ———

1½ oz (3 tbsp) gin
½ oz (1 tbsp) dry vermouth
2 dashes Benedictine
1 dash Angostura bitters
maraschino cherry

Stir liquid ingredients with ice and strain into a chilled cocktail glass. Garnish with the cherry.

Variation: Substitute Dubonnet for dry vermouth.

——— **Cactus Rose** ———

2 oz (4 tbsp) tequila
1 oz (2 tbsp) Drambuie
1 tsp lemon juice

Place ingredients in shaker with 4 or 5 ice cubes, cover, and shake vigorously several times. Strain into chilled cocktail glass.

——— **Cadiz** ———

¾ oz (1½ tbsp) dry sherry
¾ oz (1½ tbsp) blackberry brandy
½ oz (1 tbsp) Triple Sec
½ oz (1 tbsp) cream

Shake ingredients with ice and strain into a chilled old-fashioned glass over ice cubes.

——— **Café de Paris Cocktail** ———

2 oz (4 tbsp) gin
1 tsp Pernod
1 tsp cream

(continued)

Shake ingredients with ice and strain into a chilled cocktail glass.

—————   **Cajun Mimosa Punch**   —————

(serves 8)

A variation on the mimosa cocktail, and one your guests are not likely to forget. The perfect prelude to a Cajun meal.

1 qt orange juice
6 bottled jalapeño peppers, drained
2 bottles chilled champagne or other sparkling wine
crushed ice

Place orange juice in quart bottle with tight-fitting lid. Drain peppers thoroughly and pat dry. Slice into rounds and add to juice. Cap, shake well, and refrigerate 3 days. When ready to serve, strain juice and discard peppers. Fill highball glasses half full of crushed ice, then fill half full with orange juice and top off with cold champagne. Makes eight 8-oz drinks, with a little extra champagne to freshen the glasses.

—————   **Cajun Party Punch**   —————

(serves 40)

1 qt strong tea
1½ cups sugar
10 mint sprigs
4 cinnamon sticks (about 3" each)
1 tsp whole cloves
1 qt dark rum
2 cups unsweetened pineapple juice

1 cup fresh lime juice
2 qt bottles club soda, chilled
block of ice
1 lemon, thinly sliced
1 lime, thinly sliced
1 orange, thinly sliced

Place tea in 3-qt saucepan and bring heat to medium. Add sugar, mint, cinnamon, and cloves. Cook, stirring, until sugar dissolves. Cool slightly, then chill in refrigerator. When ready to serve, place block of ice in large punch bowl. Strain tea into bowl and discard spices. Add rum, juices, and soda and stir till blended. Add fruit slices. Ladle into punch cups.

California Lemonade

2 oz (4 tbsp) rye whiskey
1 dash grenadine
½ oz (1 tbsp) sugar
juice of 1 lime
juice of 1 lemon
chilled club soda
slices of fruit
maraschino cherry

Shake rye, grenadine, sugar, and fruit juices with ice. Strain into a collins glass over shaved ice and top with soda. Garnish with slices of fruit and cherry.

Calisay Cocktail

1½ oz (3 tbsp) Calisay
1½ oz (3 tbsp) sweet vermouth
3 dashes lime juice
3 dashes sugar syrup

(continued)

Shake ingredients with ice and strain into a chilled cocktail glass.

——— Calvados Cocktail ———

1½ oz (3 tbsp) calvados
1½ oz (3 tbsp) orange juice
¾ oz (1½ tbsp) Cointreau or Triple Sec
½ oz (1 tbsp) orange bitters

Shake ingredients with ice and strain into a chilled cocktail glass.

——— Campari Cocktail ———

2 oz (4 tbsp) Campari
1 oz (2 tbsp) cherry juice
½ oz (1 tbsp) orange juice
2 dashes Angostura bitters
slice of orange

Mix first 4 ingredients in a tall collins glass filled with ice; cover and shake vigorously. Garnish with orange slice.

——— Campari and Soda ———

2 oz (4 tbsp) Campari
2 oz (4 tbsp) club soda
twist of lemon

Pour ingredients into a collins glass filled with ice; cover and shake to mix. Garnish with a twist of lemon.

———— **Canadian Breeze** ————

1½ oz (3 tbsp) Canadian whisky
1 tbsp pineapple juice
1 tbsp lemon juice
1 tsp cherry juice
cherry

Pour first 4 ingredients into a collins glass filled with ice. Cover and shake to mix. Garnish with a cherry.

———— **Canadian Cherry** ————

1½ oz (3 tbsp) Canadian whisky
½ oz (1 tbsp) cherry brandy
2 tsp lemon juice
2 tsp orange juice

Sugar-rim a chilled cocktail glass by dipping it into cherry brandy and then into sugar. Shake ingredients with ice and strain into the glass.

———— **Canadian Cocktail** ————

1½ oz (3 tbsp) Canadian whisky
1½ tsp Cointreau or Triple Sec
1 dash Angostura bitters
1 tsp sugar

Shake ingredients with ice and strain into a chilled cocktail glass.

Variation: Substitute 2 dashes curaçao for the Cointreau or Triple Sec.

——— Canadian Pineapple ———

1½ oz (3 tbsp) Canadian whiskey
2 tsp pineapple juice
2 tsp lemon juice
2 tsp maraschino liqueur
stick of fresh pineapple

Shake liquid ingredients with ice and strain into a chilled cocktail glass. Garnish with the pineapple stick.

——— Cape Codder ———

2 oz (4 tbsp) vodka
4 oz (8 tbsp) cranberry juice
juice of ½ lime
chilled club soda (optional)

Shake first 3 ingredients with ice and strain into a chilled collins glass over ice cubes. Top with soda if desired.

Variation: Substitute light rum for vodka.

——— Cara Sposa ———

1 oz (2 tbsp) Tia Maria or coffee brandy
1 oz (2 tbsp) Triple Sec
1 oz (2 tbsp) cream

Shake ingredients with ice and strain into a chilled old-fashioned glass over ice cubes.

Variations: Put ingredients into a blender with ½ cup crushed ice, blend for 10 seconds, and pour into a sugar-rimmed cocktail glass. Orange curaçao can be substituted for Triple Sec.

——— Cardinal, The ———

See *Bishop*.

——— Cardinal Punch ———

(serves 16–20)

1 qt chilled club soda
1 lb sugar
juice of 12 lemons
2 qts claret
1 pt brandy
1 pt rum
8 oz sweet vermouth
1 split chilled champagne or sparkling wine
fresh fruit for garnish

Mix soda, sugar, and lemon juice and pour into a punch bowl over a block of ice. Add rest of ingredients, except champagne and fruit, and stir well. Add champagne just before serving and garnish with fruit.

Variation: Eliminate lemon juice and increase club soda to 2 qts. Add 1 pt strong black tea.

——— Caribbean Champagne ———

½ tsp light rum
½ tsp banana liqueur
1 dash Angostura or orange bitters (optional)
4 oz (8 tbsp) chilled champagne
slice of banana

Pour rum, banana liqueur, and bitters into a chilled champagne glass. Fill with champagne and stir gently. Garnish with banana slice.

─────── **Caribe Cocktail** ───────

juice of 1 orange
1/2 oz (1 tbsp) lemon juice
2 oz (4 tbsp) dark rum
1/2 oz (1 tbsp) raw sugar
orange zest (optional)

Combine juices, rum, and sugar in cocktail shaker with cracked ice. Shake well and strain into chilled cocktail glass. Garnish, if desired, with orange zest.

─────── **Carrol Cocktail** ───────

2 oz (4 tbsp) brandy
1 oz (2 tbsp) sweet vermouth
maraschino cherry or cocktail onion

Stir liquid ingredients with ice and strain into a chilled cocktail glass. Garnish with cherry or onion.

─────── **Caruso** ───────

1 1/2 oz (3 tbsp) gin
1 oz (2 tbsp) dry vermouth
1/2 oz (1 tbsp) green crème de menthe

Stir ingredients with ice and strain into a chilled cocktail glass.

Variation: Use equal parts of all 3 ingredients (1 oz [2 tbsp] of each).

─────── **Casa Blanca** ───────

2 oz (4 tbsp) light rum
1 1/2 tsp Cointreau or Triple Sec
1 1/2 tsp lime juice

1½ tsp maraschino
slice of orange (optional)

Shake liquid ingredients with ice and strain into a chilled cocktail glass. Garnish with the orange slice.

Variation: Substitute vodka for rum and Galliano for Cointreau.

–––––––– **Casino Cocktail** ––––––––

3 oz (6 tbsp) gin
¼ tsp lemon juice
¼ tsp maraschino liqueur
2 dashes orange bitters
maraschino cherry

Shake liquid ingredients with ice and strain into a chilled cocktail glass. Garnish with the cherry.

–––––––– **Champagne Cobbler** ––––––––

½ tsp lemon juice
½ tsp curaçao
thin slice of orange
chilled champagne

Fill a large goblet or wineglass half full of cracked ice. Add lemon juice, curaçao, and orange slice. Stir and fill glass with champagne. Stir again gently.

–––––––– **Champagne Cocktail** ––––––––

4–5 oz chilled champagne
1 lump sugar
1 dash Angostura bitters

(continued)

Put lump of sugar into a chilled champagne glass. Add bitters and fill with champagne.

Variation: Add twist of lemon or orange peel. Float 1 oz (2 tbsp) brandy on top of champagne. Add 1 tsp of calvados.

———— Champagne Cooler ————

1 oz (2 tbsp) brandy
1 oz (2 tbsp) Cointreau or Triple Sec
chilled champagne
sprig of fresh mint

Fill a large chilled wineglass or highball glass half full of ice cubes. Add brandy and Cointreau. Fill with champagne and stir gently. Garnish with mint.

———— Champagne Cup ————

(serves 4–6)

1 fifth chilled champagne
4 oz (8 tbsp) brandy
2 oz (4 tbsp) Benedictine
3 oz (6 tbsp) maraschino liqueur
1 qt chilled club soda
3 dashes grenadine (optional)
1 cup mixed fruit, sliced and chilled

Place fruit in a chilled pitcher or bowl and add brandy, Benedictine, maraschino liqueur, and grenadine. Add ice cubes or a block of ice and stir. Just before serving add soda and champagne and stir gently. Serve in chilled wineglasses or punch cups.

Champagne Julep

chilled champagne
1 sugar cube
2 sprigs of fresh mint
slices of fresh fruit (optional)

Put sugar cube and mint in a chilled highball glass or stemmed goblet. Add 2 cubes of ice and slowly pour in champagne while stirring constantly. Garnish with fresh fruit if desired.

Variation: Add 1 oz (2 tbsp) brandy.

Champagne Pick-Me-Up

2 oz (4 tbsp) brandy
1 oz (2 tbsp) orange juice
1/2 oz (1 tbsp) lemon juice
1 tsp grenadine
4 oz (8 tbsp) chilled champagne
twist of lemon peel

Shake brandy, fruit juices, and grenadine with ice. Strain into a large chilled wineglass. Fill with champagne and garnish with lemon peel.

Champagne Punch

(serves 10–14)

juice of 12 lemons
sugar to sweeten
1/2 cup maraschino liqueur
1 cup Triple Sec
2 cups brandy
2 cups chilled club soda
2 fifths chilled champagne
fresh fruit for garnish

(continued)

Mix first 5 ingredients in a punch bowl and add a block of ice. Just before serving pour in soda and champagne. Garnish with fruit.

Claret Punch: Substitute chilled claret for champagne.

Champagne Sherbet Punch

(serves 10–12)

1 qt frozen lemon sherbet
2 fifths chilled champagne
3/4 tsp Angostura bitters
slices of lemon

Pour champagne over sherbet in a chilled punch bowl. Add bitters and stir. Garnish with lemon slices.

Variation: Substitute pineapple sherbet for the lemon and garnish with slices of pineapple.

Champagne Velvet

See *Black Velvet.*

Champs Elysées Cocktail

1 1/2 oz (3 tbsp) brandy
1/2 oz (1 tbsp) yellow Chartreuse
juice of 1/4 lemon
1 dash Angostura bitters
1/2 tsp sugar (optional)

Shake ingredients with ice and strain into a chilled cocktail glass.

Chapala

1½ oz (3 tbsp) tequila
½ oz (1 tbsp) orange juice
½ oz (1 tbsp) lemon juice
2 tsp grenadine
1 dash orange-flower water
slice of orange

Shake liquid ingredients with ice and strain into a chilled old-fashioned glass over ice cubes. Garnish with orange slice.

Chapel Hill

1½ oz (3 tbsp) bourbon
½ oz (1 tbsp) Triple Sec
½ oz (1 tbsp) lemon juice
twist of orange peel

Shake liquid ingredients with ice and strain into a chilled cocktail glass or into an old-fashioned glass over ice cubes. Garnish with orange peel.

Cherry Blossom Cocktail

2 oz (4 tbsp) brandy
1 oz (2 tbsp) cherry brandy
1 dash grenadine
1 dash lemon juice
1 dash orange curaçao

Sugar-rim a chilled cocktail glass by dipping first into cherry brandy and then into sugar. Shake ingredients with ice and strain into the glass.

——— **Cherry Brandy Cooler** ———

2 oz (4 tbsp) cherry brandy
chilled cola
slice of lemon

Pour brandy and cola into a chilled collins or highball glass over ice and stir gently. Garnish with the lemon slice.

Variation: Substitute cherry-flavored vodka for the brandy.

——— **Cherry Cobbler** ———

1 1/2 oz (3 tbsp) gin
3/4 oz (1 1/2 tbsp) cherry brandy
1/2 oz (1 tbsp) lemon juice
1 tsp sugar
slice of lemon
maraschino cherry

Fill a chilled highball or collins glass 2/3 full of crushed ice. Add liquid ingredients and sugar and stir until sugar dissolves. Top with more ice if necessary and garnish with lemon and cherry.

——— **Cherry Fizz** ———

2 oz (4 tbsp) cherry brandy
juice of 1/2 lemon
1/2 tsp sugar (optional)
chilled club soda
maraschino cherry

Shake brandy, lemon juice, and sugar with ice and strain into a chilled collins or highball glass over ice cubes. Top with soda, stir gently, and garnish with the cherry.

─────── **Cherry Rum** ───────

1½ oz (3 tbsp) light rum
¾ oz (1½ tbsp) cherry brandy
½ oz (1 tbsp) cream

Shake ingredients with ice and strain into a chilled cocktail glass.

Variation: Put ingredients in a blender with ⅓ cup crushed ice. Blend at low speed for 15 seconds and pour into a chilled cocktail glass.

─────── **Chicago Cocktail** ───────

2 oz (4 tbsp) cognac
1 dash Triple Sec
1 dash Angostura bitters

Sugar-rim a chilled cocktail glass by rubbing with lemon and dipping into sugar. Stir ingredients with ice and strain into the glass.

Variation: Substitute curaçao for Triple Sec. Stir ingredients with ice, strain into a chilled wineglass, and top with champagne.

─────── **Chinese Cocktail** ───────

1½ oz (3 tbsp) Jamaican rum
½ oz (1 tbsp) grenadine
3 dashes Triple Sec or curaçao
3 dashes maraschino liqueur
1 dash Angostura bitters

Shake ingredients with ice and strain into a chilled cocktail glass.

——— Chiquita ———

1½ oz (3 tbsp) golden rum
½ oz (1 tbsp) banana liqueur
1 tsp grenadine
1 oz (2 tbsp) light cream

Place all ingredients in blender with ½ cup cracked ice. Cover and blend at high speed about 10 seconds or just until ice is thoroughly blended. Pour into chilled wineglass.

——— Chocolate Martini ———

See *Martini.*

——— Chocolate Rum ———

1 oz (2 tbsp) light rum
½ oz (1 tbsp) crème de cacao
½ oz (1 tbsp) white crème de menthe
½ oz (1 tbsp) cream
1 tsp 151-proof rum

Shake ingredients with ice and strain into a chilled cocktail glass or into an old-fashioned glass over ice cubes.

Variation: Float 151-proof rum on top instead of shaking it with the other ingredients.

——— Cider Cup Punch ———

(serves 2–3)

1 pt chilled apple cider
2 oz (4 tbsp) brandy
2 oz (4 tbsp) Cointreau or Triple Sec
6 oz chilled club soda

4 tsp sugar
sliced fresh fruit
mint sprigs

Mix first 5 ingredients in a pitcher with ice cubes or a chunk of ice. Garnish with fruit and mint. Serve in chilled punch cups or wineglasses.

Claret Cup: Substitute claret for cider.

———— Cinderella ————

1½ oz (3 tbsp) white rum
½ oz (1 tbsp) port wine
2 tsp fresh lemon juice
1 tsp sugar syrup

Place all ingredients in shaker with several ice cubes. Cover and shake vigorously. Strain into chilled wineglass or hollow-stemmed champagne glass.

———— Claret Cobbler ————

"Claret" is an old term for red Bordeaux wine; you can use any cabernet sauvignon or similar red wine for this recipe.

1 tsp sugar
1 tsp lemon juice (optional)
2 oz (4 tbsp) chilled club soda
4 oz (8 tbsp) chilled red wine
sliced fresh fruit in season

Dissolve sugar in soda and lemon juice in a large chilled wineglass. Add red wine and cracked ice. Garnish with fruit.

——— Claret Cup ———

See *Cider Cup Punch.*

——— Claret Lemonade I ———

$^1/_2$ oz (1 tbsp) lemon juice ($^1/_2$ lemon)
1 tsp sugar
1 cup red wine
1 thin slice of lemon

Put lemon juice and sugar in a highball glass. Stir to dissolve sugar. Fill glass halfway with cracked ice and add red wine. Stir briefly and garnish with lemon slice. Serve with a straw.

——— Claret Lemonade II ———

1 oz (2 tbsp) fresh lemon juice
2 tsp sugar syrup
2 oz (4 tbsp) red wine
club soda
thin slice lemon

Put juice and syrup into a collins glass and stir to combine. Fill glass with crushed ice and pour in soda to three-quarters full. Float wine and lemon slice atop that. Serve with long straw.

——— Claret Punch ———

See *Champagne Punch.*

——— Claridge Cocktail ———

1 oz (2 tbsp) gin
1 oz (2 tbsp) dry vermouth

½ oz (1 tbsp) Cointreau or Triple Sec
½ oz (1 tbsp) apricot brandy

Shake or stir ingredients with ice and strain into a chilled cocktail glass.

─────── **Classic Cocktail** ───────

2 oz (4 tbsp) brandy
½ oz (1 tbsp) orange curaçao
½ oz (1 tbsp) maraschino liqueur
½ oz (1 tbsp) lemon juice
twist of lemon peel

Shake liquid ingredients with ice and strain into a chilled cocktail glass. Garnish with lemon peel.

Variation: Sugar-rim the glass by rubbing with lemon and dipping into sugar.

─────── **Clover Club Cocktail** ───────

1½ oz (3 tbsp) gin
juice of ½ lime or lemon
2 tsp grenadine
sprig of fresh mint

Shake liquid ingredients with ice and strain into a chilled cocktail glass or wineglass. Garnish with mint.

─────── **Clover Leaf** ───────

2 oz (4 tbsp) gin
juice of 1 lime
1 or 2 tsp grenadine
mint sprig (optional)

(continued)

Shake first 3 ingredients vigorously with cracked ice and strain into chilled cocktail glass. Garnish, if desired, with mint sprig.

Cobbler

A tall drink made with liquor or wine, fruit juice or soda, and a large quantity of crushed ice and usually garnished with fresh fruit. For a list of cobber drinks, see *Cobbler* in **Index by Type of Drink.**

Coconut Tequila

1½ oz (3 tbsp) tequila
2 tsp cream of coconut
2 tsp lemon juice
1 tsp maraschino liqueur
½ cup crushed ice

Put ingredients in a blender and blend at low speed for 15 or 20 seconds. Pour into a chilled champagne glass.

Coffee Cocktail

2½ oz medium-dry sherry
1½ oz (3 tbsp) brandy
1 tsp sugar
nutmeg

Shake first 3 ingredients vigorously with ice and strain into a chilled wineglass. Sprinkle with nutmeg.

Variation: Substitute 1½ oz (3 tbsp) port for the sherry.

——— Coffee Flip ———

1½ oz (3 tbsp) brandy
1½ oz (3 tbsp) port
1 tsp sugar
2 tsp cream
½ tsp instant coffee
nutmeg

Shake ingredients, except nutmeg, vigorously with ice and strain into a chilled wineglass. Sprinkle with nutmeg.

Variation: Substitute 1½ oz (3 tbsp) coffee-flavored brandy for the brandy and instant coffee.

——— Coffee Grasshopper ———

See *Grasshopper Cocktail.*

——— Cognac Coupling ———

2 oz (4 tbsp) cognac
1 oz (2 tbsp) tawny port
½ oz (1 tbsp) Pernod
1 tsp lemon juice
2 dashes Peychaud's bitters (optional)

Shake ingredients with ice and strain into a chilled old-fashioned glass over ice cubes.

——— Cold Duck ———

(serves 15–18)

2 bottles German white wine
1 bottle champagne
1½ oz (3 tbsp) lemon juice

(continued)

¼–⅓ cup sugar
1 lemon thinly sliced

Mix sugar with lemon juice and pour over block of ice in large punch bowl. Add wine and champagne and stir gently. Float lemon slices.

Colleen

1½ oz (3 tbsp) Irish whiskey
1 oz (2 tbsp) Irish Mist
½ oz (1 tbsp) Cointreau
1 tsp fresh lemon juice

Place all ingredients in shaker with 4 or 5 ice cubes. Cover and shake briskly. Strain into chilled cocktail glass.

Collins

A tall drink in which any liquor can be used along with lemon or lime juice and sugar. It is topped with club soda. For a list of collins drinks, see *Collins* in **Index by Type of Drink.**

Colonial Cocktail

1½ oz (3 tbsp) gin
¾ oz (1½ tbsp) grapefruit juice
2–3 dashes maraschino liqueur
green olive

Shake liquid ingredients with ice and strain into a chilled cocktail glass. Garnish with the olive.

———— **Columbia Cocktail** ————

1½ oz (3 tbsp) light rum
¾ oz (1½ tbsp) raspberry syrup
½ oz (1 tbsp) lemon juice

Sugar-rim a chilled cocktail glass by rubbing with lemon and dipping into sugar. Shake ingredients with ice and strain into the glass.

Variation: Add 1 tsp kirschwasser.

———— **Combo** ————

2½ oz (5 tbsp) dry vermouth
1 tsp brandy
½ tsp curaçao
½ tsp sugar
1 dash Angostura bitters

Shake ingredients with ice and strain into a chilled old-fashioned glass over ice cubes.

———— **Commodore Cocktail** ————

2 oz (4 tbsp) rye whiskey
2 dashes orange bitters
1 tsp sugar
juice of ½ lime

Shake ingredients with ice and strain into a chilled cocktail glass.

Variation: Substitute juice of ¼ lemon for the lime juice.

Commuter Cocktail

1½ oz (3 tbsp) bourbon
½ oz (1 tbsp) sweet vermouth
½ oz (1 tbsp) grenadine

Shake all ingredients with cracked ice and strain into a chilled cocktail glass.

Cooler

A tall drink made with a large quantity of crushed ice or ice cubes. Various liquors or wine can be used, along with a flavoring, and it is usually topped with a carbonated beverage. A cooler is generally garnished with the peel of a fruit cut in one continuous spiral. For a list of coolers, see *Coolers* in **Index by Type of Drink.**

Cooperstown Cocktail

1½ oz (3 tbsp) gin
¾ oz (1½ tbsp) dry vermouth
¾ oz (1½ tbsp) sweet vermouth
sprig of fresh mint

Shake liquid ingredients with ice and strain into a chilled cocktail glass. Garnish with mint.

Copenhagen

1½ oz (3 tbsp) gin
1 oz (2 tbsp) aquavit
1 tsp dry vermouth
green olive (optional)

Place 4 or 5 ice cubes in shaker and add liquors. Cover and shake vigorously several times. Strain into a chilled cocktail glass and add green olive, if desired.

─────── **Corkscrew** ───────

1½ oz (3 tbsp) light rum
½ oz (1 tbsp) dry vermouth
½ oz (1 tbsp) peach brandy
slice of lime

Shake liquid ingredients with ice and strain into a chilled cocktail glass. Garnish with lime.

─────── **Cornell Cocktail** ───────

1½ oz (3 tbsp) gin
1 tsp maraschino liqueur

Shake ingredients with ice and strain into a chilled cocktail glass.

Variation: Add ½ tsp lemon juice.

─────── **Coronation Cocktail** ───────

1½ oz (3 tbsp) dry sherry
1½ oz (3 tbsp) dry vermouth
2 dashes orange bitters
1 dash maraschino liqueur

Stir ingredients with ice and strain into a chilled cocktail glass.

Variation: Add 4 oz (8 tbsp) chilled white wine to above ingredients. Stir with ice and strain into a chilled highball glass. Top with chilled club soda.

——— Corpse Reviver I ———

1 oz (2 tbsp) gin
1 oz (2 tbsp) Cointreau or Triple Sec
1 oz (2 tbsp) Swedish punch
1 oz (2 tbsp) lemon juice
1 dash Pernod

Shake ingredients with ice and strain into a large chilled cocktail glass.

——— Corpse Reviver II ———

1 oz (2 tbsp) brandy or cognac
1 oz (2 tbsp) white crème de menthe
1 oz (2 tbsp) Fernet-Branca

Shake ingredients with ice and strain into a chilled cocktail glass.

Variation: Substitute peppermint schnapps for the crème de menthe.

——— Cosmopolitan ———

See *Martini.*

——— Cossack ———

1 oz (2 tbsp) cognac
1 oz (2 tbsp) vodka
1 oz (2 tbsp) lime juice
½ tsp sugar

Shake ingredients with ice and strain into a chilled cocktail glass.

─────── **Country Club Cooler** ───────

2 oz (4 tbsp) dry vermouth
½ tsp grenadine
chilled club soda
twists of lemon and orange peel

Mix grenadine with a little soda in a chilled highball glass. Add ice cubes and vermouth. Top with soda and garnish with fruit peels.

Variation: Substitute chilled ginger ale for club soda.

─────── **Cowboy Cocktail** ───────

3 oz (6 tbsp) rye whiskey
1 oz (2 tbsp) cream

Shake ingredients with ice and strain into a chilled cocktail glass.

─────── **Cranberry Colada** ───────

See *Piña Coladas.*

─────── **Cranberry Frost** ───────

4 oz (8 tbsp) cranberry juice
½ oz (1 tbsp) calvados or other apple brandy
1 tsp lime juice
1 tsp sugar syrup

Place ingredients in shaker glass with 5 or 6 ice cubes and stir. Strain into highball glass half filled with cracked ice.

———————   **Cranberry Punch**   ———————

(serves 12–16)

1 pkg (16 oz) whole cranberries
1 cup sugar
2 cups apple juice
1 cup cranberry juice
1/2 cup lemon juice (2 large lemons)
1 cup pineapple chunks and juice
1 fifth of vodka
1 qt club soda

Combine cranberries with the sugar and 2 cups of water in a large saucepan and bring to a boil. Reduce heat and simmer until berries are soft, stirring constantly. Put through strainer, mashing skins with a wooden spoon to extract the juice, and discard the skins. Combine with other ingredients (except the soda) and refrigerate for several hours or overnight. When ready to serve, pour mixture over a block of ice in a punch bowl, add soda, and stir gently.

———————   **Cranberry Wine Punch**   ———————

(serves 15)

3 cups vodka
1 cup Burgundy (or other dry red wine)
4 cups cranberry juice
orange slices
sliced strawberries

Pour all ingredients, except fruit, into a punch bowl over a large block of ice. Garnish with fruit slices and serve in chilled punch cups.

Variation: See *Brandied Cranberry Punch.*

─────── **Creamy Orange** ───────

1 oz (2 tbsp) cream sherry
1 oz (2 tbsp) orange juice
½ oz (1 tbsp) brandy
½ oz (1 tbsp) cream

Shake ingredients with ice and strain into a chilled cocktail glass.

─────── **Creamy Screwdriver** ───────

2 oz (4 tbsp) vodka
1 oz (2 tbsp) cream
1 tsp sugar
6 oz chilled orange juice
½ cup crushed ice

Put ingredients in a blender and blend at low speed 15–20 seconds. Pour into a chilled collins glass over ice cubes.

─────── **Crème de Menthe Frappé** ───────

2 oz (4 tbsp) green crème de menthe
shaved ice

Fill a cocktail, old-fashioned, or small wineglass with the ice. Add crème de menthe and serve with short straws.

Variation: Substitute white crème de menthe for the green.

─────── **Creole** ───────

1½ oz (3 tbsp) light rum
1 tsp lemon juice

(continued)

1 dash Tabasco sauce
chilled beef bouillon
salt and pepper to taste

Shake rum, lemon, and Tabasco with ice. Strain into a chilled old-fashioned glass over ice cubes. Fill with bouillon and stir. Sprinkle with salt and pepper.

—————— Creole Champagne Punch ——————

(serves 25–30)

1 ripe pineapple, peeled and cored
1 pt lemon juice (approx. 15 lemons)
1 cup sugar
$1/2$ cup Cointreau
$1/2$ cup brandy
2 bottles chilled champagne or
other sparkling wine
1 bottle dry white wine
1 liter chilled club soda
1 cup thinly sliced strawberries
block of ice

Halve pineapple. Finely chop one half, slice the other and reserve. In large crock combine chopped pineapple, lemon juice, sugar, Cointreau, and brandy. Cover and refrigerate overnight. When ready to serve, place block of ice in large punch bowl and pour in chilled mix. Add champagne and wine and stir gently. Float pineapple slices and strawberries. Just before serving pour club soda over ice. Ladle into punch cups.

Creole Mint Julep

A milder drink than the traditional bourbon julep, but decidedly refreshing.

4–6 oz water
3–6 tsp sugar, to taste
½ oz (1 tbsp) brandy or whiskey
½ oz (1 tbsp) lemon juice
zest of lemon and/or orange
6 (or more) sprigs of mint
3 or 4 ripe strawberries

Fill highball glass half full of water, add mint sprigs and 3 tsp sugar. With bar spoon, bruise mint leaves and stir till sugar dissolves. Add liquor and stir well. Add zest and fill glass with crushed ice. Decorate with another sprig or two of mint and the strawberries. Sprinkle with sugar before serving.

Crusta

2 oz (4 tbsp) brandy
½ oz (1 tbsp) lemon juice
1 tsp maraschino liqueur
1 tsp curaçao
2 dashes Angostura bitters
peel of 1 whole lemon cut in a continuous spiral

Sugar-rim a chilled wineglass by rubbing with lemon and dipping into sugar. Place the lemon peel around the rim. Shake liquid ingredients with ice and strain into the glass.

Variation: Substitute gin for the brandy.

——— **Cuban Cocktail** ———

2 oz (4 tbsp) brandy
1 oz (2 tbsp) apricot brandy
1 oz (2 tbsp) lime juice

Shake ingredients with ice and strain into a chilled
cocktail glass.

Variation: Add 1 tsp light rum.

——— **Culross** ———

1 1/2 oz (3 tbsp) light rum
1/2 oz (1 tbsp) apricot brandy
1/2 oz (1 tbsp) Lillet
1 tsp lemon juice

Shake ingredients with ice and strain into a chilled
cocktail glass or into an old-fashioned glass over ice
cubes.

——— **Cup** ———

See *Champagne Cup.*

——— **Czarina** ———

2 oz (4 tbsp) vodka
1/2 oz (1 tbsp) dry vermouth
1/2 oz (1 tbsp) apricot brandy
dash bitters

Add all ingredients to shaker with half cup of cracked
ice. Cover and shake vigorously several times. Strain
into a chilled cocktail glass.

D

─────── **Daiquiri** ───────

The daiquiri was invented around 1900 in Daiquiri, Cuba, and has become one of the most popular rum drinks in the United States. The following is the original version, but with the invention of the blender the frozen daiquiri (usually made with fresh fruit) has gained almost as much popularity. Recipes for a *Frozen Daiquiri* and a variety of variations follow below.

2 oz (4 tbsp) light rum
juice of ½ lime
1 tsp sugar

Shake ingredients vigorously with ice and strain into a chilled cocktail glass.

Variations: Add 1 tsp Cointreau or Triple Sec.

─────── **Apricot Daiquiri** ───────

2 oz (4 tbsp) light rum
1 oz (2 tbsp) apricot brandy
1 tsp Triple Sec
cherry

Shake first 3 ingredients vigorously with ice and strain into an old-fashioned glass with ice. Garnish with cherry.

─────── **Derby Daiquiri** ───────

1½ oz (3 tbsp) rum
1 oz (2 tbsp) orange juice

(continued)

½ oz (1 tbsp) lime juice
½ cup crushed ice

Blend all ingredients at medium speed for 20 seconds. Pour into a chilled wine or old-fashioned glass.

─────── **Frozen Daiquiri** ───────

2 oz (4 tbsp) light rum
2 oz (4 tbsp) lime juice
1 tsp Cointreau or Triple Sec
¾ cup crushed ice

Put all ingredients in blender and blend at medium speed for 20 seconds. Pour into a chilled wine or old-fashioned glass.

─────── **Frozen Banana Daiquiri** ───────

1½ oz (3 tbsp) rum
1½ oz (3 tbsp) lime juice
½ oz (1 tbsp) Cointreau or Triple Sec
1 cup crushed ice
1 medium ripe banana

Blend all ingredients at medium speed for 15 seconds and serve in a chilled wine or old-fashioned glass.

─────── **Frozen Kiwi Daiquiri** ───────

2 oz (4 tbsp) white rum
2 oz (4 tbsp) water
1 oz (2 tbsp) Galliano
½ kiwi fruit, peeled
½ oz (1 tbsp) sugar
1 tsp lemon juice
½ cup crushed ice
slice of kiwi

Blend first 7 ingredients at high speed for 20–30 seconds. Pour into a chilled wine or old-fashioned glass and garnish with a kiwi slice.

——— Frozen Mint Daiquiri ———

2 oz (4 tbsp) rum
$1/2$ oz (1 tbsp) Rose's lime juice
6 mint leaves, crushed
$1/2$ cup crushed ice

Blend all ingredients at medium speed for 15–20 seconds. Pour into a chilled wine or old-fashioned glass.

——— Frozen Peach Daiquiri ———

$1^1/2$ oz (3 tbsp) rum
$1/2$ fresh peach, peeled or $1/2$ canned peach
$1^1/2$ tsp sugar (if using fresh peach)
$1/2$ cup crushed ice

Blend all ingredients at medium speed for 15 seconds. Pour into a chilled wine or old-fashioned glass.

——— Frozen Pineapple Daiquiri ———

$1^1/2$ oz (3 tbsp) rum
1 tsp Rose's lime juice
4 chunks very ripe fresh or canned pineapple
$1/2$ cup crushed ice

Blend all ingredients at medium speed for 20 seconds. Pour into a chilled wine or old-fashioned glass.

Frozen Raspberry Daiquiri

1½ oz (3 tbsp) rum
2 tsp Rose's lime juice
¾ cup fresh or frozen raspberries
½ cup crushed ice

Blend all ingredients at medium speed for 20 seconds. Pour into a chilled wine or old-fashioned glass.

Frozen Strawberry Daiquiri

1 oz (2 tbsp) rum
½ oz (1 tbsp) strawberry liqueur
¼ cup strawberries
1 oz (2 tbsp) Rose's lime juice
⅓ cup crushed ice

Blend all ingredients at medium speed for 20 seconds. Pour into a chilled wine or old-fashioned glass.

Frozen Watermelon Daiquiri

1½ oz (3 tbsp) rum
½ oz (1 tbsp) Rose's lime juice
½ cup seeded watermelon pieces
1 tsp Cointreau or Triple Sec
⅓ cup crushed ice

Blend all ingredients at medium speed for 20 seconds. Pour into a chilled wine or old-fashioned glass.

Grapefruit Daiquiri

2 oz (4 tbsp) light rum
1 oz (2 tbsp) grapefruit juice
1 tsp sugar

Shake ingredients vigorously with ice and strain into
an old-fashioned glass with ice.

DAISY

A daisy is served over ice cubes and is made with a
liquor, raspberry syrup (or grenadine), and fruit juice.
For a list of daisy drinks, see *Daisy* in **Index by Type
of Drink.**

Danish Gin Fizz

1½ oz (3 tbsp) gin
½ oz (1 tbsp) Peter Heering
1 tsp kirschwasser
½ oz (1 tbsp) lime juice
1 tsp sugar
chilled club soda
slice of lime
maraschino cherry

Shake first 5 ingredients vigorously with ice. Strain
into a chilled highball glass over ice cubes. Top with
soda and garnish with cherry and lime.

Dark & Stormy

2 oz (4 tbsp) rum
4 oz (8 tbsp) ginger beer

Put 2 or 3 ice cubes in a chilled highball glass or copper mug. Add rum, fill with ginger beer, and stir.

Deauville Cocktail

¾ oz (1½ tbsp) brandy
½ oz (1 tbsp) apple brandy
½ oz (1 tbsp) Triple Sec
½ oz (1 tbsp) lemon juice

Shake ingredients with ice and strain into a chilled cocktail glass.

Delmonico

1½ oz (3 tbsp) gin
½ oz (1 tbsp) dry vermouth
½ oz (1 tbsp) sweet vermouth
½ oz (1 tbsp) brandy
dash bitters
zest of lemon

In shaker with 5 or 6 ice cubes place liquors and bitters. Cover and shake vigorously several times. Strain into a chilled cocktail glass. Twist lemon zest over the drink to release oils and drop into drink.

Delta Blues

1½ oz (3 tbsp) blended whiskey
½ oz (1 tbsp) Southern Comfort
1 tsp lime juice
1 tsp sugar syrup
orange slice and peach slice

In shaker add liquid ingredients with several ice cubes. Cover and shake vigorously, then strain into an old-fashioned glass half filled with crushed ice. Garnish with peach slice and orange slice.

——— **Dempsey Cocktail** ———

1 oz (2 tbsp) gin
1 oz (2 tbsp) calvados or apple brandy
1/2 tsp Pernod
2 dashes grenadine

Stir ingredients with ice and strain into a chilled cocktail glass.

——— **Depth Bomb I** ———

1 1/2 oz (3 tbsp) brandy
1 1/2 oz (3 tbsp) apple brandy
2 dashes lemon juice
1 dash grenadine

Shake ingredients with ice and strain into a chilled old-fashioned glass over ice cubes. Also called a Depth Charge.

——— **Depth Bomb II** ———

This drink was a special favorite of servicemen during World War II.

1 shot glass of whiskey
1 glass of beer

Serve ingredients separately. Carefully drop the glass of whiskey into the glass of beer, and the drink is ready.

——— **Derby Cocktail** ———

1 1/2 oz (3 tbsp) bourbon
1/2 oz (1 tbsp) B & B
1/2 oz (1 tbsp) pineapple juice

(continued)

Place ingredients in shaker with ½ cup cracked ice. Cover and shake briefly. Strain into chilled cocktail glass.

─────── **Derby Daiquiri** ───────

See *Daiquiri.*

─────── **Derby Fizz** ───────

1½ oz (3 tbsp) rye whiskey
juice of ½ lemon
1 tsp sugar
3 dashes curaçao
chilled club soda

Shake ingredients, except soda, with ice. Strain into a chilled highball glass over ice cubes and top with soda.

Variation: Substitute Scotch for rye and Cointreau or Triple Sec for curaçao.

─────── **Derby Special** ───────

2 oz (4 tbsp) white or golden rum
½ oz (1 tbsp) Cointreau
2 tsp lime juice
1 oz (2 tbsp) orange juice

Place ingredients in blender with ½ cup cracked ice and blend at high speed 10–15 seconds. Pour into a chilled wineglass.

─────── **Desert Rose** ───────

See *Tequila Solo.*

——— **Devil's Cocktail** ———

1½ oz (3 tbsp) port
1½ oz (3 tbsp) dry vermouth
½ tsp lemon juice

Stir ingredients with ice and strain into a chilled cocktail glass.

——— **Devil's Tail** ———

1½ oz (3 tbsp) light rum
1 oz (2 tbsp) vodka
¼ oz apricot brandy
½ oz (1 tbsp) lime juice
2–3 dashes grenadine
½ cup crushed ice
twist of lemon peel

Put first 6 ingredients in a blender and blend at low speed for 15 seconds. Pour into a chilled wine or champagne glass and garnish with lemon peel.

——— **Diablo** ———

1½ oz (3 tbsp) dry white port
1 oz (2 tbsp) dry vermouth
¼ tsp lemon juice
twist of lemon peel (optional)

Shake liquid ingredients with ice and strain into a chilled cocktail glass. Garnish with lemon peel.

Variation: Substitute sweet vermouth for dry.

——— **Diana Cocktail** ———

2 oz (4 tbsp) white crème de menthe
3 tsp brandy

(continued)

Fill a cocktail glass or small wineglass with crushed ice and pour in crème de menthe. Float brandy on top.

Variation: Substitute peppermint schnapps for the crème de menthe.

——————— **Diplomat Cocktail** ———————

2 oz (4 tbsp) dry vermouth
1 oz (2 tbsp) sweet vermouth
2 dashes maraschino liqueur
1 dash Angostura bitters (optional)
twist of lemon peel
maraschino cherry

Stir liquid ingredients with ice and strain into a chilled cocktail glass. Garnish with lemon peel and cherry.

——————— **Dirty Martini** ———————

See *Martini.*

——————— **Dixie Cocktail** ———————

1 oz (2 tbsp) gin
1/2 oz (1 tbsp) dry vermouth
1/2 oz (1 tbsp) Pernod
juice of 1/4 orange
2 dashes grenadine (optional)

Shake ingredients with ice and strain into a chilled cocktail glass.

———— Dolores Cocktail ————

Said to have been created in tribute to the beautiful Mexican actress Dolores Del Rio.

¾ oz (1½ tbsp) Spanish brandy
¾ oz (1½ tbsp) cherry brandy
¾ oz (1½ tbsp) white or dark crème de cacao
maraschino cherry (optional)

Shake ingredients with ice and strain into a chilled cocktail glass. Garnish with the cherry if desired.

———— Dream Cocktail ————

1½ oz (3 tbsp) brandy
¾ oz Cointreau or Triple Sec
1 dash Pernod

Shake ingredients with ice and strain into a chilled cocktail glass.

Variation: Substitute curaçao for the Cointreau.

———— Dubarry Cocktail ————

1½ oz (3 tbsp) gin
¾ oz (1½ tbsp) dry vermouth
½ tsp Pernod
1 dash Angostura bitters
thin slice of orange

Stir liquid ingredients with ice and strain into a chilled cocktail glass. Garnish with orange slice.

—————— **Dubonnet Cocktail** ——————

2 oz (4 tbsp) red Dubonnet
1 oz (2 tbsp) gin
twist of lemon peel

Stir liquid ingredients with ice and strain into a chilled cocktail glass. Garnish with lemon peel.

Variation: Add a fresh dash of orange bitters, omit the lemon twist, and rub the rim of the glass with an orange peel (do not add the orange peel to the drink).

—————— **Dubonnet Fizz** ——————

2 oz (4 tbsp) red Dubonnet
1 oz (2 tbsp) cherry brandy
1 oz (2 tbsp) orange juice
1/2 oz (1 tbsp) lemon juice
1 tsp kirschwasser (optional)
chilled club soda
slice of lemon

Shake Dubonnet, brandy, juices, and kirschwasser with ice. Strain into a chilled highball glass and top with soda. Garnish with lemon slice.

—————— **Dubonnet Martini** ——————

See *Martini.*

—————— **Duchess** ——————

1 oz (2 tbsp) Pernod
1 oz (2 tbsp) dry vermouth
1 oz (2 tbsp) sweet vermouth

Shake ingredients with ice and strain into a chilled cocktail glass.

———— **Duke Cocktail** ————

½ oz (1 tbsp) Cointreau
2 tsp lemon juice
1 tsp orange juice
½ tsp white maraschino liqueur
cold champagne

Shake first 4 ingredients vigorously with several ice cubes. Strain into chilled Burgundy wineglass and top with champagne.

E

———— **Earthquake** ————

1 oz (2 tbsp) rye or bourbon
1 oz (2 tbsp) gin
1 oz (2 tbsp) Pernod

Shake ingredients with ice and strain into a chilled cocktail glass.

———— **Edwardian** ————

1½ oz (3 tbsp) vodka
1½ oz (3 tbsp) Dubonnet
1 tsp fresh lime juice
1 tsp grenadine

Place ingredients in shaker with ice cubes, cover, and shake briskly. Strain into chilled cocktail glass.

——— **Eggnog I** ———

(serves 1)

2 oz (4 tbsp) rye whiskey
1 whole egg
1 tsp sugar
4 oz (8 tbsp) chilled milk
nutmeg

Shake first 4 ingredients with ice and strain into a chilled collins glass or large wineglass. Sprinkle with nutmeg.

Variation: Add 1½ oz (3 tbsp) Jamaican rum.

Baltimore Eggnog: Substitute 1 oz (2 tbsp) brandy or cognac and 1 oz (2 tbsp) Jamaican rum for the whiskey and add 1 oz (2 tbsp) Madeira wine and 2 oz (4 tbsp) heavy cream.

Brandy Eggnog: Substitute brandy for whiskey.

Breakfast Eggnog: Substitute 2 oz (4 tbsp) brandy or apricot brandy for the whiskey and ½ oz (1 tbsp) Cointreau or Triple Sec for the sugar.

Hot Eggnog: Substitute 1 oz (2 tbsp) rum and 1 oz (2 tbsp) brandy for the whiskey and 6–8 oz hot milk for the chilled milk. Mix egg and sugar in a heated mug, add rum, brandy, and milk, stirring constantly. Sprinkle with nutmeg.

——— **Eggnog II** ———

(serves 12)

10 whole eggs (separated)
⅓ cup sugar
1 qt chilled heavy cream
1 pt chilled milk

1 fifth rye or bourbon whiskey
2 oz (4 tbsp) Jamaican rum (optional)
nutmeg

Beat egg whites with all but 1 oz (2 tbsp) of the sugar until thick and foamy. In a separate bowl beat egg yolks. Add egg white mixture to this and beat together until thoroughly combined. Put heavy cream (with 1 oz [2 tbsp] sugar) in a punch bowl and beat until cream doubles in volume. While continuing to beat, slowly add egg mixture. When thoroughly combined continue beating while adding whiskey, rum (is desired), and milk. Sprinkle with nutmeg and chill for 2–3 hours (overnight is fine). Eggnog will thicken as it chills.

———— Egg Toddy ————

A hot drink, similar to eggnog.

2 egg yolks
½ oz (1 tbsp) brown sugar
½ cup hot milk
½ oz (1 tbsp) golden or dark rum
nutmeg (optional)

Whisk egg yolks with sugar till creamy. Gradually whisk in hot milk, then the rum. Pour into a warmed mug and, if desired, sprinkle top with a few gratings of nutmeg.

———— El Diablo ————

1½ oz (3 tbsp) tequila
½ oz (1 tbsp) crème de cassis
juice and rind of ½ lime
chilled ginger ale

(continued)

Put lime juice and rind into a chilled collins glass over ice cubes. Add tequila and crème de cassis. Fill with ginger ale and stir gently.

See also *Diablo.*

──────── El Presidente ────────

3 oz (6 tbsp) light rum
½ oz (1 tbsp) dry vermouth
1 dash Angostura bitters

Stir ingredients with ice and strain into a chilled cocktail glass.

Variation: Substitute sweet vermouth or the juice of 1 lime for the dry vermouth. Add ½ oz (1 tbsp) curaçao. Add a dash of grenadine.

──────── Elk (Elk's Own) Cocktail ────────

1½ oz (3 tbsp) rye whiskey
¾ oz (1½ tbsp) port
1 tsp sugar
juice of ¼ lemon
small wedge of fresh pineapple

Shake first 4 ingredients vigorously with ice and strain into a chilled cocktail glass. Garnish with pineapple.

──────── Embassy Royal ────────

1 oz (2 tbsp) bourbon
1 oz (2 tbsp) Drambuie
½ oz (1 tbsp) sweet vermouth
2 dashes orange juice
twist of orange peel

Shake liquid ingredients with ice and strain into a chilled cocktail glass. Garnish with orange peel.

Emerald Isle Cocktail

2½ oz (5 tbsp) gin
1 tsp green crème de menthe
3 dashes Angostura bitters
green cherry (optional)

Stir liquid ingredients with ice and strain into a chilled cocktail glass. Garnish with the cherry.

English Bolo

4 oz (8 tbsp) dry sherry
1 tsp sugar
1½ oz (3 tbsp) lemon juice
1 stick cinnamon

Muddle the cinnamon, sugar, and lemon juice in an old-fashioned glass. Add sherry and stir.

See also *Bolo.*

English Rose

1½ oz (3 tbsp) gin
½ oz (1 tbsp) dry vermouth
½ oz (1 tbsp) apricot brandy
1 tsp lemon juice
1 tsp grenadine
maraschino cherry (optional)

Combine all ingredients in shaker with ½ cup cracked ice. Cover and shake vigorously several times. Strain into chilled cocktail glass and garnish, if desired.

Everybody's Irish Cocktail

2 oz (4 tbsp) Irish whiskey
1 tsp green Chartreuse
3 dashes green crème de menthe
green olive

Stir liquid ingredients with ice and strain into a chilled cocktail glass. Garnish with the olive.

Executive Suite

2 oz (4 tbsp) brandy
1 oz (2 tbsp) Grand Marnier
1–2 dashes orange bitters
cold champagne

To chilled hollow-stemmed champagne glass add ingredients in order given. Stir gently.

Eye-Opener Cocktail

1½ oz (3 tbsp) light rum
1 tsp white crème de cacao
1 tsp orange curaçao
1 tsp Pernod
1 egg yolk
½ tsp sugar

Shake ingredients vigorously with ice and strain into a chilled cocktail glass.

F

--------- **Fair-and-Warmer Cocktail** ---------

2 oz (4 tbsp) light rum
1 oz (2 tbsp) sweet vermouth
3 dashes curaçao
twist of lemon peel (optional)

Stir liquid ingredients with ice and strain into a chilled cocktail glass. Garnish with lemon peel if desired.

--------- **Fallen Angel Cocktail** ---------

1 1/2 oz (3 tbsp) gin
1/2 oz (1 tbsp) white crème de menthe
1/2 oz (1 tbsp) lemon juice
1 dash Angostura bitters
maraschino cherry (optional)

Shake liquid ingredients with ice and strain into a chilled cocktail glass. Garnish with the cherry if desired.

Variation: Substitute lime juice for lemon.

--------- **Fandango** ---------

2 oz (4 tbsp) fino (dry sherry)
1 oz (2 tbsp) golden rum
1–2 dashes orange bitters

Place ingredients in shaker with 5 or 6 ice cubes, cover, and shake vigorously several times. Strain into chilled cocktail glass.

——— Fantasia ———

1½ oz (3 tbsp) brandy
1 oz (2 tbsp) dry vermouth
1 tsp white crème de menthe
1 tsp maraschino liqueur
maraschino cherry (optional)

Shake first 4 ingredients together with cracked ice and strain into chilled cocktail glass. Garnish, if desired, with cherry.

——— Favorite Cocktail ———

1 oz (2 tbsp) gin
1 oz (2 tbsp) apricot brandy
½ oz (1 tbsp) dry vermouth
½ tsp fresh lemon juice

Shake all ingredients with cracked ice and strain into a chilled cocktail glass.

——— Fernet Cocktail ———

1½ oz (3 tbsp) Fernet-Branca
1½ oz (3 tbsp) brandy
1 tsp sugar
1 dash Angostura bitters (optional)
twist of lemon or orange peel

Stir liquid ingredients with ice and strain into a chilled cocktail glass. Garnish with lemon or orange peel.

——— Fifth Avenue ———

1 oz (2 tbsp) dark crème de cacao
1 oz (2 tbsp) apricot brandy
½ oz (1 tbsp) cream

Pour ingredients carefully and slowly, in the order given, into a cordial or pousse-café glass. Ingredients should be in layers.

Fifty-Fifty Cocktail

1½ oz (3 tbsp) gin
1½ oz (3 tbsp) dry vermouth
green olive

Stir liquid ingredients with ice and strain into a chilled cocktail glass. Garnish with the olive.

Fine-and-Dandy Cocktail

1½ oz (3 tbsp) gin
¾ oz (1½ tbsp) Cointreau or Triple Sec
½ oz (1 tbsp) lemon juice
1 dash Angostura bitters
maraschino cherry

Stir liquid ingredients with ice and strain into a chilled cocktail glass. Garnish with the cherry.

Fino Martini

See *Martini.*

Firemen's Sour

2 oz (4 tbsp) rum
juice of 1 lime
½ tsp sugar
½ oz (1 tbsp) grenadine
slice of lemon
maraschino cherry

(continued)

Shake liquid ingredients with ice and strain into a chilled cocktail glass. Garnish with lemon and cherry.

——————— **Fish House Punch** ———————

(serves 18–24)

1½ cups sugar
3 cups lemon juice (12 large lemons)
2 qts Jamaican rum
6 cups chilled water
6 oz peach brandy
1 qt brandy
1 cup sliced peaches (optional)

Dissolve sugar in lemon juice in a large punch bowl. Add rum, water, and brandies and stir. Allow to stand at room temperature for several hours, stirring occasionally. Before serving, add block of ice and peaches.

Variation: Substitute light rum for Jamaican rum for a less "heavy" punch.

FIX

A tall drink similar to a cobbler, in which sugar, water, and lemon juice are added to a liquor. For a list of fix drinks, see *Fix* in **Index by Type Drink.**

FIZZ

A tall drink in which a liquor, fruit juice, and sugar are shaken together and strained into a glass over ice cubes. It is topped with club soda. For a list of fizz drinks, see *Fizz* in **Index by Type Drink.**

—————   **Flamingo Cocktail**   —————

1½ oz (3 tbsp) gin
½ oz (1 tbsp) apricot brandy
½ oz (1 tbsp) lime juice
1 tsp grenadine

Shake ingredients with ice and strain into a chilled cocktail glass.

FLIP

Similar to eggnog, a flip is a combination of liquor, egg, and sugar shaken vigorously with ice and strained into a stemmed glass. Heavy cream can be substituted for the egg. For a list of flip drinks, see *Flip* in **Index by Type Drink.**

—————   **Florida**   —————

½ oz (1 tbsp) gin
1½ tsp kirschwasser
1½ tsp Cointreau or Triple Sec
1½ oz (3 tbsp) orange juice
1 tsp lemon juice

Shake ingredients with ice and strain into a chilled cocktail glass or into an old-fashioned glass over ice cubes.

——————   **Florida Special**   ——————

1½ oz (3 tbsp) light rum
1 tsp dry vermouth
1 tsp sweet vermouth
1 oz (2 tbsp) grapefruit juice

Stir ingredients with ice and strain into a chilled cocktail glass.

——————   **Flying Dutchman**   ——————

3 oz (6 tbsp) gin
1 dash Triple Sec or curaçao
1 dash orange bitters (optional)

Stir ingredients with ice and strain into a chilled cocktail glass.

——————   **Flying Grasshopper Cocktail**   ——————

1 oz (2 tbsp) vodka
¾ oz (1½ tbsp) green crème de menthe
¾ oz (1½ tbsp) white crème de menthe

Stir ingredients with ice and strain into a chilled cocktail glass.

——————   **Flying Scotchman Cocktail**   ——————

1½ oz (3 tbsp) Scotch
1½ oz (3 tbsp) sweet vermouth
¼ tsp sugar syrup
1 dash Angostura bitters

Stir ingredients with ice and strain into a chilled cocktail glass.

Fog Cutter

1½ oz (3 tbsp) light rum
⅔ oz (1⅓ tbsp) brandy
½ oz (1 tbsp) gin
⅔ oz (1⅓ tbsp) orange juice
1 oz (2 tbsp) lemon juice
1 tsp orgeat syrup
1 tsp sweet sherry

Shake all ingredients, except sherry, with ice and strain into a chilled collins glass over ice cubes. Float sherry on top.

Fog Horn

2 oz (4 tbsp) gin
juice of 1 lime
chilled ginger ale

In chilled highball glass with 4 or 5 ice cubes squeeze lime juice and add the squeezed halves. Pour in gin and top with chilled ginger ale. Stir before serving.

Fort Lauderdale

1½ oz (3 tbsp) light rum
¾ oz (1½ tbsp) sweet vermouth
juice of ¼ lime
juice of ¼ orange
slice of orange
maraschino cherry (optional)

Shake liquid ingredients with ice and strain into a chilled old-fashioned glass over ice cubes. Garnish with orange and cherry.

——— **Foxhound** ———

1½ oz (3 tbsp) brandy
¾ oz cranberry juice
1 tsp kümmel
1 dash lemon juice
slice of lemon

Shake liquid ingredients with ice and strain into a chilled old-fashioned glass over ice cubes. Garnish with lemon slice.

——— **Fox River Cocktail** ———

2 oz (4 tbsp) rye whiskey
½ oz (1 tbsp) crème de cacao
3–4 dashes Angostura bitters
twist of lemon peel

Stir liquid ingredients with ice and strain into a chilled cocktail glass. Garnish with lemon peel.

Variation: Substitute peach bitters for Angostura.

——— **Fraise Fizz** ———

1½ oz (3 tbsp) gin
1 oz (2 tbsp) strawberry liqueur
½ oz (1 tbsp) lemon juice
1 tsp sugar
chilled club soda
twist of lemon peel
1 fresh strawberry

Shake gin, liqueur, lemon juice, and sugar with ice. Strain into a chilled highball glass (with or without ice cubes) and top with soda. Stir and garnish with lemon peel and strawberry.

FRAPPÉ

A short drink in which a liquor is poured into an old-fashioned glass over shaved or crushed ice. It is served with a short straw. For examples, see *All White Frappé* and *Crème de Menthe Frappé*.

——— **French Connection** ———

2 oz (4 tbsp) brandy
1 oz (2 tbsp) amaretto

Pour ingredients into an old-fashioned or sour glass half-filled with cracked ice. Serve with small straw.

——— **French Manhattan** ———

See *Manhattan*.

——— **French Rose** ———

3 oz (6 tbsp) rosé wine
1/2 oz (1 tbsp) cherry brandy
1/2 oz (1 tbsp) cherry liqueur

Put ingredients in shaker with cracked ice. Cover and shake quickly 2 or 3 times. Strain into chilled champagne glass.

——— **French "75"** ———

1 oz (2 tbsp) lemon juice
1 tsp sugar
1 oz (2 tbsp) gin or cognac
3 oz (6 tbsp) chilled champagne

(continued)

Stir lemon and sugar together in a tall chilled glass, add 3–4 cubes of ice, gin or cognac, and champagne.

Variation: Mix lemon, sugar, gin, and champagne with 1 egg white, ½ oz (1 tbsp) heavy cream, and ice. Shake vigorously and strain into a large chilled champagne or wineglass. Add twist of lemon peel and/or a cherry as garnish.

——— Frisco Sour ———

2½ oz (5 tbsp) rye whiskey
¾ oz (1½ tbsp) Benedictine
¼ oz (½ tbsp) lemon juice
¼ oz (½ tbsp) lime juice
slice of lime and lemon

Shake liquid ingredients with ice and strain into a chilled cocktail or sour glass. Garnish with lemon and lime.

——— Frobisher ———

1½ oz (3 tbsp) gin
2 or 3 dashes bitters
cold champagne
zest of lemon (optional)

In highball glass with 6 or 8 ice cubes add gin and bitters. Top very slowly with champagne. Garnish with lemon zest, if desired.

——— Froupe Cocktail ———

1½ oz (3 tbsp) brandy
1½ oz (3 tbsp) sweet vermouth
1 tsp Benedictine

Stir ingredients with ice and strain into a chilled cock-tail glass.

--------   **Frozen Apple**   --------

(serves 2)

3 oz (6 tbsp) applejack
1 oz (2 tbsp) lime juice
2 tsp sugar
1 cup crushed ice

Put ingredients into a blender and blend at low speed for 15 seconds. Pour into chilled old-fashioned or champagne glasses.

--------   **Frozen Brandy & Rum**   --------

1½ oz (3 tbsp) brandy
1 oz (2 tbsp) light rum
½ oz (1 tbsp) lemon juice
1 tsp sugar
½ cup crushed ice

Put ingredients into a blender and blend at low speed for 15 seconds. Pour into a chilled old-fashioned or champagne glass.

--------   **Frozen Citron**   --------

See *Vodka.*

--------   **Frozen Daiquiri**   --------

See *Daiquiri.*

————— **Fruitini** —————

See *Martini.*

————— **Fuzzy Navel** —————

1½ oz (3 tbsp) peach schnapps
orange juice, to taste

Pour schnapps into an ice-filled collins glass. Fill with orange juice and stir to combine.

G

————— **Gauguin** —————

2 oz (4 tbsp) light rum
½ oz (1 tbsp) passionfruit syrup
½ oz (1 tbsp) lemon juice
½ oz (1 tbsp) lime juice
½ cup crushed ice
maraschino cherry

Put first 5 ingredients in a blender and blend at low speed for 15 seconds. Pour into a chilled old-fashioned or champagne glass. Garnish with the cherry.

————— **Gazebo** —————

A delicious drink named for the summertime retreat.

1½ oz (3 tbsp) gin
½ oz (1 tbsp) Cointreau
½ oz (1 tbsp) blue curaçao
dash or two of bitters

zest of lemon and maraschino cherry (optional)

In shaker combine liquors and bitters with 4 or 5 ice cubes. Cover and shake vigorously several times. Strain into a cocktail glass filled with crushed ice. Add zest and cherry if desired.

--------- **Genoa** ---------

³/₄ oz (1½ tbsp) gin
³/₄ oz (1½ tbsp) grappa
2 tsp Sambuca
2 tsp dry vermouth
green olive

Stir liquid ingredients with ice and strain into a chilled cocktail glass or into an old-fashioned glass over ice cubes. Garnish with the olive.

Variation: Eliminate the gin and increase the grappa to 1½ oz (3 tbsp).

--------- **Georgia Peach** ---------

1½ oz (3 tbsp) vodka
½ oz (1 tbsp) peach schnapps
1 dash grenadine
lemonade

Pour first three ingredients into a collins glass filled with ice. Fill with lemonade; cover and shake to mix.

--------- **Gibson** ---------

See *Martini.*

———— **Gilroy Cocktail** ————

1 oz (2 tbsp) gin
1 oz (2 tbsp) cherry brandy
½ oz (1 tbsp) dry vermouth
2 tsp lemon juice
1–2 dashes bitters

Shake together with cracked ice and strain into a chilled cocktail glass.

———— **Gimlet** ————

2 oz (4 tbsp) gin
1 oz (2 tbsp) Rose's lime juice
1 slice lime (optional)

Shake liquid ingredients with ice and strain into a chilled cocktail glass. Garnish with lime slice.

Variation: Substitute fresh lime juice for Rose's and add ½ tsp sugar.

Vodka Gimlet: Substitute vodka for the gin.

GIN

Invented in the Netherlands in the 17th century, gin is made from distilled fermented grains, chiefly rye but also corn, barley, and oats, and is usually flavored with juniper berries. (The name *gin* is an anglicized and abbreviated form of *jenever,* one of the terms that the Dutch used for gin. The Dutch term is an altered form of the French *genièvre,* meaning juniper.) Gin does not require aging and can be drunk immediately, but some London dry gins are aged, and the aging process gives them a pale golden color. All gins are dry, but there are distinctive characteristics about the three basic types. London dry gin, made primarily in the United States, is the best known of all gins and is usually distilled from a mash composed mostly of corn. In addition to juniper berries, other botanicals are also added in varying proportions (caraway, cassis bark, angelica, licorice roots, etc.), and these flavorings account for the differences among the various brands. Genever gin is a Dutch gin with a strong malty aroma and is more heavily flavored with juniper than London dry. It is not aged, which accounts for its lack of color, and because of its strong aroma is usually drunk straight instead of being mixed in a cocktail. Plymouth gin, made solely in Plymouth, England, is somewhat sweeter than London gin, and its juniper flavor ranks midway between the other two types of gin.

--------- **Gin & Bitters** ---------

2–3 oz (6 tbsp) gin
3 dashes Angostura bitters

Put bitters into a cocktail glass and swirl the bitters to coat the inside of the glass. Shake out any excess and add the gin.

Variation: Ice is not usually used in this drink but can be added if desired. Chilled gin can be used.

--------- **Gin & It** ---------

British slang for a sweet Martini.

2 oz (4 tbsp) gin
1 oz (2 tbsp) sweet vermouth

Place ingredients in a cocktail glass and stir. No ice is used.

(continued)

Variation: Use equal parts of gin and vermouth (1½ oz [3 tbsp] each). Garnish with a maraschino cherry.

——— Gin & Sin ———

1 oz (2 tbsp) gin
1 oz (2 tbsp) orange juice
1 oz (2 tbsp) lemon juice
1 dash grenadine

Shake ingredients with ice and strain into a chilled cocktail glass.

——— Gin & Tonic ———

3 oz (6 tbsp) gin
4–6 oz cold tonic (quinine) water
slice or wedge of lemon or lime

Put 2 ice cubes in a highball glass, add gin, and fill glass with tonic water. Do not stir. Garnish with lemon or lime.

Vodka & Tonic: Substitute vodka for gin.

——— Gin Buck ———

2 oz (4 tbsp) gin
juice of ½ lemon
chilled ginger ale

Pour gin and lemon juice over ice cubes in a chilled highball glass. Top with ginger ale.

Variation: Substitute lime juice for lemon.

─────── **Gin Daisy** ───────

2 oz (4 tbsp) gin
1 oz (2 tbsp) lemon juice
$\frac{1}{2}$ tsp sugar
1 tsp raspberry syrup (or grenadine)
fresh fruit

Shake liquid ingredients with ice and strain into a chilled collins glass over ice cubes. Garnish with fresh fruit.

─────── **Gin Fizz** ───────

2 oz (4 tbsp) gin
1 tsp sugar
1 oz (2 tbsp) lemon juice
chilled club soda

Shake gin, sugar, and lemon juice with ice and strain into a chilled highball glass over ice cubes. Top with soda.

Sloe Gin Fizz: Substitute sloe gin for the gin and use only $\frac{1}{2}$ tsp sugar.

─────── **Gin Rickey** ───────

2 oz (4 tbsp) gin
juice of $\frac{1}{2}$ lime
chilled club soda
maraschino cherry

Pour gin and lime into a chilled highball glass over ice cubes. Top with soda and stir gently. Garnish with maraschino cherry.

Sloe Gin Rickey: Substitute sloe gin for the gin.

——— **Gin Sangaree** ———

See *Sangaree.*

——— **Gin Sling** ———

See *Sling.*

——— **Gin Smash** ———

See *Brandy Smash.*

——— **Gin Sour** ———

See *Whiskey Sour.*

——— **Gin Stinger** ———

See *Stinger.*

——— **Gin Swizzle** ———

See *Swizzle.*

——— **Gin Toddy, Hot** ———

See *Hot Toddy.*

——— **Glogg** ———

(serves 10)

Sometimes called the Swedish national drink, and a
special Christmas drink throughout Scandinavia.

2 qts dry red wine

1 pt sweet vermouth
15 whole cloves
2 cinnamon sticks
20 cardamom seeds (crushed)
2 oz (4 tbsp) dried orange peel
1½ cups blanched almonds
1½ cups raisins
½ lb sugar lumps
1 cup aquavit

Put all ingredients, except sugar and aquavit, in a pan and boil slowly for 20 minutes, stirring occasionally. Place a rack on top of the pan and spread the sugar lumps on it. Warm the aquavit and thoroughly saturate the sugar. Ignite and let the sugar melt into the glogg mixture. Stir again. Serve in heated mugs or punch cups with a few almonds and raisins in each. Leftover glogg can be bottled and reheated.

Gloom Chaser

¾ oz (1½ tbsp) Grand Marnier
¾ oz (1½ tbsp) curaçao
¾ oz (1½ tbsp) lemon juice
¾ oz (1½ tbsp) grenadine
twist of orange peel (optional)

Shake liquid ingredients with ice and strain into a chilled cocktail glass. Garnish with orange peel.

Gloom Lifter

(serves 2)

4 oz (8 tbsp) rye whiskey
juice of 1 lemon
1 tsp sugar

(continued)

Shake ingredients vigorously with ice and strain into chilled cocktail glasses.

Variation: Add 1 oz (2 tbsp) brandy. Add 2 tsp raspberry syrup.

Gloom Raiser

2½ oz (5 tbsp) gin
½ oz (1 tbsp) dry vermouth
2 dashes Pernod
2 dashes grenadine

Stir ingredients with ice and strain into a chilled cocktail glass.

Variation: Float Pernod on top of drink.

Godfather

2 oz (4 tbsp) Scotch
1 oz (2 tbsp) amaretto or almond liqueur

Pour ingredients into a chilled old-fashioned glass over ice cubes and stir gently.

Variation: Substitute bourbon for Scotch.

Godmother

2 oz (4 tbsp) vodka
1 oz (2 tbsp) amaretto or almond liqueur

Pour ingredients into a chilled old-fashioned glass over ice cubes and stir gently.

───────── **Golden Cadillac** ─────────

³/₄ oz (1¹/₂ tbsp) Galliano
³/₄ oz (1¹/₂ tbsp) white crème de cacao
³/₄ oz (1¹/₂ tbsp) cream
¹/₃ cup crushed ice

Put ingredients into a blender and blend at low speed for 10 seconds. Pour into a chilled cocktail or champagne glass.

───────── **Golden Dawn** ─────────

1¹/₂ oz (3 tbsp) gin
³/₄ oz (1¹/₂ tbsp) apricot brandy
³/₄ oz (1¹/₂ tbsp) orange juice

Shake ingredients with ice and strain into a chilled cocktail glass or into an old-fashioned glass over ice cubes.

Variation: Add ³/₄ oz (1¹/₂ tbsp) apple brandy.

───────── **Golden Dream** ─────────

1¹/₂ oz (3 tbsp) Galliano
³/₄ oz (1¹/₂ tbsp) Cointreau or Triple Sec
¹/₂ oz (1 tbsp) orange juice
¹/₂ oz (1 tbsp) cream

Shake ingredients with ice and strain into a chilled cocktail glass.

───────── **Golden Fizz** ─────────

2 oz (4 tbsp) gin
1 oz (2 tbsp) lemon juice
³/₄ tsp sugar
chilled club soda

(continued)

Shake first 3 ingredients with ice and strain into a chilled collins or large wineglass. Top with soda.

——— Golden Gate ———

1 oz (2 tbsp) light rum
$^{1}/_{2}$ oz (1 tbsp) gin
$^{1}/_{2}$ oz (1 tbsp) lemon juice
$^{1}/_{2}$ oz (1 tbsp) white crème de cacao
pinch of ginger
slice of orange

Shake first 5 ingredients with ice and strain into a chilled old-fashioned glass over ice cubes. Garnish with orange slice.

Variations: Use equal parts ($^{3}/_{4}$ oz each) rum and gin. Substitute dark rum and dark crème de cacao for the light varieties.

——— Golden Lemonade ———

1 oz (2 tbsp) orange-flavored brandy
1 oz (2 tbsp) fresh lemon juice
2 tsp sugar syrup
club soda
orange slice
maraschino cherry

Place first 3 ingredients in shaker with 5 or 6 ice cubes. Cover and shake vigorously. Strain into chilled collins glass and top with soda. Stir and garnish with orange and cherry.

Variation: Substitute dry white wine or champagne for the soda.

——— Golden Tang ———

1½ oz (3 tbsp) vodka
¾ oz (1½ tbsp) Strega
½ oz (1 tbsp) banana liqueur
½ oz (1 tbsp) orange juice

Shake ingredients with ice and strain into a chilled cocktail glass.

——— Golf Cocktail ———

2 oz (4 tbsp) gin
1 oz (2 tbsp) dry vermouth
2 dashes Angostura bitters

Stir ingredients with ice and strain into a chilled cocktail glass.

——— Granada ———

1 oz (2 tbsp) dry sherry
1 oz (2 tbsp) brandy
½ oz (1 tbsp) orange curaçao
chilled tonic water
slice of orange

Shake sherry, brandy, and curaçao with ice and pour into a chilled highball glass. Top with tonic and garnish with orange slice.

——— Grand Marnier Cocktail ———

2 oz (4 tbsp) Grand Marnier
½ oz (1 tbsp) sweet vermouth
1–2 dash bitters
cherry for garnish

(continued)

Shake liquid ingredients with ice and pour into an old-fashioned glass. Top with cherry.

Grand Passion

2 oz (4 tbsp) gin
1 oz (2 tbsp) passionfruit juice
1 dash Angostura bitters

Shake ingredients with ice and strain into a chilled cocktail glass.

Variations: Add juice of 1/2 lemon. Substitute light rum or tequila for gin. Substitute peach bitters for Angostura.

Grand Royal Fizz

1/2 oz (1 tbsp) fresh lemon juice
1/2 oz (1 tbsp) orange juice
2 oz (4 tbsp) gin
1 tsp sugar syrup
1 tsp maraschino liqueur
1 egg white
chilled club soda

Add all ingredients but soda to shaker with 5 or 6 ice cubes. Cover and shake vigorously several times. Strain into a chilled highball glass and top with soda. Stir gently.

Variation: Substitute 1 tbsp heavy cream for egg white.

Grand Slam

1 1/2 oz (3 tbsp) Swedish punch
3/4 oz (1 1/2 tbsp) sweet vermouth
3/4 oz (1 1/2 tbsp) dry vermouth

Stir ingredients with ice and strain into a chilled cocktail glass.

Grape Crush

See **Shooters.**

Grapefruit Cocktail

2 oz (4 tbsp) gin
1 oz (2 tbsp) grapefruit juice

Shake ingredients with ice and strain into a chilled cocktail glass.

Variation: Add 1 tsp maraschino liqueur and garnish with a cherry.

Grapefruit Nog

1½ oz (3 tbsp) brandy
4 oz (8 tbsp) unsweetened grapefruit juice
1 oz (2 tbsp) lemon juice
½ oz (1 tbsp) honey
1 whole egg
½ cup crushed ice

Put ingredients in a blender and blend at low speed for 15–20 seconds. Pour into a chilled collins glass and add ice cubes.

Grappa Strega

1 oz (2 tbsp) grappa
1 oz (2 tbsp) Strega
1 tsp lemon juice

(continued)

1 tsp orange juice
twist of lemon peel

Shake liquid ingredients with ice and strain into a chilled cocktail glass. Garnish with lemon peel.

—————— **Grasshopper Cocktail** ——————

1 oz (2 tbsp) white crème de menthe
1 oz (2 tbsp) green crème de menthe
1 oz (2 tbsp) cream

Shake ingredients with ice and strain into a chilled cocktail glass.

Variations: Garnish with finely grated chocolate. Substitute white crème de cacao for white crème de menthe.

Coffee Grasshopper: Substitute 1 oz (2 tbsp) coffee brandy for the green crème de menthe.

See also *Flying Grasshopper Cocktail.*

—————— **Greek Buck** ——————

1½ oz (3 tbsp) Metaxa brandy
2 tsp lemon juice
chilled ginger ale
1 tsp ouzo
slice of lemon (optional)

Shake Metaxa and lemon juice with ice. Strain into a chilled collins glass over ice cubes. Top with ginger ale and stir gently. Float ouzo on top and garnish with lemon if desired.

Green Apple Martini

See *Martini.*

Greenbriar

2 oz (4 tbsp) dry sherry
1 oz (2 tbsp) dry vermouth
1 dash Angostura or peach bitters
sprig of fresh mint

Stir liquid ingredients with ice and strain into a chilled
cocktail glass or into an old-fashioned glass over ice
cubes. Garnish with mint.

Green Devil

1½ oz (3 tbsp) gin
2 tsp green crème de menthe
½ oz (1 tbsp) lime juice
fresh mint leaves

Shake liquid ingredients with ice and strain into an
old-fashioned glass over ice cubes. Garnish with mint.

Green Dragon Cocktail

1½ oz (3 tbsp) gin
¾ oz (1½ tbsp) kümmel
¾ oz (1½ tbsp) green crème de menthe
½ oz (1 tbsp) lemon juice
4 dashes orange or peach bitters

Shake ingredients with ice and strain into a chilled
cocktail glass.

─────── **Green Lady** ───────

1½ oz (3 tbsp) gin
½ oz (1 tbsp) yellow Chartreuse
½ oz (1 tbsp) green Chartreuse
½ oz (1 tbsp) lime juice
twist of lime peel

Shake liquid ingredients with ice and strain into a chilled cocktail glass. Garnish with lime peel.

Variation: Substitute lemon juice for lime and garnish with lemon peel.

─────── **Greyhound** ───────

2½ oz (5 tbsp) vodka
5 oz (10 tbsp) grapefruit juice

Fill highball glass with ice and pour in vodka and grapefruit; cover and shake to mix.

Variation: Substitute lemon (citron) vodka for regular vodka.

─────── **Grog** ───────

1 slice lemon
4 whole cloves
1 tsp or 1 lump sugar
½ cinnamon stick
2 oz (4 tbsp) Jamaican rum
3 oz (6 tbsp) boiling water

Stick cloves into lemon slice. Put lemon and other ingredients into heated mug or glass and stir to dissolve sugar.

See also *Navy Grog.*

Gypsy Life

2 oz (4 tbsp) vodka
1 oz (2 tbsp) Benedictine
1–2 dashes orange bitters

Shake ingredients with ice and strain into a chilled cocktail glass.

H

Hair Raiser Cocktail

1½ oz (3 tbsp) vodka
½ oz (1 tbsp) Rock & Rye
juice of ½ lemon

Shake ingredients with ice and strain into a chilled cocktail glass.

Variation: Substitute 1 oz (2 tbsp) Dubonnet for Rock & Rye.

Hairy Navel

1 oz (2 tbsp) peach schnapps
1 oz (2 tbsp) vodka
6 oz (12 tbsp) orange juice

Fill old-fashioned glass with ice, pour in ingredients; cover and shake to mix.

Happy Youth

1 oz (2 tbsp) cherry brandy
3 oz (6 tbsp) chilled orange juice

(continued)

1 tsp sugar
chilled champagne
slice of orange

Pour ingredients, except champagne and orange slice, into a highball or large stemmed glass over ice cubes. Stir gently and top with champagne. Garnish with orange slice.

─────── **Harvard Cocktail** ───────

1½ oz (3 tbsp) brandy
1½ oz (3 tbsp) sweet vermouth
2 dashes Angostura bitters
1 dash sugar syrup
twist of lemon peel (optional)

Shake liquid ingredients with ice and strain into a chilled cocktail glass. Garnish with lemon peel.

Variation: Use only ¾ oz (1½ tbsp) vermouth. Add 1–2 tsp lemon juice.

─────── **Harvard Cooler** ───────

2 oz (4 tbsp) applejack or apple brandy
1 tsp sugar
chilled club soda
twist of lemon peel

Dissolve sugar in brandy in a chilled collins glass. Add ice and top with soda. Stir gently and garnish with lemon peel.

Variation: Add juice of ½ lemon.

——— **Harvey Wallbanger** ———

Simply a screwdriver with a few dashes of Galliano, this drink has a colorful history. According to the story, a young California surfer named Harvey often consoled himself after losing a contest by consuming numerous screwdrivers laced with Galliano. As he left the bar he would bang into the walls. Hence the name Harvey Wallbanger. The story may or may not be true, but it was used successfully to promote the sale of Galliano, and the drink gained sudden popularity in the 1960s.

2 oz (4 tbsp) vodka
4 oz (8 tbsp) orange juice
1/2–1 oz (1–2 tbsp) Galliano

Pour vodka and orange juice into a chilled collins glass over ice cubes and stir. Float Galliano on top.

Variation: Shake vodka and orange juice with ice and strain into a chilled cocktail glass. Float Galliano.

——— **Hasty Cocktail** ———

1 1/2 oz (3 tbsp) gin
3/4 oz (1 1/2 tbsp) dry vermouth
1/4 tsp Pernod
3 dashes grenadine

Shake ingredients with ice and strain into a chilled cocktail glass.

——— **Havana (Beach) Cocktail** ———

1 1/2 oz (3 tbsp) light rum
1 1/2 oz (3 tbsp) pineapple juice
1/2 tsp lemon juice

(continued)

Shake ingredients with ice and strain into a chilled cocktail glass.

Variation: Eliminate the lemon juice and add 1 tsp sugar, ½ lime cut in pieces, and ½ cup crushed ice. Put ingredients in a blender and blend at medium speed for 15 seconds. Pour into a highball glass and top with chilled ginger ale. Garnish with a sliver of lime.

--------- **Hawaiian Cocktail** ---------

2 oz (4 tbsp) gin
½ oz (1 tbsp) Cointreau or Triple Sec
½ oz (1 tbsp) pineapple juice

Shake ingredients with ice and strain into a chilled cocktail glass.

Variation: Substitute orange juice for pineapple. Add 1 egg white.

--------- **Heavenly Express** ---------

1½ oz (3 tbsp) brandy
½ oz (1 tbsp) cherry brandy (kirsch)
½ oz (1 tbsp) slivovitz

Pour ingredients in the order given into an old-fashioned glass filled with cracked ice. Stir gently.

--------- **Helen of Troy** ---------

1½ oz (3 tbsp) vodka
1 oz (2 tbsp) cherry brandy
1–2 dashes orange bitters

Place ingredients in shaker with 5 or 6 ice cubes and stir briefly. Strain into a wineglass half filled with crushed ice.

Hennessy Martini

See *Martini.*

HIGHBALL

A long drink of whiskey or other liquor (approximately 2 oz) poured into a tall glass over 2 or 3 ice cubes and topped with chilled soda water, branch water, etc. For a list of highball drinks, see *Highball* in **Index by Type of Drink.**

Highland Cooler

2 oz (4 tbsp) Scotch
1 tsp sugar
2 oz (4 tbsp) chilled club soda
chilled ginger ale
twist of lemon peel

Dissolve sugar in club soda in a chilled highball glass. Add ice cubes and Scotch. Top with ginger ale and stir gently.

Variation: Add juice of ½ lemon.

Highland Fling Cocktail

2 oz (4 tbsp) Scotch
1 oz (2 tbsp) sweet vermouth

(continued)

2–3 dashes orange bitters
green olive (optional)

Shake liquid ingredients with ice and strain into a chilled cocktail glass. Add a liquid green olive, if desired.

Hole-in-One

2 oz (4 tbsp) Scotch
1 oz (2 tbsp) dry vermouth
2 dashes lemon juice
1 dash orange bitters

Shake ingredients with ice and strain into a chilled cocktail glass.

Hollywood Boulevard

2 oz (4 tbsp) orange juice
1 oz (2 tbsp) vodka
chilled white wine
sprig of mint
orange slice

To highball glass filled with cracked ice add orange juice and vodka and stir well. Top with wine and stir briefly. Garnish with mint and affix orange slice to rim of glass.

Homestead Cocktail

2 oz (4 tbsp) gin
1 oz (2 tbsp) sweet vermouth
slice of orange

Stir gin and vermouth with ice and strain into a chilled cocktail glass. Garnish with orange slice.

———— Honolulu Cocktail ————

1½ oz (3 tbsp) gin
1 dash Angostura bitters
½ tsp sugar
¼ tsp orange juice
¼ tsp lemon juice
¼ tsp pineapple juice

Shake ingredients with ice and strain into a chilled cocktail glass.

———— Hopscotch ————

1½ oz (3 tbsp) Scotch whiskey
1 oz (2 tbsp) sweet vermouth
½ tsp sugar syrup
1–2 dashes orange bitters
maraschino cherry (optional)

Shake first 4 ingredients with cracked ice and strain into a chilled cocktail glass. Add cherry, if desired.

———— Hop Toad ————

1½ oz (3 tbsp) light rum
1½ oz (3 tbsp) apricot brandy
2 tsp fresh lime juice

Shake all ingredients with cracked ice and strain into a chilled cocktail glass.

———— Horse's Neck (with a Kick) ————

2 oz (4 tbsp) rye or bourbon
peel of 1 lemon cut in a continuous spiral
chilled ginger ale

(continued)

Put lemon peel in a chilled collins glass, allowing it to curl over the edge, and add ice cubes. Pour in whiskey and top with ginger ale. Stir gently.

Variation: Substitute brandy for whiskey.

——— **Hot Brick Toddy** ———

1½ oz (3 tbsp) rye whiskey
1 tsp butter
1 tsp brown or powdered sugar
dash of cinnamon
1 oz (2 tbsp) hot water
4–6 oz boiling water

In heated whiskey glass dissolve butter, sugar, and cinnamon in hot water. Add whiskey and stir in boiling water to desired strength.

——— **Hot Buttered Rum** ———

1 lump sugar
½ cinnamon stick
2 cloves (optional)
slice of lemon
6 oz boiling water
½ oz (1 tbsp) butter
2 oz (4 tbsp) rum
nutmeg

Put sugar and spices, except nutmeg, in a heated mug and add boiling water. Add butter and rum and stir. Sprinkle with nutmeg.

Variations: Add 1 tsp maple syrup.

Hot Rum Cow: Substitute 8 oz hot milk for the boiling water.

Hot Rum Cow

See *Hot Buttered Rum.*

Hot Spiced Wine (Vin Chaud)

(serves 2)

1 pt Burgundy wine
1½–2 oz (2–3 tbsp) sugar
5 whole cloves
stick of cinnamon
2 slices of lemon
2 dashes orange curaçao

Heat ingredients almost to a boiling point, stirring occasionally. Serve in heated wineglasses or mugs.

Hot Toddy

1 lump sugar
½ stick cinnamon
slice of lemon
3 whole cloves
2 oz (4 tbsp) rye whiskey
4–6 oz boiling water
nutmeg

Dissolve sugar in boiling water in a heated mug. Add cinnamon, cloves, and rye and stir. Sprinkle with nutmeg.

Variations: Eliminate cinnamon and cloves and simply mix together the rye, water, sugar, and lemon. Sprinkle with nutmeg.

Hot Gin Toddy: Substitute gin for rye.

Hot Rum Toddy: Substitute light rum for rye.

Hudson Bay

1 oz (2 tbsp) gin
1/2 oz (1 tbsp) cherry brandy
1 tsp 151-proof rum
1/2 oz (1 tbsp) orange juice
1 tsp lime juice
slice of lime (optional)

Shake liquid ingredients with ice and strain into a chilled cocktail glass. Garnish with lime if desired.

Hurricane

1 oz (2 tbsp) dark rum
1 oz (2 tbsp) light rum
juice of 1/2 lime
1/2 oz (1 tbsp) passionfruit juice

Shake ingredients with ice and strain into a chilled cocktail glass.

Variation: Shake 1 1/2 oz (3 tbsp) dark rum, 1 1/2 oz (3 tbsp) lemon juice, 2 oz (4 tbsp) passionfruit juice, and 1 tsp sugar with ice. Strain into a chilled highball glass over ice cubes.

I

Ice Pick

2 1/2 oz (5 tbsp) vodka
1 oz (2 tbsp) sours mix
6 oz iced tea, unsweetened

Fill shaker with ice and ingredients; shake vigorously. Pour into a tall collins glass filled with ice.

——— **Ideal Cocktail** ———

1½ oz (3 tbsp) gin
1 oz (2 tbsp) dry vermouth
2 dashes maraschino
1 tsp grapefruit juice
maraschino cherry

Shake liquid ingredients with ice and strain into a chilled cocktail glass. Garnish with the cherry.

Variations: Substitute lemon juice for grapefruit. Substitute sweet vermouth for dry.

——— **Imperial Fizz** ———

1½ oz (3 tbsp) rye or bourbon
1 tsp sugar
juice of ½ lemon
chilled club soda

Shake ingredients, except soda, with ice and strain into a chilled highball glass. Top with soda.

Variation: Add ½ oz (1 tbsp) light rum. Substitute chilled champagne for soda.

——— **Imperial (Martini) Cocktail** ———

See *Martini.*

——— **Inca** ———

¾ oz (1½ tbsp) gin
¾ oz (1½ tbsp) dry vermouth
¾ oz (1½ tbsp) sweet vermouth
¾ oz (1½ tbsp) dry sherry

(continued)

1 dash Angostura or orange bitters
1 dash orgeat syrup

Stir ingredients with ice and strain into a chilled cocktail glass.

Income Tax Cocktail

1½ oz (3 tbsp) gin
½ oz (1 tbsp) dry vermouth
½ oz (1 tbsp) sweet vermouth
1 dash Angostura bitters
juice of ¼ orange

Shake ingredients with ice and strain into a chilled cocktail glass.

Ink Street

1 oz (2 tbsp) rye whiskey
1 oz (2 tbsp) lemon juice
1 oz (2 tbsp) orange juice

Shake ingredients with ice and strain into a chilled cocktail glass.

Irish Blackthorn

1½ oz (3 tbsp) Irish whiskey
1 oz (2 tbsp) dry vermouth
3 dashes Pernod
3 dashes Angostura bitters

Stir ingredients with ice and strain into a chilled old-fashioned glass over ice cubes.

See also *Blackthorn.*

Irish Cooler

2 oz (4 tbsp) Irish whiskey
chilled club soda
peel of ½ lemon cut in a continuous spiral

Pour whiskey into a chilled collins or highball glass over ice cubes. Fill with soda, stir gently, and garnish with lemon peel.

Irish Shillelagh

Packs the wallop of a shillelagh, but with an agreeable aftertaste.

2 oz (4 tbsp) Irish whiskey
½ oz (1 tbsp) light rum
½ oz (1 tbsp) sloe gin
½ oz (1 tbsp) fresh lemon juice
1 tsp sugar syrup
peach slice
maraschino cherry

Place first 5 ingredients in shaker with 5 or 6 ice cubes. Cover and shake vigorously. Strain into large old-fashioned glass half-filled with cracked ice. Garnish as desired and serve with short straw.

Irish Whiskey Cream

(serves 8)

1 cup heavy cream
1 can (14 oz) sweetened condensed milk
3 large eggs, lightly beaten
1 oz (2 tbsp) chocolate syrup
½ tsp coconut extract
1 cup Irish whiskey

(continued)

In bowl whisk together ingredients in the order given. Cover and refrigerate several hours or overnight. Serve in chilled punch cups or small old-fashioned glasses. Makes eight 4-oz servings.

J

———— Jack Frost ————

1 oz (2 tbsp) rye whiskey
1 oz (2 tbsp) dry sherry
1 oz (2 tbsp) port
orange and lemon slices

Add ingredients to an old-fashioned glass half-filled with cracked ice. Stir and garnish with orange and lemon slices. Serve with short straw.

———— Jack-in-the-Box Cocktail ————

1½ oz (3 tbsp) apple brandy
1½ oz (3 tbsp) pineapple juice
1 dash Angostura bitters

Shake ingredients with ice and strain into a chilled cocktail glass.

———— Jack Rose Cocktail ————

2 oz (4 tbsp) calvados or apple brandy
juice of ½ lime
2 dashes grenadine
lemon twist (optional)

Shake ingredients with ice and strain into a chilled cocktail glass. Garnish with lemon.

Variation: Substitute ³/₄ oz (1¹/₂ tbsp) lemon juice for the lime juice.

─────── **Jade** ───────

1¹/₂ oz (3 tbsp) dark rum
¹/₂ oz (1 tbsp) green crème de menthe
¹/₂ oz (1 tbsp) Triple Sec
¹/₂ oz (1 tbsp) lime juice
1 tsp sugar
slice of lime

Shake first 5 ingredients with ice and strain into a chilled cocktail glass. Garnish with lime slice.

Variation: Substitute light rum for dark.

─────── **Jamaica Glow** ───────

1¹/₂ oz (3 tbsp) gin
¹/₂ oz (1 tbsp) dark rum
¹/₂ oz (1 tbsp) dry red wine
¹/₂ oz (1 tbsp) orange juice

Shake ingredients with cracked ice and strain into a chilled cocktail glass.

─────── **Jamaican Cocktail** ───────

1 oz (2 tbsp) Jamaican rum
1 oz (2 tbsp) Tia Maria or other coffee brandy
1 oz (2 tbsp) lime juice
1 dash Angostura bitters (optional)

Shake ingredients with ice and strain into a chilled cocktail glass.

——— Jamaican Breeze ———

2 oz (4 tbsp) dark Jamaican rum
1/2 oz (1 tbsp) peach brandy
1/2 oz (1 tbsp) curaçao
2 tsp lime juice
1–2 dashes orange bitters
pineapple stick (optional)

Place first 5 ingredients in shaker, cover, and shake vigorously. Strain into highball glass three-quarters filled with cracked ice. Garnish with pineapple stick, if desired.

——— Jamaican Doubloon ———

1 oz (2 tbsp) white or light rum
1 oz (2 tbsp) dark Jamaican rum
1 oz (2 tbsp) 151-proof rum
1 oz (2 tbsp) orange juice
1 oz (2 tbsp) grapefruit juice
1 tsp Pernod or Ricard
1 tsp orange curaçao
orange slice
maraschino cherry

In mixing glass with several ice cubes pour first 7 ingredients and stir to combine. Strain into highball glass half-filled with cracked ice and garnish with orange slice and cherry.

——— Jamaican Rumba ———

2 oz (4 tbsp) dark Jamaican rum
1 oz (2 tbsp) Tia Maria
2 or 3 dashes orange bitters
1 oz (2 tbsp) heavy cream

Shake all ingredients with ice. Strain into a chilled wineglass.

———— **Java Cooler** ————

2 oz (4 tbsp) gin
1/2 oz (1 tbsp) fresh lime juice
1–2 dashes bitters
tonic water

Place 4 or 5 ice cubes in a highball glass. Add gin, lime juice, and bitters and stir gently to combine. Top off with tonic water and stir again before serving.

———— **Jewel Cocktail** ————

1 oz (2 tbsp) gin
1 oz (2 tbsp) sweet vermouth
1 oz (2 tbsp) green Chartreuse
1–2 dashes orange bitters
maraschino cherry

Shake first 4 ingredients with cracked ice and strain into a chilled cocktail glass. Garnish with cherry.

———— **Jocose Julep** ————

2 1/2 oz bourbon
1/2 oz (1 tbsp) green crème de menthe
1 oz (2 tbsp) lime juice
1 tsp sugar
5 mint leaves
chilled club soda
1/2 cup crushed ice
2 sprigs of mint

(continued)

Put ingredients, except club soda and mint sprigs, into a blender and blend at low speed for 15 seconds. Pour into a thoroughly frosted collins glass or metal mug over ice cubes. Top with soda and garnish with mint sprigs.

——— **John Collins** ———

See *Tom Collins*.

——— **Joulouville** ———

1 oz (2 tbsp) gin
1/2 oz (1 tbsp) apple brandy
1/4 oz (1/2 tbsp) sweet vermouth
1/2 oz (1 tbsp) lemon juice
2 dashes grenadine

Shake ingredients with ice and strain into a chilled cocktail glass.

——— **Judge Jr. Cocktail** ———

1 oz (2 tbsp) gin
1 oz (2 tbsp) light rum
1 oz (2 tbsp) lemon juice
2 dashes grenadine
1/2 tsp sugar

Shake ingredients with ice and strain into a chilled cocktail glass.

——— **Judgette Cocktail** ———

1 oz (2 tbsp) gin
1 oz (2 tbsp) peach brandy
1 oz (2 tbsp) dry vermouth

3 dashes lime juice
maraschino cherry (optional)

Shake liquid ingredients with ice and strain into a chilled cocktail glass. Garnish with the cherry.

JULEP

A tall, mint-flavored drink served in a well-frosted glass, often made of silver, pewter, or other metal. A julep can be made with a variety of liquors, but bourbon is traditional. For a list of julep drinks, see *Julep* in the **Index by Type of Drink.**

Jungfrau Cocktail

As refreshing as its namesake, the Swiss mountain peak.

2 oz (4 tbsp) rye whiskey
1 oz (2 tbsp) dry vermouth
1 tsp Pernod or Ricard
1–2 dashes bitters

In mixing glass stir all ingredients with cracked ice and strain into a chilled cocktail glass.

Jungle Juice

1 oz (2 tbsp) vodka
1 oz (2 tbsp) rum
1/2 oz (1 tbsp) Triple Sec
1 splash sours mix
1 oz (2 tbsp) cranberry juice
1 oz (2 tbsp) orange juice
1 oz (2 tbsp) pineapple juice

(continued)

Pour all ingredients in a shaker filled with ice, shake and pour into a tall collins glass.

K

-------- ### Kahlúa Cocktail --------

2 oz (4 tbsp) Kahlúa
2 dashes crème de noyaux
½ tsp cream

Fill a chilled old-fashioned glass half full of crushed ice. Pour in Kahlúa and crème de noyaux and float cream on top. Serve with a short straw.

-------- ### Kamikaze --------

1 oz (2 tbsp) vodka
1 oz (2 tbsp) Triple Sec
1 oz (2 Tbps) Rose's lime juice
lime slice

Shake liquid ingredients with ice. Serve over ice in an old-fashioned glass. Garnish with lime.

See also **Shooters.**

-------- ### Kangaroo Cocktail --------

1½ oz (3 tbsp) vodka
¾ oz (1½ tbsp) dry vermouth
twist of lemon peel

Stir vodka and vermouth with ice and strain into a chilled cocktail glass or into an old-fashioned glass over ice cubes. Garnish with lemon peel.

——— **Kentucky Cocktail** ———

1½ oz (3 tbsp) bourbon
¾ oz pineapple juice

Shake ingredients with ice and strain into a chilled cocktail glass.

Variation: Sugar-rim the glass by rubbing with lemon and dipping into sugar. Add ½ oz (1 tbsp) lemon juice and 2 dashes maraschino.

——— **Kentucky Colonel Cocktail** ———

1½ oz (3 tbsp) bourbon
2 tsp Benedictine
twist of lemon peel (optional)

Stir liquid ingredients with ice and strain into a chilled cocktail glass or into an old-fashioned glass over ice cubes. Garnish with lemon peel.

——— **Kerry Cooler** ———

2 oz (4 tbsp) Irish whiskey
1 oz (2 tbsp) dry sherry
½ oz (1 tbsp) orgeat syrup or almond extract
1 oz (2 tbsp) lemon juice
chilled club soda
slice of lemon

Shake whiskey, sherry, orgeat, and lemon juice with ice. Strain into a chilled collins glass over ice cubes. Top with soda and garnish with lemon slice.

——— **K.G.B. Cocktail** ———

2 oz (4 tbsp) gin
1/2 oz (1 tbsp) kümmel or kirsch
1 tsp apricot brandy
1/2 tsp lemon juice
twist of lemon

Shake first 4 ingredients with cracked ice and strain into chilled cocktail glass. Twist peel over glass to activate oils and drop in.

——— **King Cole Cocktail** ———

2 oz (4 tbsp) bourbon
1/2 tsp sugar
1 slice orange
1 slice pineapple

Muddle sugar, orange, and pineapple in an old-fashioned glass. Add ice and bourbon and stir well.

——— **Kingston** ———

1 oz (2 tbsp) Jamaican rum
1 oz (2 tbsp) gin
1/2 oz (1 tbsp) lemon or lime juice
3 dashes grenadine

Shake ingredients with ice and strain into a chilled cocktail glass.

Variation: Substitute curaçao for gin.

——— **Kir Cocktail** ———

Said to have been named after a former mayor of Dijon, France.

6 oz chilled dry white wine
1/2 oz (1 tbsp) crème de cassis
twist of lemon peel

Pour wine and crème de cassis into a large chilled wineglass over ice cubes and stir. Garnish with lemon peel.

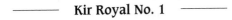

Kir Royal No. 1

6 oz chilled champagne
1/2 oz (1 tbsp) crème de cassis
twist of lemon

Pour champagne and crème de cassis into a champagne flute. Garnish with lemon peel.

Kir Royal No. 2

While the original Kir Royal is made with crème de cassis, in the past decade bartenders have been using Chambord.

6 oz chilled champagne
1/2 oz (1 tbsp) Chambord
twist of lemon

Pour Chambord and then the champagne into a champagne flute. Garnish with lemon peel.

Klondike Cooler

2 oz (4 tbsp) rye whiskey
peel of 1 orange cut in a continuous spiral
1 tsp sugar
chilled ginger ale or club soda

(continued)

Dissolve sugar in a small amount of ginger ale in a chilled highball glass. Add orange peel, ice cubes, and rye. Top with ginger ale.

——————— Knickerbocker Cocktail ———————

1½ oz (3 tbsp) gin
¾ oz (1½ tbsp) dry vermouth
2 dashes sweet vermouth
twist of lemon peel

Stir liquid ingredients with ice and strain into a chilled cocktail glass. Garnish with lemon peel.

——————— Knickerbocker Special Cocktail ———————

2 oz (4 tbsp) light rum
½ tsp Triple Sec
1 tsp raspberry syrup
1 tsp pineapple juice
1 tsp orange juice
1 tsp lemon or lime juice
small slice of fresh pineapple

Shake liquid ingredients vigorously with ice and strain into a chilled cocktail glass. Garnish with pineapple slice.

——————— Knock-Out Cocktail ———————

¾ oz (1½ tbsp) gin
¾ oz (1½ tbsp) Pernod
¾ oz (1½ tbsp) dry vermouth
1 tsp white crème de menthe
sprig of fresh mint or a maraschino cherry

Stir liquid ingredients with ice and strain into a chilled cocktail glass. Garnish with mint or cherry.

———— **Kretchma Cocktail** ————

1 oz (2 tbsp) vodka
1 oz (2 tbsp) white crème de cacao
½ oz (1 tbsp) lemon juice
1 dash grenadine

Shake ingredients with ice and strain into a chilled cocktail glass.

———— **Kup's Indispensable Cocktail** ————

2 oz (4 tbsp) gin
1 oz (2 tbsp) sweet vermouth
1 oz (2 tbsp) dry vermouth
1 dash Angostura bitters
twist of orange peel (optional)

Stir liquid ingredients with ice and strain into a chilled cocktail glass. Garnish with orange peel.

Variation: Use only ½ oz (1 tbsp) sweet vermouth.

L

———— **Ladies' Cocktail** ————

2 oz (4 tbsp) bourbon
½ tsp Pernod
½ tsp anisette
2 dashes Angostura bitters
slice of fresh pineapple

Stir liquid ingredients with ice and strain into a chilled cocktail glass. Garnish with pineapple.

—————— **Lady Be Good** ——————

1½ oz (3 tbsp) brandy
¾ oz (1½ tbsp) white crème de menthe
¾ oz (1½ tbsp) sweet vermouth

Shake ingredients with ice and strain into a chilled cocktail glass.

—————— **Lady Finger** ——————

1½ oz (3 tbsp) gin
¾ oz (1½ tbsp) kirsch
¾ oz (1½ tbsp) cherry brandy

Shake ingredients with ice and strain into a chilled cocktail glass.

—————— **Lady Macbeth** ——————

2 oz (4 tbsp) Scotch
1 tsp white curaçao
1 tsp amaretto
2 tsp lemon juice
1 tsp sugar
1–2 dashes orange bitters

Place ingredients in shaker with 5 or 6 ice cubes, cover, and shake vigorously several times. Strain into a chilled cocktail glass.

—————— **Lawhill Cocktail** ——————

1½ oz (3 tbsp) rye whiskey
¾ oz (1½ tbsp) dry vermouth
2 dashes Pernod
2 dashes maraschino
1 dash Angostura bitters

Stir ingredients with ice and strain into a chilled cocktail glass.

─────── **Lazy Afternoon** ───────

dry white wine, chilled
$\frac{1}{2}$ oz (1 tbsp) peach brandy
1 tsp anisette
1 tsp fresh lemon juice

In a highball glass filled with cracked ice pour brandy, anisette, and lemon juice. Stir briefly and top with wine. Serve with a long straw.

─────── **Leave-It-to-Me Cocktail I** ───────

1 oz (2 tbsp) gin
$\frac{1}{2}$ oz (1 tbsp) apricot brandy
$\frac{1}{2}$ oz (1 tbsp) dry vermouth
2 dashes lemon juice
1 dash grenadine

Shake ingredients with ice and strain into a chilled cocktail glass.

─────── **Leave-It-to-Me Cocktail II** ───────

2 oz (4 tbsp) gin
1 tsp raspberry syrup
1 tsp lemon juice
1 dash grenadine
1 egg white (optional)

Shake ingredients vigorously with ice and strain into a chilled cocktail glass.

——— Leeward ———

1½ oz (3 tbsp) light rum
½ oz (1 tbsp) calvados
½ oz (1 tbsp) sweet vermouth
twist of lemon peel

Shake liquid ingredients with ice and strain into a chilled cocktail glass or into an old-fashioned glass over ice cubes. Garnish with lemon peel.

——— Liberty Cocktail ———

1½ oz (3 tbsp) apple brandy
¾ oz (1½ tbsp) light rum
1 dash sugar syrup

Stir ingredients with ice and strain into a chilled cocktail glass.

——— Lillet Cocktail ———

1½ oz (3 tbsp) Lillet
¾ oz (1½ tbsp) gin
twist of lemon peel

Stir gin and Lillet with ice and strain into a chilled cocktail glass. Garnish with peel.

Variation: Add 1–2 dashes crème de noyaux.

——— Lillet Royal ———

¾ oz (1½ tbsp) brandy
¾ oz (1½ tbsp) Cointreau or Triple Sec
¾ oz (1½ tbsp) Lillet
¾ oz (1½ tbsp) lemon juice

Shake ingredients with ice and strain into a large chilled cocktail glass.

─────── **Lime Cocktail** ───────

1 oz (2 tbsp) light rum
1 oz (2 tbsp) lime liqueur
2 tsp Triple Sec
2 tsp lime juice
½ cup crushed ice
twist of lemon peel

Put first 5 ingredients into a blender and blend at low speed for 15 seconds. Pour into a large chilled wine or champagne glass. Garnish with lemon peel.

─────── **Lime Colada** ───────

See *Piña Colada.*

─────── **Linstead Cocktail** ───────

1 oz (2 tbsp) Scotch
1 oz (2 tbsp) pineapple juice
1 dash Pernod
½ tsp sugar
2 dashes lemon juice

Shake ingredients with ice and strain into a chilled cocktail glass.

Variation: Substitute rye whiskey for Scotch.

─────── **Little Devil Cocktail** ───────

1 oz (2 tbsp) gin
1 oz (2 tbsp) light rum

(continued)

3/4 oz Cointreau or Triple Sec
juice of 1/4 lemon

Shake ingredients with ice and strain into a chilled
cocktail glass.

–––––––– **Little Princess Cocktail** ––––––––

1 1/2 oz (3 tbsp) light rum
1 1/2 oz (3 tbsp) sweet vermouth

Stir ingredients with ice and strain into a chilled cocktail glass.

–––––––– **Loch Lomond** ––––––––

2 oz (4 tbsp) Scotch
1 tsp sugar
2–3 dashes Angostura bitters

Shake ingredients with ice and strain into a chilled
cocktail glass.

–––––––– **London Buck** ––––––––

2 oz (4 tbsp) gin
1/2 oz (1 tbsp) lemon juice
ginger ale, chilled
thin slice lemon (optional)

In chilled highball glass filled with ice cubes, pour
gin and lemon juice. Top with ginger ale and float
lemon slice, if desired.

–––––––– **London Cocktail** ––––––––

2 oz (4 tbsp) gin
2 dashes sugar syrup

2 dashes maraschino
2 dashes orange bitters
twist of lemon peel

Stir liquid ingredients with ice and strain into a chilled cocktail glass. Garnish with lemon peel.

London Special

cold champagne
lump of sugar
1–2 dashes orange bitters
strip of orange peel

Place sugar in bottom of chilled champagne glass and dash with bitters. Rub rim of glass with peel, twist to release oils, and add to glass. Fill with champagne, stir gently, and serve with a small straw.

Lone Tree Cocktail

2 oz (4 tbsp) gin
1 oz (2 tbsp) sweet vermouth

Stir gin and vermouth with ice and strain into a chilled cocktail glass.

Variation: Decrease sweet vermouth to ½ oz (1 tbsp) and add ½ oz (1 tbsp) dry vermouth and 2 dashes orange bitters.

Love Cocktail

2 oz (4 tbsp) sloe gin
2 dashes raspberry syrup
2 dashes lemon juice
1 egg white

(continued)

Shake ingredients vigorously with ice and strain into a chilled cocktail glass.

Lover's Delight

1 oz (2 tbsp) Cointreau
1 oz (2 tbsp) brandy or cognac
1 oz (2 tbsp) Forbidden Fruit

Shake ingredients with ice and strain into a chilled cocktail glass.

Loving Cup

(serves 2)

2 cups dry red wine
2 oz (4 tbsp) peach brandy
1 oz (2 tbsp) Cointreau or Triple Sec
½ oz (1 tbsp) sugar
6 oz club soda
orange slices
mint sprigs

Fill 2-qt glass pitcher with ice cubes. Pour in liquors, sugar, soda, and orange slices. Stir several times and garnish pitcher with mint and orange slices.

Lynchburg Lemonade

2 oz (4 tbsp) whiskey
2 oz (4 tbsp) sours mix
1 oz (2 tbsp) Triple Sec
4 oz (8 tbsp) 7-Up
slice of lemon
cherry

Fill shaker with ice cubes and pour in first 3 ingredients; cover and shake vigorously. Pour into a tall collins glass and fill with 7-Up. Garnish with lemon and cherry.

M

——— ## Madeira Mint Flip ———

1½ oz (3 tbsp) Madeira
¾ oz (1½ tbsp) chocolate mint liqueur
1 tsp sugar
grated dark chocolate or nutmeg

Shake first 3 ingredients with ice and strain into a chilled cocktail glass. Garnish with chocolate or nutmeg.

——— ## Madras ———

2 oz (4 tbsp) vodka
2 oz (4 tbsp) cranberry juice
2 oz (4 tbsp) orange juice
orange slice

Fill an old-fashioned glass with ice and pour in ingredients. Garnish with orange slice.

——— ## Magna Carta ———

1½ oz (3 tbsp) well-chilled tequila
1 oz (2 tbsp) well-chilled Triple Sec
champagne
lime juice
salt

(continued)

Dip the rim of a chilled goblet in lime juice, then in salt, shaking off excess. Pour in tequila and Triple Sec, then fill with champagne and stir gently.

——— **Magnolia Cocktail** ———

1 oz (2 tbsp) lemon juice
3 oz (6 tbsp) gin
½ tsp grenadine
1 tsp heavy cream

Place all ingredients in shaker with cracked ice. Cover and shake vigorously several times. Strain into a chilled cocktail glass.

——— **Maiden's Blush Cocktail** ———

1½ oz (3 tbsp) gin
1 tsp Cointreau or Triple Sec
1 tsp grenadine
2 dashes lemon juice

Shake ingredients with ice and strain into a chilled cocktail glass.

——— **Maiden's Prayer** ———

1½ oz (3 tbsp) gin
1½ oz (3 tbsp) Cointreau or Triple Sec
½ oz (1 tbsp) lemon juice

Shake ingredients with ice and strain into a chilled cocktail glass.

Variation: Substitute orange juice for lemon.

Mai-Tai

Trader Vic claims to have invented this drink at his Oakland, California, restaurant in 1944. When he served it to a Tahitian friend, the comment was "Mai Tai—Roa Aé," which means "out of this world—the best" in Tahitian.

2 oz (4 tbsp) dark Jamaican rum
$1/2$ oz (1 tbsp) curaçao
$1/2$ oz (1 tbsp) apricot brandy
juice of $1/2$ lime
1 tsp grenadine
wedge of fresh pineapple
maraschino cherry
twist of lime peel

Shake liquid ingredients with ice and strain into a chilled collins or large old-fashioned glass over crushed ice. Garnish with pineapple, cherry, and lime peel.

Variation: Substitute 1 oz (2 tbsp) light and 1 oz (2 tbsp) dark rum for the 2 oz (4 tbsp) dark Jamaican rum.

Mamie Taylor

2 oz (4 tbsp) Scotch
juice of $1/2$ lime
chilled ginger ale

Pour Scotch and lime juice into a chilled collins glass over ice cubes. Top with ginger ale and stir.

——————— **Mañana** ———————

2 oz (4 tbsp) golden rum
½ oz (1 tbsp) apricot brandy
1 tsp lemon juice

Place ingredients in shaker with 4 or 5 ice cubes. Cover and shake vigorously several times. Strain into an old-fashioned glass two-thirds full of cracked ice.

——————— **Mandeville** ———————

1½ oz (3 tbsp) light rum
1½ oz (3 tbsp) dark rum
1 tsp Pernod
¼ tsp grenadine
½ oz (1 tbsp) lemon juice (optional)
½ oz (1 tbsp) chilled cola

Shake ingredients with ice and strain into a chilled old-fashioned glass over ice cubes.

——————— **Manhasset** ———————

1½ oz (3 tbsp) rye whiskey
¼ oz (½ tbsp) dry vermouth
¼ oz (½ tbsp) sweet vermouth
½ oz (1 tbsp) lemon juice
twist of lemon peel (optional)

Shake liquid ingredients with ice and strain into a chilled cocktail glass. Garnish with lemon peel if desired.

——————— **Manhasset Mauler** ———————

2 oz (4 tbsp) gin
1 oz (2 tbsp) sloe gin
lemon zest

Place gins in shaker with 4 or 5 ice cubes, cover, and shake vigorously several times. Strain into a chilled cocktail glass after rubbing the rim with lemon zest. Twist zest over drink to release oils and drop in.

MANHATTAN

The manhattan, named for the New York City borough, is thought to have been invented (in New York City, of course) around 1890. The original version, which did not contain bitters or a garnish, was simply 2 parts rye to 1 part vermouth. Around 1919, gin was substituted for the whiskey and a new drink, the Bronx, was born. The Rob Roy is a manhattan made with Scotch. The standard manhattan is sweet. For other types of manhattans, see variations below.

> 2 oz (4 tbsp) rye whiskey
> 1 oz (2 tbsp) sweet vermouth
> 1 dash Angostura bitters
> maraschino cherry

Stir liquid ingredients with ice and strain into a chilled cocktail glass. Garnish with the cherry.

———— Bourbon Manhattan ————

> 2 oz (4 tbsp) bourbon
> 1 oz (2 tbsp) sweet vermouth
> 1 dash Angostura bitters
> maraschino cherry

Stir liquid ingredients with ice and strain into a chilled cocktail glass. Garnish with the cherry.

Dry Manhattan

2 oz (4 tbsp) rye whiskey
½ oz (1 tbsp) dry vermouth
1 dash Angostura bitters
maraschino cherry

Stir liquid ingredients with ice and strain into a chilled cocktail glass. Garnish with the cherry.

French Manhattan

2 oz (4 tbsp) rye whiskey
½ oz (1 tbsp) dry vermouth
1 dash Angostura bitters
1 dash Cointreau
maraschino cherry

Stir liquid ingredients with ice and strain into a chilled cocktail glass. Garnish with the cherry.

Perfect Manhattan

2 oz (4 tbsp) rye whiskey
½ oz (1 tbsp) dry vermouth
½ oz (1 tbsp) sweet vermouth
1 dash Angostura bitters
maraschino cherry

Stir liquid ingredients with ice and strain into a chilled cocktail glass. Garnish with the cherry.

Scotch Manhattan

See *Rob Roy.*

──────── **Margarita** ────────

1 1/2 oz (3 tbsp) tequila
1/2 oz (1 tbsp) Cointreau or Triple Sec
juice of 1/2 lime

Salt-rim a chilled cocktail glass by rubbing the rim
with lime and dipping into salt. Shake ingredients
with ice and strain into the glass.

Frozen Margarita: In blender combine 1 oz (2
tbsp) frozen limeade concentrate, 1/2 oz (1 tbsp) Triple
Sec, 1 oz (2 tbsp) tequila, and 1/3 cup cracked ice and
blend till smooth. Rim chilled champagne glass with
lime wedge and dip in salt to coat. Pour frappéed
drink into glass.

──────── **Margarita Impériale** ────────

1 oz (2 tbsp) Mandarine Napoléon
(orange-flavored brandy)
1 oz (2 tbsp) tequila
2 tsp fresh lemon juice
dash of curaçao

Fill an old-fashioned glass with cracked ice. Add
liquors and juice and stir gently before serving.

──────── **Martinez Cocktail** ────────

1 1/2 oz (3 tbsp) London dry gin
1 oz (2 tbsp) dry vermouth
1 tsp curaçao
dash orange bitters
maraschino cherry

Place first 4 ingredients in mixing glass and stir several times to combine. Pour onto a chilled cocktail
glass and garnish with cherry, if desired.

MARTINI

The exact origin of both the martini and its name are obscure. The cocktail seems to have appeared in the United States in the 1860s, when it consisted of 2 parts gin to 1 part vermouth. It was attributed to a bartender named Martinez, or may have been named after a town of that name. Later, the name somehow got linked with the Italian firm of Martini and Rossi, vermouth manufacturers. With the passage of time, the martini has become drier and drier; 6–1 is no longer considered dry; 10–1 (below) has become standard, and some faddists either merely rinse the glass with vermouth before adding gin or dip the ice cubes in vermouth before placing them in the shaker with the gin. There are many variations on the drink, and vodka has become a popular subtitute for gin and can be used in any of the recipes below. It is customary to serve martinis with a garnish to compliment the ingredients.

SOME HINTS

1. Use nothing but the best liquor. Most confirmed martini drinkers specify the gin or vodka when ordering in public. A cheap vermouth can ruin an otherwise fine martini. This is particularly unnecessary since even the finest vermouth is not expensive.

2. Buy vermouth in small bottles unless you consume a lot of it. Once opened, vermouth gradually loses its strength and flavor.

3. Pour the gin or vodka over the ice cubes for quicker chilling. Cracked or crushed ice will turn the martini into a watery mush.

4. To chill the martini glass, fill it with ice and cold water before beginning to mix the martini. After the martini has been mixed, empty the glass of ice and water and strain the martini into the glass.

5. When making clear martinis, mix the martini by stirring. Shaking will turn it cloudy.

6. When shaking the martini, let it sit for a moment before straining to settle.

Here is the dry martini, with the proportions 10 to 1. The classic martini is made with gin.

> 2½ oz (5 tbsp) gin or vodka
> ¼–½ tsp dry vermouth
> twist of lemon peel or olive

Stir liquid ingredients with ice and strain into a chilled cocktail glass, the rim of which has been rubbed with the cut edge of the lemon peel. Garnish with lemon peel or olive.

Variations: For a drier martini, decrease the amount of vermouth; some individuals prefer only a drop or two, going so far as to add it with an eye-dropper.

Martini-on-the-Rocks: Strain ingredients into an old-fashioned glass over ice cubes.

Apple Martini

> 2 oz (4 tbsp) vodka
> 1 oz (2 tbsp) apple brandy
> ¼–½ tsp Cointreau or Triple Sec
> slice of an apple

Combine liquid ingredients with ice and stir until chilled. Strain into a chilled cocktail glass. Garnish with apple slice.

——— **Berritini** ———

2 oz (4 tbsp) raspberry vodka
1 oz cranberry juice
2 raspberries

Combine liquid ingredients with ice and stir until chilled. Strain into a chilled cocktail glass. Garnish with raspberries.

——— **Blue Martini (Yale Cocktail)** ———

1½ oz (3 tbsp) gin
½ oz (1 tbsp) dry vermouth
2 dashes orange bitters
2 dashes blue curaçao

Shake ingredients with ice and strain into a chilled martini glass.

——— **Boston Bullet** ———

2½ oz (5 tbsp) gin
¼ oz (½ tbsp) dry vermouth
twist of lemon peel
almond-stuffed olive

Stir liquid ingredients with ice and strain into a chilled cocktail glass, the rim of which has been rubbed with the cut edge of the lemon peel. Garnish with olive.

——— **Brandy Martini** ———

Not gin or vodka but brandy, and surprisingly popular.

2 oz (4 tbsp) Hennessy V.S. or other brandy
squeeze of lemon juice
zest of lemon peel

Combine liquid ingredients with ice and stir until chilled. Rub rim of chilled martini glass with lemon zest and add to glass. Strain liquid into chilled cocktail glass.

—— **Chocolate Martini** ——

2 oz (4 tbsp) vodka
1 oz (2 tbsp) chocolate liqueur
1 tsp sweetened chocolate powder
cherry

Combine liquid ingredients with ice and stir until chilled. Before straining liquid into martini glass, dust entire top portion of martini glass with chocolate powder. Carefully strain liquid into martini glass and garnish with a cherry.

—— **Cosmopolitan** ——

2 oz (4 tbsp) vodka
1 tsp Cointreau or Triple Sec
2 tsp lime juice
1 oz (2 tbsp) cranberry juice
slice of lime or twist of lemon

Combine liquid ingredients with ice and stir until chilled. Strain into a chilled cocktail glass. Garnish with lime slice or twist of lemon.

—— **Dirty Martini** ——

This martini gets its name from the color the olive juice gives the martini.

2½ oz (5 tbsp) gin or vodka
½ oz (1 tbsp) olive juice
2 olives

(continued)

Combine liquid ingredients with ice and stir until chilled. Strain into a chilled cocktail glass. Garnish with olives.

———— Dubonnet Martini ————

1½ oz (3 tbsp) Dubonnet
1 oz (2 tbsp) gin
¼–½ tsp dry vermouth
twist of lemon peel

Combine liquid ingredients with ice and stir until chilled. Rub rim of chilled martini glass with lemon zest and add to glass. Strain liquid into chilled cocktail glass and garnish with lemon twist.

———— Espresso Martini ————

1½ oz (3 tbsp) vodka
1 oz (2 tbsp) Sambuca
3 coffee beans

Combine liquid ingredients with ice and stir until chilled. Strain into a chilled cocktail glass. Garnish with coffee beans.

———— Fino Martini ————

2 oz (4 tbsp) gin
1 tsp fino sherry
twist of lemon peel

Stir liquid ingredients with ice and strain into a chilled cocktail glass, the rim of which has been rubbed with the cut edge of the lemon peel. Garnish with lemon peel.

———— **Fruitini** ————

2 oz (4 tbsp) currant vodka
1 oz (2 tbsp) cranberry juice
lime slice

Stir liquid ingredients with ice and strain into a chilled cocktail glass. Garnish with lime slice.

———— **Gibson Martini** ————

Dry martini garnished with 2–3 cocktail onions.

———— **Green Apple Martini** ————

2 oz (4 tbsp) vodka
1 oz (2 tbsp) green apple schnapps
green apple slice

Stir liquid ingredients with ice and strain into a chilled cocktail glass. Garnish with apple slice.

———— **Imperial (Martini) Cocktail** ————

1½ oz (3 tbsp) gin
1½ oz (3 tbsp) dry vermouth
1 dash Angostura bitters
2 dashes maraschino
maraschino cherry

Combine liquid ingredients with 3 or 4 ice cubes and stir gently. Strain liquid into a chilled martini glass and garnish with cherry.

——— Lemon Pepper Martini ———

1½ oz pepper vodka
½ oz citrus vodka
¼ tsp vermouth
twist of lemon or caperberry

Combine liquid ingredients with ice and stir until chilled. Rub rim of chilled martini glass with lemon zest and add to glass. Pour in strained liquid. Garnish with caperberry.

——— Melon Martini ———

2 oz (4 tbsp) vodka
1 oz (2 tbsp) melon liqueur
twist of lemon peel

Combine liquid ingredients with ice and stir until chilled. Strain into a chilled cocktail glass. Garnish with lemon peel.

——— Orange Martini ———

2 oz (4 tbsp) orange vodka
½ oz (1 tbsp) Grand Mariner
¼ tsp sweet vermouth
twist of orange peel

Combine liquid ingredients with ice and stir until chilled. Strain into a chilled cocktail glass. Garnish with orange peel.

——— Paisley Martini ———

2 oz (4 tbsp) gin
¼ oz dry vermouth

1 tsp Scotch
twist of lemon

Stir liquid ingredients with ice and strain into a chilled cocktail glass, the rim of which has been rubbed with the cut edge of the lemon peel. Garnish with lemon peel.

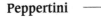

Peppertini

2 oz (4 tbsp) pepper vodka
1/2 oz (1 tbsp) dry sherry
caperberry

Stir liquid ingredients with ice and strain into a chilled cocktail glass. Garnish with caperberry.

Perfect Martini

1 1/2 oz (3 tbsp) gin
1/2 oz (1 tbsp) sweet vermouth
1/2 oz (1 tbsp) dry vermouth
twist of orange peel or an olive

Stir liquid ingredients with ice and strain into a chilled cocktail glass, the rim of which has been rubbed with the cut edge of the orange peel. Garnish with orange peel or olive.

Rum Martini

2 oz (4 tbsp) light rum
1/4 oz dry vermouth
dash of orange bitters
twist of lemon

(continued)

Stir liquid ingredients with ice and strain into a chilled cocktail glass, the rim of which has been rubbed with the cut edge of the lemon peel. Garnish with lemon peel.

———— Saketini ————

2 oz (4 tbsp) vodka
1 oz (2 tbsp) sake
cucumber slice

Combine liquid ingredients with ice and stir until chilled. Strain into a chilled cocktail glass. Garnish with cucumber.

———— Spanish Martini ————

2 oz (4 tbsp) vodka
1 oz (2 tbsp) sherry
twist of lemon peel

Combine liquid ingredients with ice and stir until chilled. Strain into a chilled cocktail glass. Garnish with twist.

———— Sweet Martini ————

1 oz (2 tbsp) gin or vodka
1 oz (2 tbsp) sweet vermouth
twist of orange peel or a cherry

Stir liquid ingredients with ice and strain into a chilled cocktail glass, the rim of which has been rubbed with the cut edge of the orange peel. Garnish with orange peel or cherry.

──────── **Tequini** ────────

2½ oz (5 tbsp) tequila
¼–½ tsp dry vermouth
twist of lemon peel

Stir liquid ingredients with ice and strain into a chilled cocktail glass, the rim of which has been rubbed with the cut edge of the lemon peel. Garnish with lemon peel.

──────── **Vampire Martini** ────────

2 oz (4 tbsp) vodka
1 oz (2 tbsp) Chambord
½ oz (1 tbsp) cranberry juice
2 raspberries

Combine liquid ingredients with ice and stir until chilled. Strain into a chilled cocktail glass. Garnish with raspberries.

──────── **Mary Garden Cocktail** ────────

Perhaps invented by the famous opera diva, but at least a fitting tribute.

2 oz (4 tbsp) Dubonnet
1 oz (2 tbsp) dry vermouth

Shake ingredients with cracked ice and strain into a chilled cocktail glass.

Variation: Rub rim of glass with lemon peel before filling. Twist peel over drink to release oils and drop in.

——————   **Mary Pickford**   ——————

1 oz (2 tbsp) light rum
1 oz (2 tbsp) pineapple juice
1/3 tsp grenadine
1 or 2 dashes maraschino (optional)

Shake ingredients with ice and strain into a chilled cocktail glass.

——————   **Matador**   ——————

1 oz (2 tbsp) tequila
2 oz (4 tbsp) pineapple juice
juice of 1/2 lime

Shake ingredients with ice and strain into a chilled cocktail glass.

Frozen Matador: Put ingredients, with 1/2 cup ice, into a blender and blend at low speed for 15 seconds. Pour into a chilled old-fashioned glass and garnish with a stick of fresh pineapple.

——————   **Matelot**   ——————

Takes its name from the French word for "sailor."

2 oz (4 tbsp) Pernod, Ricard, or pastis
1/2 oz (1 tbsp) anisette
1–2 dashes bitters

In a highball glass filled with ice cubes pour in the liquors and bitters. Stir to mix.

─────── **Matinee** ───────

(serves 2)

2 oz (4 tbsp) gin
1 oz (2 tbsp) Sambuca
4 dashes lime juice
1 oz (2 tbsp) cream
nutmeg

Shake first 4 ingredients vigorously with ice and strain into chilled cocktail glasses. Sprinkle with nutmeg.

─────── **Maui Cocktail** ───────

2 oz (4 tbsp) gin
1 oz (2 tbsp) pineapple juice
½ oz (1 tbsp) Cointreau

Place ingredients in shaker with 4 or 5 ice cubes. Cover and shake vigorously several times. Strain into a chilled cocktail glass.

─────── **Maurice** ───────

1½ oz (3 tbsp) gin
¾ oz (1½ tbsp) sweet vermouth
¾ oz (1½ tbsp) dry vermouth
juice of ¼ orange
1 dash Angostura bitters

Shake ingredients with ice and strain into a chilled cocktail glass.

───── **Mayfair** ─────

spiral peel of half orange
1 cube sugar
1–2 dashes bitters
cold champagne or other sparkling wine

To chilled tulip champagne glass add sugar cube, orange peel, and bitters. Fill with champagne and stir gently.

───── **Megabyte Cocktail** ─────

1½ oz (3 tbsp) gin
½ oz (1 tbsp) dry vermouth
½ oz (1 tbsp) sweet vermouth
½ oz (1 tbsp) orange juice

Shake all ingredients with cracked ice and strain into a chilled cocktail glass.

───── **Melon Breeze** ─────

1½ oz (3 tbsp) light rum
¼ cup diced cantaloupe
½ oz (1 tbsp) lime juice
½ oz (1 tbsp) orange juice
½ tsp sugar (optional)
cube of cantaloupe

Put first 5 ingredients in a blender and blend at low speed for 15 seconds. Pour into a chilled old-fashioned glass over ice cubes. Garnish with the cantaloupe cube on a toothpick.

——— **Melon Cocktail** ———

2 oz (4 tbsp) London dry gin
1 tsp white maraschino
$\frac{1}{2}$ tsp lemon juice
maraschino cherry

Shake first 3 ingredients with cracked ice and strain into chilled cocktail glass. Garnish with cherry, if desired.

——— **Merry Widow Cocktail I** ———

1$\frac{1}{2}$ oz (3 tbsp) sherry
1$\frac{1}{2}$ oz (3 tbsp) sweet vermouth
twist of lemon peel

Stir liquid ingredients with ice and strain into a chilled cocktail glass. Garnish with lemon peel.

Variation: For a drier Merry Widow, substitute Dubonnet for sherry and dry vermouth for the sweet.

——— **Merry Widow Cocktail II** ———

1$\frac{1}{2}$ oz (3 tbsp) cherry brandy
1$\frac{1}{2}$ oz (3 tbsp) maraschino
maraschino cherry

Stir liquid ingredients with ice and strain into a chilled cocktail glass. Garnish with the cherry.

——— **Merry Widow Fizz** ———

2 oz (4 tbsp) gin
juice of $\frac{1}{2}$ orange
juice of $\frac{1}{2}$ lemon
chilled club soda

(continued)

Shake ingredients, except soda, vigorously with ice.
Strain into a chilled highball or collins glass over ice
cubes and top with soda.

Variation: Substitute sloe gin or Dubonnet for gin.

——— Metropolitan ———

1½ oz (3 tbsp) brandy
1½ oz (3 tbsp) sweet vermouth
½ tsp sugar syrup
dash bitters
maraschino cherry

Shake with ice and strain into an old-fashioned glass
half-filled with cracked ice. Garnish with cherry.

——— Miami ———

2 oz (4 tbsp) light rum
1 oz (2 tbsp) white crème de menthe
2 dashes lemon juice

Shake ingredients with ice and strain into a chilled
cocktail glass.

——— Miami Beach ———

2 oz (4 tbsp) Scotch whisky
2 oz (4 tbsp) dry vermouth
2 oz (4 tbsp) grapefruit juice

Pour into a highball glass half-filled with cracked ice
and stir gently. Top off, if desired, with a little more
grapefruit juice before serving.

Mikado

2 oz (4 tbsp) brandy
1 tsp crème de cacao
1/2 tsp crème de noyaux
1/2 tsp orgeat
1–2 dashes bitters

Shake all ingredients with cracked ice and strain into a chilled cocktail glass.

Milk Punch

2 oz (4 tbsp) rye whiskey
8 oz chilled milk
1 tsp sugar
nutmeg

Shake first 3 ingredients with ice and strain into a chilled cocktail glass. Sprinkle with nutmeg.

Variations: Substitute brandy for rye or substitute 1 oz (2 tbsp) brandy and 1 oz (2 tbsp) rum for rye. A milk punch can also be served hot. Mix the sugar and liquor in a heated mug or glass and add hot milk. Sprinkle with nutmeg.

Millionaire Cocktail

1 1/2 oz (3 tbsp) rye or bourbon
1/2 oz (1 tbsp) curaçao
2 dashes grenadine

Shake ingredients vigorously with ice and strain into a chilled cocktail glass.

Million Dollar Cocktail

1½ oz (3 tbsp) gin
¾ oz (1½ tbsp) sweet vermouth
1–2 tsp pineapple juice
1 tsp grenadine

Shake ingredients vigorously with ice and strain into a chilled cocktail glass.

Mimosa

4 oz (8 tbsp) chilled champagne
4 oz (8 tbsp) chilled orange juice

Pour ingredients into a chilled collins or balloon wineglass over ice cubes and stir gently.

Variation: Using equal parts of champagne and orange juice, pour ingredients into a chilled champagne glass but do not use ice.

See also *Cajun Mimosa.*

Mint Collins

2 oz (4 tbsp) gin
5 sprigs of fresh mint
juice of ½ lemon
1 tsp sugar
chilled club soda
slice of lemon

In a chilled collins glass crush 4 mint leaves in the gin, lemon, and sugar. Add ice cubes and top with soda. Garnish with the remaining mint and lemon slice.

Mint Cooler

2 oz (4 tbsp) Scotch
2–3 dashes white crème de menthe
chilled club soda
sprig of fresh mint

Pour Scotch and crème de menthe into a chilled collins or highball glass over ice cubes. Top with soda, stir gently, and garnish with mint sprig.

Minted Brandy Ice

(serves 6–8)

A rich dessert beverage.

6 oz brandy
4 oz (8 tbsp) white crème de cacao
2 oz (4 tbsp) white crème de menthe
1 qt vanilla ice cream
6–8 mint sprigs

Combine ingredients, except mint, in blender with 8–10 ice cubes and blend until smooth. Serve in brandy snifters or large old-fashioned glasses, garnished with mint.

Mint Julep

Although mint juleps are customarily associated with Kentucky bourbon, the mint julep was an American term for nearly 40 years before Kentucky bourbon became popular. Juleps were originally nonalcoholic minted fruited drinks.

2¹/₂ oz (5 tbsp) bourbon
1 tsp sugar
2–3 dashes cold water or club soda

(continued)

8 sprigs fresh mint
crushed or shaved ice

Muddle sugar, water, and 5 mint sprigs in a glass. Pour into a thoroughly frosted collins glass or mug and pack with ice. Add bourbon and mix (with a chopping motion using a long-handled bar spoon). Some variations suggest not stirring. Garnish with remaining mint and serve with a straw.

SOME HINTS

1. Clipping the ends of the mint used as a garnish will release the juices. If a less pronounced mint flavor is desired, muddle only lightly.

2. A silver mug will frost better than a glass. If a glass is used, it is best to use one with a handle to avoid a warm hand touching the surface of the glass. The finished drink can be additionally frosted by placing it in the refrigerator for an hour.

Variations: Garnish with 1–2 slices of lemon. Float 2–3 drops of brandy or rum on top before serving.

See also *Creole Mint Julep.*

Mo Bay Special

"Mo Bay" is the nickname for Montego Bay, resort capital of Jamaica.

1½ oz (3 tbsp) Jamaican rum
1 tsp lime juice
½ oz (1 tbsp) pineapple juice
1 tsp grenadine

Shake all ingredients with 4 or 5 ice cubes and strain into an old-fashioned glass filled with cracked ice.

———— Mocha Mint ————

³/₄ oz (1½ tbsp) coffee brandy
³/₄ oz (1½ tbsp) white crème de menthe
³/₄ oz (1½ tbsp) white crème de cacao

Shake ingredients with ice and strain into a chilled cocktail glass.

———— Modern Cocktail ————

2 oz (4 tbsp) Scotch
½ tsp Jamaican rum
¼ tsp Pernod
½ tsp lemon juice
1 dash orange bitters
maraschino cherry

Shake liquid ingredients with ice and strain into a chilled cocktail glass. Garnish with the cherry.

———— Mojito ————

Its origin is unknown, but this drink is popular enough to be served at nearly every bar in the West Indies.

2 oz (4 tbsp) light rum
1 tsp sugar
4–5 fresh mint leaves
1–2 dashes Angostura bitters

Shake ingredients with ice. Strain into a chilled cocktail glass or into a collins glass that has been packed with crushed ice.

Variation: Add ½ lime, both the juice and the squeezed rind.

——— Monkey Gland ———

1½ oz (3 tbsp) gin
1 oz (2 tbsp) orange juice
2 dashes Benedictine
2 dashes grenadine

Stir or shake ingredients with ice. Strain into a chilled cocktail glass or into an old-fashioned glass over ice cubes.

Variation: Substitute 1 oz (2 tbsp) Pernod for the Benedictine and grenadine.

——— Montana ———

2 oz (4 tbsp) brandy
¾ oz (1½ tbsp) port
¾ oz (1½ tbsp) dry vermouth

Stir ingredients with ice and strain into a chilled old-fashioned glass over ice cubes.

Variation: Add 2 dashes Angostura bitters and 2 dashes anisette.

——— Montmartre Cocktail ———

1½ oz (3 tbsp) gin
½ oz (1 tbsp) sweet vermouth
½ oz (1 tbsp) Triple Sec

Shake all ingredients with cracked ice and strain into a chilled cocktail glass.

─────── **Moonlight** ───────

2 oz (4 tbsp) calvados or apple brandy
juice of 1 lemon
1 tsp sugar

Shake ingredients with ice and strain into a chilled old-fashioned glass over ice cubes.

Variation: Strain into a chilled collins glass over ice cubes and top with chilled club soda.

─────── **Morning Fizz** ───────

(serves 2)

4 oz (8 tbsp) rye whiskey
1 oz (2 tbsp) Pernod
1 oz (2 tbsp) lemon juice
2 tsp sugar
chilled club soda

Shake ingredients, except soda, vigorously with ice. Strain into chilled collins glasses over ice cubes. Top with soda and stir.

─────── **Morning Glory** ───────

2 oz (4 tbsp) brandy
$1/2$ oz (1 tbsp) curaçao
$1/2$ oz (1 tbsp) lemon juice (optional)
2 dashes Pernod
2 dashes Angostura bitters
twist of lemon peel

Shake liquid ingredients with ice and strain into a chilled cocktail glass. Garnish with lemon peel.

Variation: Strain into a collins glass over ice cubes and top with chilled club soda. Decrease brandy to 1 oz (2 tbsp) and add 1 oz (2 tbsp) rye whiskey.

——— **Morning Glory Fizz** ———

2 oz (4 tbsp) Scotch
½ tsp Pernod
1 tsp sugar
1½ oz (3 tbsp) lemon or lime juice
1 dash Angostura bitters (optional)
chilled club soda

Shake all ingredients, except soda, vigorously with ice and strain into a chilled highball or collins glass over ice cubes. Top with soda.

——— **Morro** ———

1 oz (2 tbsp) gin
½ oz (1 tbsp) dark rum
½ oz (1 tbsp) lime juice
½ oz (1 tbsp) pineapple juice
½ tsp sugar

Sugar-rim a chilled cocktail glass by rubbing the rim with lime and dipping into sugar. Shake ingredients with ice and strain into the glass.

——— **Moscow Mule** ———

3 oz (6 tbsp) vodka
juice of ½ lime
chilled ginger beer
slice of lime

Pour lime juice and vodka into a chilled collins glass or beer mug over ice cubes. Fill with ginger beer and garnish with lime slice.

Variation: Substitute ginger ale for ginger beer.

Mothers Milk

(serves 16–18)

1 qt vodka or gin
1 qt pineapple juice
1 qt grapefruit juice
thin slices of orange or lemon (optional)

Pour ingredients over a block of ice in a large punch bowl. Garnish with fruit slices if desired.

Mountain Cocktail

2 oz (4 tbsp) rye whiskey
$\frac{1}{2}$ oz (1 tbsp) dry vermouth
$\frac{1}{2}$ oz (1 tbsp) sweet vermouth
$\frac{1}{2}$ oz (1 tbsp) lemon juice
1 egg white

Shake ingredients vigorously with ice and strain into a chilled cocktail glass.

Mudslide

See **Shooters.**

Mull

See *Mulled Wine, Glogg.*

Mulled Wine I

(serves 8)

2 fifths dry red wine
6 oz brandy
6 oz port
8 whole cloves
8 sticks cinnamon
peel of 1 orange cut in pieces
peel of 1 lemon cut in pieces
1 tsp nutmeg
1 oz (2 tbsp) brown sugar

Combine ingredients in a large pan and bring almost to a boil. Simmer 5 minutes. Serve in heated glasses or mugs with a few spices and fruit peels in each.

See also *Glogg*.

Mulled Wine II

For 1 serving of mulled wine, the following is a simplified version.

5 oz dry red wine
1 tsp sugar
juice of ½ lemon
¼ tsp nutmeg
¼ tsp cinnamon
¼ tsp clove

Put ingredients into a metal mug. Put all ingredients into a saucepan. Heat until they boil. Carefully pour into metal mug.

Murray Hill

2 oz (4 tbsp) gin
2 tsp lime juice

½ tsp sugar syrup
½ oz (1 tbsp) grenadine
chilled club soda
long-stemmed maraschino cherry

Shake first 4 ingredients with ice cubes. Strain into collins glass filled with cracked ice. Top with soda and stir. Garnish with cherry.

N

Napobitter

1 oz (2 tbsp) Mandarine Napoléon
(orange-flavored brandy)
bitter lemon
thin slice lime (optional)

Fill an old-fashioned glass with cracked ice. Pour in brandy and top off with the bitter lemon. Stir gently and garnish with lime slice, if desired.

Napoleon Cocktail

2 oz (4 tbsp) gin
2 dashes curaçao
2 dashes Dubonnet
twist of lemon peel

Stir liquid ingredients with ice and strain into a chilled cocktail glass. Garnish with lemon peel.

Navy Grog

1 oz (2 tbsp) light rum
1 oz (2 tbsp) Jamaican rum

(continued)

1 oz (2 tbsp) demerara rum (86-proof)
juice of 1 lime
3/4 oz (1 1/2 tbsp) grapefruit juice
3/4 oz (1 1/2 tbsp) sugar syrup
rind of 1/2 lime
sprig of fresh mint

Shake ingredients, except lime rind and mint, with ice and strain into a chilled collins or highball glass over shaved ice. Garnish with lime rind and mint sprig and serve with a straw.

───────── **Negroni** ─────────

1 1/2 oz (3 tbsp) gin
1 1/2 oz (3 tbsp) Campari
1 1/2 oz (3 tbsp) sweet vermouth
twist of lemon peel

Put 2–3 ice cubes in a large chilled old-fashioned glass or balloon wineglass. Add liquid ingredients and stir. Garnish with lemon peel.

Variation: Stir liquid ingredients with ice and strain into a chilled cocktail glass. Garnish with lemon peel.

Variation: Substitute vodka for gin

───────── **Nevada Cocktail** ─────────

1 1/2 oz (3 tbsp) dark rum
1 1/2 oz (3 tbsp) grapefruit juice
1/2 oz (1 tbsp) lime juice
1 tsp sugar
1 dash Angostura bitters (optional)

Shake ingredients with ice and strain into a chilled cocktail glass.

─────── **Nevins** ───────

1½ oz (3 tbsp) bourbon
¼ oz (1½ tsp) apricot brandy
½ oz (1 tbsp) grapefruit juice
¼ oz (1½ tsp) lemon juice
1 dash Angostura bitters

Shake ingredients with ice and strain into a chilled cocktail glass.

Variation: Sugar-rim the glass by rubbing with lemon and dipping into sugar.

─────── **New Orleans Buck** ───────

1½ oz (3 tbsp) rum
½ oz (1 tbsp) lime juice
½ oz (1 tbsp) orange juice
chilled ginger ale
slice of lime

Shake first 3 ingredients with ice and strain into a chilled collins glass over ice cubes. Top with ginger ale and stir. Garnish with lime.

─────── **New Orleans Gin Fizz** ───────

2 oz (4 tbsp) gin
juice of ½ lemon
juice of ½ lime
1 tsp sugar
½ oz (1 tbsp) cream
1 egg white
chilled club soda
slice of lime or lemon

(continued)

Shake first 6 ingredients with ice. Strain into a chilled highball or collins glass over ice cubes. Top with soda, stir, and garnish with lime or lemon.

New York(er) Cocktail

2 oz (4 tbsp) rye or bourbon
juice of ½ lime
2 dashes grenadine
twist of orange peel

Shake liquid ingredients with ice and strain into a chilled cocktail glass. Garnish with orange peel.

New York Sour

2 oz (4 tbsp) rye whiskey
juice of ½ lemon
1 tsp sugar
chilled dry red wine
small slice of lemon

Shake rye, lemon, and sugar with ice. Strain into a chilled sour glass and top with wine. Stir and garnish with lemon slice.

Nightcap

2 oz (4 tbsp) brandy
1 tsp sugar or ½ oz (1 tbsp) honey
6 oz warm milk

Put brandy and sugar into a warmed mug. Add milk and stir.

Variation: To serve cold, mix cold milk and sugar in a tall glass. Add brandy and stir.

——— **Night Owl** ———

2 oz (4 tbsp) bourbon
½ oz (1 tbsp) lemon juice
½ oz (1 tbsp) Triple Sec
dash of bitters
chilled club soda

To highball glass filled with cracked ice add first 4 ingredients and stir gently. Top with soda and stir again.

——— **Ninotchka** ———

1½ oz (3 tbsp) vodka
½ oz (1 tbsp) white crème de cacao
½ oz (1 tbsp) lemon juice

Shake ingredients with ice and strain into a chilled cocktail glass.

——— **Nob Hill** ———

2 oz (4 tbsp) whiskey
1 oz (2 tbsp) grapefruit juice
1 tsp honey

Shake ingredients with cracked ice and strain into a chilled cocktail glass.

O

——— **Ocho Rios** ———

1½ oz (3 tbsp) dark rum
1 oz (2 tbsp) guava nectar *or*
½ cup diced guava

(continued)

½ oz (1 tbsp) lime juice
½ tsp sugar
½ oz (1 tbsp) cream (optional)
⅓ cup crushed ice

Put ingredients in a blender and blend at low speed for 15 seconds. Pour into a chilled champagne glass.

─────── **Old Etonian** ───────

1½ oz (3 tbsp) gin
1½ oz (3 tbsp) Lillet
2 dashes orange bitters
2 dashes crème de noyaux
twist of orange peel

Stir liquid ingredients with ice and strain into a chilled cocktail glass. Garnish with orange peel.

─────── **Old-Fashioned** ───────

As in the case of numerous other cocktails, the origin of the old-fashioned is uncertain. Some say it was invented at the Pendennis Club, Louisville, Kentucky, in the late 1880s, the result of a bartender's being asked to make a "good old-fashioned cocktail." There are countless variations on this classic cocktail. Some "authorities" insist on sugar syrup instead of a cube; others may instruct the bartender to "hold the garbage," that is, to eliminate the fruit.

2 oz (4 tbsp) rye or bourbon
½ cube sugar
1 dash Angostura bitters
1 tsp water
twist of lemon peel
maraschino cherry
1 slice lemon, lime, or orange

Muddle sugar and bitters in water in a chilled old-fashioned glass. Add whiskey slowly, while stirring. Add ice and garnish with the lemon peel and fruit.

Variations: Add 1 dash curaçao. Soak fruit slices overnight in whiskey. Various liquors can be substituted for the whiskey (rum, Scotch, tequila, etc.), and the old-fashioned is then named after the liquor used (Rum Old-Fashioned).

———————   **Old Pal Cocktail**   ———————

1 oz (2 tbsp) rye whiskey
1 oz (2 tbsp) Campari
1 oz (2 tbsp) dry vermouth

Stir ingredients with ice and strain into a chilled cocktail glass.

Variation: For a sweeter drink, substitute sweet vermouth for the dry and grenadine for the Campari.

———————   **Olympic Cocktail**   ———————

1 oz (2 tbsp) brandy
1 oz (2 tbsp) curaçao
1 oz (2 tbsp) orange juice
twist of orange peel (optional)

Shake liquid ingredients with ice and strain into a chilled cocktail glass. Garnish with orange peel.

———————   **Opal Cocktail**   ———————

1½ oz (3 tbsp) London dry gin
½ oz (1 tbsp) Cointreau
½ oz (1 tbsp) orange juice

(continued)

½ tsp orange-flower water
½ tsp sugar

Shake all ingredients with cracked ice and strain into a chilled cocktail glass.

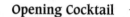

Opening Cocktail

2 oz (4 tbsp) rye whiskey
1 oz (2 tbsp) sweet vermouth
½ oz (1 tbsp) grenadine

Shake ingredients with ice and strain into a chilled cocktail glass or into an old-fashioned glass over ice cubes.

Opera Cocktail

1½ oz (3 tbsp) gin
½ oz (1 tbsp) Dubonnet
1 tsp maraschino

Stir or shake ingredients with ice and strain into a chilled cocktail glass.

Variation: Add 1 dash orange juice and garnish with a twist of orange peel.

Orange Bloom

1½ oz (3 tbsp) gin
3 tsp Cointreau or Triple Sec
2 tsp sweet vermouth

Shake ingredients with ice and strain into a chilled cocktail glass.

———— Orange Blossom Cocktail ————

2 oz (4 tbsp) gin
1 oz (2 tbsp) orange juice
1/4 tsp sugar (optional)

Shake ingredients with ice and strain into a chilled cocktail glass.

Variation: Add 2 tsp curaçao and 1 egg white and put in a blender at low speed for 15 seconds. Pour into a chilled sour or wineglass over ice cubes. Garnish with slice of orange.

———— Orange Buck ————

1 1/2 oz (3 tbsp) gin
1 oz (2 tbsp) orange juice
1/2 oz (1 tbsp) lemon or lime juice
chilled ginger ale
slice of lime (optional)

Shake gin and juices with ice. Strain into a chilled collins glass over ice cubes. Top with ginger ale and stir. Garnish with lime slice if desired.

———— Orange Fizz ————

2 oz (4 tbsp) gin
2 tsp Cointreau or Triple Sec (optional)
1 tsp sugar
juice of 1/2 orange
juice of 1/2 lemon
chilled club soda
slice of orange

Shake first 5 ingredients with ice and strain into a chilled highball glass over ice cubes. Top with soda and garnish with orange slice.

Orange Gin Cooler

2 oz (4 tbsp) orange-flavored gin
1/2 oz (1 tbsp) fresh lemon juice
1/2 oz (1 tbsp) Triple Sec
chilled club soda
maraschino cherry

Shake together first 3 ingredients with 4 or 5 ice cubes. Strain into a collins glass half-filled with cracked ice and top with soda. Stir briefly and garnish with cherry before serving.

Orange Oasis

1 1/2 oz (3 tbsp) gin
1/2 oz (1 tbsp) cherry brandy
4 oz (8 tbsp) chilled orange juice
chilled ginger ale

Pour gin, brandy, and orange juice into a chilled highball glass over ice cubes. Top with ginger ale and stir.

Orient Express

1 oz (2 tbsp) gin
1 oz (2 tbsp) bourbon
1 oz (2 tbsp) brandy

In mixing glass stir ingredients with cracked ice and strain into chilled cocktail glass.

Ostend Fizz

3/4 oz (1 1/2 tbsp) crème de cassis
3/4 oz (1 1/2 tbsp) kirschwasser
chilled club soda

Shake crème de cassis and kirschwasser with ice. Strain into a chilled collins or highball glass over ice cubes and top with soda.

Variation: Add ½ oz (1 tbsp) lemon juice and 1 tsp sugar and shake with other ingredients. Garnish with slice of lemon.

P

Paddy Cocktail

1½ oz (3 tbsp) Irish whiskey
1½ oz (3 tbsp) sweet vermouth
1 dash Angostura bitters

Stir ingredients with ice and strain into a chilled cocktail glass.

Paisley Martini

See *Martini.*

Pall Mall

1½ oz (3 tbsp) gin
½ oz (1 tbsp) dry vermouth
½ oz (1 tbsp) sweet vermouth
1 tsp white crème de menthe
1 dash orange bitters (optional)

Stir ingredients with ice and strain into a chilled cocktail glass or into an old-fashioned glass over ice cubes.

--------- **Palm Beach Cooler** ---------

(serves 15)

2 bottles dry white wine
¼ cup sugar syrup
2 cups cubed pineapple
6 orange slices
6 lemon slices
block of ice
1 liter club soda, chilled
mint sprigs

In large punch bowl with block of ice add first 5 ingredients and stir to combine. Just before serving pour soda over ice. Ladle into punch cups and garnish each with mint sprig.

--------- **Palmer Cocktail** ---------

2 oz (4 tbsp) rye or bourbon
2 dashes lemon juice
1 dash Angostura bitters

Stir ingredients with ice and strain into a chilled cocktail glass.

--------- **Panama Cocktail** ---------

1 oz (2 tbsp) rum
1 oz (2 tbsp) crème de cacao
1 oz (2 tbsp) cream

Shake ingredients with ice and strain into a chilled cocktail glass.

Variation: Substitute brandy for rum.

Panama Hattie

1½ oz (3 tbsp) white rum
1 oz (2 tbsp) banana liqueur
½ oz (1 tbsp) curaçao
1 tsp lemon juice

Place all ingredients in blender with 1 cup cracked ice. Cover and blend at high speed 10 to 15 seconds. Pour into a chilled wineglass.

Paradise Cocktail

1½ oz (3 tbsp) gin
1 oz (2 tbsp) apricot brandy
juice of ¼ orange
slice of orange (optional)

Shake liquid ingredients with ice and strain into a chilled cocktail glass. Garnish with orange slice.

Parisian

1 oz (2 tbsp) gin
1 oz (2 tbsp) dry vermouth
1 oz (2 tbsp) crème de cassis

Shake ingredients with ice and strain into a chilled cocktail glass.

Park Avenue

2 oz (4 tbsp) gin
1 oz (2 tbsp) sweet vermouth
1 oz (2 tbsp) pineapple juice
1–2 dashes curaçao (optional)

Shake ingredients with ice and strain into a large chilled cocktail glass or wineglass.

———— **Park West** ————

2 oz (4 tbsp) gin
2 oz (4 tbsp) pineapple juice
2 oz (4 tbsp) grapefruit juice

Place ingredients in shaker with 5 or 6 ice cubes, cover, and shake briskly several times. Pour immediately into a chilled highball glass.

Variation: Substitute vodka for gin.

———— **Peach Blossom** ————

2 oz (4 tbsp) gin
$\frac{1}{2}$ oz (1 tbsp) peach brandy
1 tsp lemon juice
1 tsp sugar syrup
$\frac{1}{2}$ ripe peach

Put all ingredients in blender with $\frac{1}{2}$ cup cracked ice. Blend 10–15 seconds at high speed till thoroughly puréed. Pour into a chilled wineglass.

———— **Peach Blow Fizz** ————

2 oz (4 tbsp) gin
$\frac{1}{4}$ peach
juice of $\frac{1}{2}$ lemon
$\frac{2}{3}$ oz (1$\frac{1}{3}$ tbsp) cream
$\frac{1}{2}$ tsp powdered sugar
chilled club soda
2 fresh strawberries

Shake first 5 ingredients with ice. Strain into a chilled highball glass over ice cubes and top with soda. Garnish with strawberries.

Peach Buck

1½ oz (3 tbsp) vodka
½ oz (1 tbsp) peach brandy
½ oz (1 tbsp) lemon juice
chilled ginger ale

Place liquors and juice in shaker with 5 or 6 ice cubes, cover, and shake vigorously several times. Strain into a highball glass three-quarters filled with cracked ice. Top with ginger ale and stir gently.

Peaches & Cream

2 oz (4 tbsp) golden rum
1 oz (2 tbsp) peach brandy
½ oz (1 tbsp) heavy cream

Place ingredients in shaker with 4 or 5 ice cubes. Cover and shake briskly several times. Strain into a chilled sour glass.

Peach Fizz

2 oz (4 tbsp) cognac (brandy)
2 tsp peach brandy
2 tsp lemon juice
1½ tsp sugar syrup
1 tsp banana liqueur
cold champagne or sparkling wine
peach slice

In shaker with 4 or 5 ice cubes place first 5 ingredients. Cover and shake quickly 3 or 4 times. Strain immediately into a chilled wineglass and top with champagne. Decorate glass with peach slice or add to drink.

———— **Peach Melba** ————

1 oz (2 tbsp) peach schnapps
1/2 oz (1 tbsp) black raspberry schnapps
2 oz (4 tbsp) cream

In a shaker with ice, pour ingredients and shake vigorously. Pour into an old-fashioned glass.

———— **Peach Sangaree** ————

2 oz (4 tbsp) peach brandy
chilled club soda
1/2 oz (1 tbsp) port
grated nutmeg (optional)

In highball glass place 3 or 4 ice cubes and add brandy. Top with soda and stir. Carefully float port on top and, if desired, sprinkle lightly with nutmeg.

———— **Pendennis Cocktail** ————

From Louisville's famed Pendennis Club.

1 1/2 oz (3 tbsp) gin
1/2 oz (1 tbsp) apricot brandy
1/2 oz (1 tbsp) lime juice
1–2 dashes Peychaud's bitters

Add all ingredients to shaker with 4 or 5 ice cubes. Cover and shake vigorously several times. Strain into chilled cocktail glass.

———— **Perfect Manhattan** ————

See *Manhattan.*

——— **Perfect Martini** ———

See *Martini.*

——— **Pernod Frappé** ———

2½ oz (5 tbsp) Pernod
½ oz (1 tbsp) anisette (optional)
½ oz (1 tbsp) cream

Shake ingredients vigorously with ice and strain into
a chilled cocktail glass or wineglass.

——— **Petite Fleur** ———

1 oz (2 tbsp) light rum
1 oz (2 tbsp) Cointreau or Triple Sec
1 oz (2 tbsp) grapefruit juice
twist of orange peel (optional)

Shake liquid ingredients with ice and strain into a
chilled cocktail glass. Garnish with orange peel.

——— **Philly Mainliner** ———

2 oz (4 tbsp) cognac (brandy)
1 oz (2 tbsp) curaçao
dash anisette
stemmed maraschino cherry (optional)

Place liquors in shaker with ½ cup cracked ice. Cover and shake vigorously several times. Strain into a
chilled cocktail glass and garnish with cherry, if desired.

———   **Phoebe Snow**   ———

1½ oz (3 tbsp) Dubonnet
1½ oz (3 tbsp) brandy
1–2 dashes Pernod

Place liquors in shaker with ½ cup cracked ice. Cover and shake briskly several times. Strain into an old-fashioned glass two-thirds full of cracked ice.

———   **Picador**   ———

3 oz (6 tbsp) very dry sherry, chilled
½ oz (1 tbsp) Cointreau
lemon zest

Add liquors to chilled sherry glass and stir gently. Twist zest over drink to release oils and add.

———   **Piccadilly Cocktail**   ———

1½ oz (3 tbsp) gin
¾ oz (1½ tbsp) dry vermouth
1 dash Pernod
1 dash grenadine

Stir ingredients with ice and strain into a chilled cocktail glass.

———   **Picon Cocktail**   ———

See *Amer Picon Cocktail.*

———   **Pike's Peak**   ———

2 oz (4 tbsp) gin
½ oz (1 tbsp) lemon juice

½ oz (1 tbsp) white maraschino
whipped cream

Shake first 3 ingredients vigorously with ice cubes and strain into chilled wineglass. Top with whipped cream.

———— **Pimm's Cup** ————

3 oz (6 tbsp) Pimm's No. 1
1 tsp Cointreau (optional)
1 tsp sugar
juice of 1 lime
6 oz chilled lemon soda or 7-Up
2 lengthwise peels of cucumber
sprig of fresh mint
slice of lemon

Dissolve sugar in lime juice in a large chilled mug or highball glass. Add ice, Pimm's, and Cointreau. Top with lemon soda and stir gently. Stand cucumber peels upright in the glass and garnish with mint and lemon slice.

PIÑA COLADA

2½ oz (5 tbsp) light rum
3 oz (6 tbsp) pineapple juice or
crushed pineapple (canned)
2 oz (4 tbsp) coconut cream
¾ cup crushed ice
2 pieces fresh pineapple for garnish

Put ingredients, except fresh pineapple pieces, in a blender and blend at medium-high speed for 15 seconds. Pour into a chilled collins glass or stemmed goblet. Garnish with fresh pineapple.

Variation: Substitute tequila for rum.

Banana Colada

2½ oz (5 tbsp) light rum
1 very ripe banana, mashed
2 oz (4 tbsp) coconut cream
1 oz (2 tbsp) banana liqueur
¾ cup crushed ice
whipped cream
cherry

Put first 5 ingredients in a blender and blend at medium-high speed for 15 seconds. Pour into a chilled collins glass or stemmed goblet. Garnish with whipped cream and cherry.

Cranberry Colada

2½ oz (5 tbsp) light rum
2 oz (4 tbsp) cranberry juice
2 oz (4 tbsp) coconut cream
¾ cup crushed ice
lime

Put ingredients, except lime, in a blender and blend at medium-high speed for 15 seconds. Pour into a chilled collins glass or stemmed goblet. Garnish with lime wedge.

Lime Colada

2½ oz (5 tbsp) light rum
2 oz (4 tbsp) Rose's lime juice
2 oz (4 tbsp) coconut cream
¾ cup crushed ice
lime

Put ingredients, except lime, in a blender and blend at medium-high speed for 15 seconds. Pour into a chilled collins glass or stemmed goblet. Garnish with lime wedge.

Piña Fría

2 oz (4 tbsp) light rum
2 oz (4 tbsp) pineapple juice
½ oz (1 tbsp) lemon juice
1 dash sugar syrup
2 slices fresh pineapple
½ cup crushed ice

Put ingredients into a blender and blend at medium speed for 10–15 seconds. Pour into a chilled stemmed goblet.

Pineapple Cooler

3 oz (6 tbsp) chilled dry white wine
3 oz (6 tbsp) pineapple juice
1 dash lemon juice
½ tsp sugar
peel of ½ lemon cut in a continuous spiral

Dissolve sugar in juice in a chilled collins glass or stemmed goblet. Add ice cubes and wine. Garnish with lemon peel.

Pineapple Fizz

2 oz (4 tbsp) rum
1 tsp sugar
1 oz (2 tbsp) pineapple juice
chilled club soda

Shake rum, sugar, and juice with ice. Strain into a chilled collins glass over ice cubes and top with club soda.

——— **Pine Valley Cocktail** ———

juice of 1 lime
2 oz (4 tbsp) gin
2 or 3 sprigs fresh mint
½ tsp sugar

In shaker add all ingredients (first bruising the mint) along with several ice cubes. Cover and shake vigorously, then strain into a chilled cocktail glass.

——— **Pink Almond** ———

1 oz (2 tbsp) rye whiskey
½ oz (1 tbsp) crème de noyaux
½ oz (1 tbsp) orgeat
½ oz (1 tbsp) kirsch
½ oz (1 tbsp) lemon juice
slice of lemon

Shake liquid ingredients with ice and strain into a chilled old-fashioned glass over ice cubes. Garnish with lemon slice.

——— **Pink Creole** ———

1½ oz (3 tbsp) light rum
½ oz (1 tbsp) lime juice
1 tsp grenadine
1 tsp cream
1 black cherry soaked in rum

Shake liquid ingredients with ice and strain into a chilled cocktail glass. Garnish with black cherry.

——— **Pink Gin** ———

See *Gin & Bitters*.

————— **Pink Lady Cocktail** —————

2 oz (4 tbsp) gin
1 tsp grenadine
1 tsp cream
1 tsp lemon juice (optional)

Shake ingredients vigorously with ice and strain into a chilled cocktail glass.

————— **Pink Panther** —————

2 oz (4 tbsp) grain alcohol
4 oz (8 tbsp) cranberry juice
2 or 3 ice cubes

Place 2 or 3 ice cubes in a chilled highball glass. Add alcohol, fill with cranberry juice, and stir.

Variation: Place all ingredients, including ice cubes, in a blender and blend at high speed for 20–30 seconds. Pour into a chilled goblet.

————— **Pink Rose** —————

1 1/2 oz (3 tbsp) gin
1 tsp lemon juice
1 tsp heavy cream
1/2 oz (1 tbsp) egg white
1/2 tsp grenadine

Place all ingredients in shaker with 5 or 6 ice cubes. Cover and shake vigorously. Strain into a chilled cocktail glass or into an old-fashioned glass filled with crushed ice.

———— Pink Rose Fizz ————

2 oz (4 tbsp) gin
½ oz (1 tbsp) lemon juice
1 tsp grenadine
½ oz (1 tbsp) heavy cream
1 tsp sugar syrup
chilled club soda

Place all ingredients but soda in shaker with 4 or 5 ice cubes. Cover and shake vigorously. Strain into a chilled highball glass. Top with soda and stir gently.

———— Pink Squirrel Cocktail ————

1 oz (2 tbsp) créme de noyaux
1 oz (2 tbsp) white crème de cacao
1 oz (2 tbsp) light cream

Shake ingredients with ice and strain into a chilled cocktail glass.

———— Pisco Punch ————

2 oz (4 tbsp) pisco brandy
1 tsp lemon or lime juice
1 tsp sugar
2–3 drops Angostura bitters

Shake ingredients, except bitters, with ice and strain into a chilled cocktail glass. Shake bitters on top.

Variation: Sugar-rim the glass by rubbing with lemon or lime and dipping into sugar.

--------   **Pisco Sour (Pisco Cooler)**   --------

Although the addition of club soda actually makes
this a cooler, it is commonly known as a sour.

2 oz (4 tbsp) pisco brandy
1/2–3/4 oz (1–1 1/2 tbsp) lemon juice
1 tsp sugar
2–3 dashes Angostura bitters
chilled club soda
slice of lemon

Stir first 4 ingredients with ice cubes in a chilled highball glass. Top with soda and garnish with lemon
slice.

--------   **Plantation Cocktail**   --------

2 oz (4 tbsp) bourbon
1/2 tsp crème de menthe
1/2 tsp sugar syrup
3 or 4 drops curaçao
dash bitters

Combine all ingredients in mixing glass. Pour over
cracked ice in an old-fashioned glass.

--------   **Plantation Punch**   --------

1 1/2 oz (3 tbsp) Southern Comfort
3/4 oz (1 1/2 tbsp) lemon juice
2 dashes light rum
1 tsp sugar
chilled club soda
maraschino cherry
twist of orange peel

(continued)

Mix first 4 ingredients in a large old-fashioned glass. Add ice cubes and top with soda. Garnish with cherry and orange peel.

--------   **Planter's Cocktail**   --------

1½ oz (3 tbsp) light rum
¾ oz (1½ tbsp) lemon juice
½ tsp sugar
¾ oz (1½ tbsp) orange juice (optional)

Shake ingredients with ice and strain into a chilled cocktail glass.

--------   **Planter's Punch**   --------

3 oz (6 tbsp) Jamaican rum
juice of 1 lime
1 tsp sugar
1 oz (2 tbsp) chilled club soda
slices of orange and lime
maraschino cherry

Dissolve sugar in lime juice in a frosted collins glass. Add rum and fill with crushed ice. Top with soda, stir, and garnish with fruit.

Variation: Add juice of ½ orange and top drink with 2 dashes Triple Sec.

--------   **Platinum Blonde**   --------

1 oz (2 tbsp) light rum
1 oz (2 tbsp) Cointreau
½ oz (1 tbsp) cream

Shake ingredients with ice and strain into a chilled cocktail glass.

Variation: Substitute Grand Marnier for Cointreau.

——— Poinsettia ———

1½ oz (3 tbsp) cranberry juice, chilled
½ oz (1 tbsp) apple brandy
cold champagne or other sparkling wine

To chilled champagne flute add ingredients in order given. Top off with champagne and stir briefly.

——— Pollyanna Cocktail ———

2 oz (4 tbsp) gin
²/₃ oz (1⅓ tbsp) sweet vermouth
½ tsp grenadine
3 slices of orange
3 slices of pineapple

Muddle orange and pineapple slices. Add other ingredients and shake with ice. Strain into a chilled cocktail glass.

——— Polo Cocktail ———

1½ oz (3 tbsp) gin
¾ oz (1½ tbsp) orange juice
¾ oz (1½ tbsp) lemon juice

Shake ingredients with ice and strain into a chilled cocktail glass.

Variation: Substitute grapefruit juice for lemon juice.

——— **Polonaise** ———

1½ oz (3 tbsp) brandy
½ oz (1 tbsp) blackberry brandy
½ oz (1 tbsp) dry sherry
2 dashes lemon juice
1 dash orange bitters (optional)

Shake ingredients with ice and strain into a chilled cocktail glass or into an old-fashioned glass over ice cubes.

——— **Polynesia Cocktail** ———

1½ oz (3 tbsp) light rum
1½ oz (3 tbsp) passionfruit juice
½ oz (1 tbsp) lime juice
1 egg white
½ cup crushed ice

Put ingredients into a blender and blend at low speed for 10–15 seconds. Pour into a chilled champagne glass.

——— **Pompano** ———

1½ oz (3 tbsp) gin
¾ oz (1½ tbsp) dry vermouth
1½ oz (3 tbsp) grapefruit juice
2 dashes orange bitters (optional)

Shake ingredients with ice and strain into a chilled cocktail glass.

——— **Pope, The** ———

See *Bishop.*

——— **Port in a Storm** ———

3 oz (6 tbsp) port
1 oz (2 tbsp) brandy
½ oz (1 tbsp) lemon juice
twist of lemon peel

Stir liquid ingredients with ice and pour into a wine-glass. Add more ice if necessary and garnish with lemon peel.

Variation: Add 2 oz (4 tbsp) dry red wine.

——— **Port Wine Cocktail** ———

2 oz (4 tbsp) port
½ oz (1 tbsp) brandy
twist of orange peel (optional)

Stir port and brandy with ice and strain into a chilled cocktail glass. Garnish with orange peel.

——— **Port Wine Eggnog** ———

4 oz (8 tbsp) port
1 whole egg
1 tsp sugar
nutmeg

Shake ingredients, except nutmeg, vigorously with ice and strain into a chilled wineglass or flip glass. Sprinkle with nutmeg.

Variation: Shake with cracked ice and pour into the glass. Add 2 tsp cream.

─────   **Port Wine Flip**   ─────

4 oz (8 tbsp) port
2 tsp cream
1 tsp sugar
nutmeg

Shake all ingredients, except nutmeg, vigorously with ice and strain into a chilled wine or flip glass. Sprinkle with nutmeg.

─────   **Port Wine Sangaree**   ─────

2 oz (4 tbsp) port
1 tsp sugar
chilled club soda
1/2 oz (1 tbsp) brandy
slice of lemon
nutmeg

Dissolve sugar in port in a chilled highball glass. Add ice and top with soda. Float brandy on top. Garnish with lemon slice and sprinkle with nutmeg.

See also *Sangaree.*

─────   **Pousse-Café**   ─────

An after-dinner drink consisting of 2 or more liqueurs served in a tall cordial glass in separate layers. Carefully made, the drink can present a spectacular rainbow effect. The number of liqueurs combined usually varies from 2 to 7, and, since liqueurs vary in density, they should be poured heavy-to-light in ascending order of lightness. The best method of keeping them separate is to pour them slowly over the back of a spoon held inside the glass.

Listed below are several suggested variations of

pousse-cafés, but the combinations are almost limit-less.

Variation 1:

    ½ oz (1 tbsp) parfait d'amour
    ½ oz (1 tbsp) crème Yvette

Variation 2:

    ¼ oz (1½ tsp) orange curaçao
    ¼ oz (1½ tsp) kirschwasser
    ¼ oz (1½ tsp) cognac
    ¼ oz (1½ tsp) green Chartreuse

Variation 3:

    ¼ oz (1½ tsp) green crème de menthe
    ¼ oz (1½ tsp) yellow Chartreuse
    ¼ oz (1½ tsp) Peter Heering
    ¼ oz (1½ tsp) cognac

Variation 4:

    ⅙ oz (1 tsp) grenadine
    ⅙ oz (1 tsp) yellow Chartreuse
    ⅙ oz (1 tsp) crème de cassis
    ⅙ oz (1 tsp) white crème de menthe
    ⅙ oz (1 tsp) green Chartreuse
    ⅙ oz (1 tsp) cognac

Variation 5:

    ⅙ oz (1 tsp) grenadine
    ⅙ oz (1 tsp) dark crème de cacao
    ⅙ oz (1 tsp) maraschino
    ⅙ oz (1 tsp) orange curaçao
    ⅙ oz (1 tsp) green crème de menthe
    ⅙ oz (1 tsp) parfait d'amour
    ⅙ (1 tsp) oz cognac

——— **Prado** ———

(serves 2)

3 oz (6 tbsp) tequila
1 1/2 oz (3 tbsp) lime or lemon juice
1 oz (2 tbsp) maraschino
4 dashes grenadine
2 small slices of lemon
2 maraschino cherries

Shake first 4 ingredients with ice and strain into chilled sour glasses. Garnish with lemon slices and cherries.

——— **Presbyterian** ———

See *Whiskey Highball.*

——— **Prince Edward** ———

1 1/2 oz (3 tbsp) Scotch
1/2 oz (1 tbsp) dry vermouth
1/4 oz Drambuie
slice of orange

Shake liquid ingredients with ice and strain into a chilled old-fashioned glass over ice cubes. Garnish with orange slice.

Variation: Substitute Lillet for vermouth.

——— **Princeton Cocktail** ———

2 oz (4 tbsp) gin
1 oz (2 tbsp) port
1–2 dashes orange bitters
twist of lemon peel

Stir liquid ingredients with ice and strain into a chilled cocktail glass. Garnish with lemon peel.

Variation: Eliminate orange bitters, add juice of ½ lime, and substitute dry vermouth for the port.

——————— **Puerto Apple** ———————

1½ oz (3 tbsp) applejack
¾ oz (1½ tbsp) light rum
½ oz (1 tbsp) lime juice
2 tsp orgeat
slice of lime

Shake liquid ingredients with ice and strain into a chilled old-fashioned glass over ice cubes. Garnish with lime slice.

——————— **Punch** ———————

A drink that can easily be made in quantity to serve large groups of people. Typically it contains liquor (brandy, rum, vodka, etc.), fruit juice, and soda or ginger ale. A recipe usually serves 8–12 people, making it a simple matter to double or triple the recipe for large numbers. For a list of punches, see *Punch* in **Index by Type of Drink.**

——————— **Purple Jesus** ———————

1 oz (2 tbsp) grain alcohol
4 oz (8 tbsp) Concord grape juice

Put 2 or 3 ice cubes in a chilled highball glass. Pour in alcohol, fill with grape juice and stir.

Variation: Substitute 2 oz (4 tbsp) vodka for the grain alcohol.

Q

-------- **Quaker's Cocktail** --------

1 oz (2 tbsp) brandy
1 oz (2 tbsp) light rum
$\frac{1}{2}$ oz (1 tbsp) lemon juice
1$\frac{1}{2}$ tsp raspberry syrup
twist of lemon peel (optional)

Shake liquid ingredients with ice and strain into a chilled cocktail glass. Garnish with lemon peel.

-------- **Quarter Deck Cocktail** --------

2 oz (4 tbsp) dark rum
1 oz (2 tbsp) dry sherry
2 dashes lime juice

Stir ingredients with ice and strain into a chilled cocktail glass.

Variation: Substitute sweet sherry for dry.

-------- **Quebec** --------

1$\frac{1}{2}$ oz (3 tbsp) Canadian whiskey
$\frac{1}{2}$ oz (1 tbsp) dry vermouth
1 tsp Amer Picon
1 tsp maraschino

Shake or stir ingredients with ice and strain into a chilled cocktail glass.

Variation: Sugar-rim the glass by rubbing with lemon and dipping into sugar.

——— **Queen of Denmark** ———

1½ oz (3 tbsp) Cherry Heering
½ oz (1 tbsp) heavy cream

Pour liqueur into cordial glass. Carefully float cream on top.

——— **Queen of Spades** ———

2 oz (4 tbsp) dark Jamaican rum
1 oz (2 tbsp) Tia Maria
1 oz (2 tbsp) heavy cream

Blend with ½ cup cracked ice at high speed 10–15 seconds. Pour into chilled wineglass.

——— **Queens** ———

¾ oz (1½ tbsp) gin
¾ oz (1½ tbsp) dry vermouth
¾ oz (1½ tbsp) sweet vermouth
¾ oz (1½ tbsp) pineapple juice

Shake ingredients with ice and strain into a chilled cocktail glass.

Variation: Muddle a slice of fresh pineapple in place of the pineapple juice.

——— **Quelle Vie** ———

Pronounced "kell vee," and as the French say, "What a life!"

1½ oz (3 tbsp) brandy
¾ oz kümmel

(continued)

Stir ingredients with ice and strain into a chilled cocktail glass.

R

——— **Racquet Club Cocktail** ———

2 oz (4 tbsp) gin
1 oz (2 tbsp) dry vermouth
1 dash orange bitters

Stir ingredients with ice and strain into a chilled cocktail glass.

——— **Rainbow Ridge** ———

1 oz (2 tbsp) apricot brandy
1/2 oz (1 tbsp) cherry brandy
1 tsp fresh lemon juice
1/2 oz (1 tbsp) heavy cream
1/2 ripe banana peeled and sliced

Place all ingredients into blender with 1/2 cup cracked ice. Blend at high speed for 10–15 seconds or until just puréed. Pour into chilled wineglass.

——— **Ramos Gin Fizz I** ———

2 oz (4 tbsp) gin
2 oz (4 tbsp) light cream or milk
juice of 1/2 lemon
1 tsp sugar
1 tsp orange-flower water

Shake ingredients with ice and strain into a chilled cocktail glass. Add ice cubes if desired.

————— **Ramos Gin Fizz II** —————

1½ oz (3 tbsp) gin
1 oz (2 tbsp) powdered sugar
juice of ½ lemon and ½ lime
½ tsp orange-flower water
1 oz (2 tbsp) heavy cream
crushed ice
club soda or seltzer

In bottom of cocktail shaker add all ingredients except soda, including ½ cup or more of crushed ice. Shake vigorously and strain into a chilled highball glass. Top with a jigger of club soda or seltzer.

————— **Rancho Grande** —————

2 oz (4 tbsp) light rum
1 oz (2 tbsp) dry sherry
½ oz (1 tbsp) brandy
1 tsp curaçao

Pour all ingredients into an old-fashioned glass half-filled with cracked ice. Stir gently.

————— **Raspberry Cream** —————

2 oz (4 tbsp) white rum
1 oz (2 tbsp) crème de framboise
½ oz (1 tbsp) heavy cream
1–2 dashes orange bitters

Place ingredients in shaker with ice cubes. Cover and shake briskly several times. Strain into a chilled cocktail glass.

——— **Red Apple** ———

1 oz (2 tbsp) vodka
1 oz (2 tbsp) apple juice
¹/₂ oz (1 tbsp) lemon juice
2–3 dashes grenadine

Shake ingredients with ice and strain into a chilled cocktail glass.

——— **Red Cloud** ———

1¹/₂ oz (3 tbsp) gin
¹/₂ oz (1 tbsp) apricot brandy
¹/₂ oz (1 tbsp) lemon juice
1 tsp grenadine
1 dash Angostura bitters (optional)

Shake ingredients with ice and strain into a chilled cocktail glass.

——— **Red-Eye Special** ———

Favored by some as a pick-me-up and by others as a morning-after remedy.

6 oz tomato juice
6 oz beer
1 tsp Worcestershire sauce
1 tsp lemon juice
1–2 dashes Tabasco sauce

Combine all ingredients in a large glass with several ice cubes. Stir to mix.

——— Red Lion ———

1½ oz (3 tbsp) Grand Marnier
¾ oz (1½ tbsp) gin
1 oz (2 tbsp) lemon juice
1 oz (2 tbsp) orange juice
1 dash orange bitters (optional)
twist of orange peel

Shake liquid ingredients vigorously with ice and strain into a chilled cocktail glass. Garnish with orange peel.

——— Renaissance Cocktail ———

1½ oz (3 tbsp) gin
1 oz (2 tbsp) dry sherry
¾ oz (1½ tbsp) cream
nutmeg

Shake liquid ingredients with ice and strain into a chilled cocktail glass. Sprinkle with nutmeg.

——— Resolute Cocktail ———

1½ oz (3 tbsp) gin
¾ oz (1½ tbsp) apricot brandy
½ oz (1 tbsp) lemon juice

Stir or shake ingredients with ice and strain into a chilled cocktail glass.

——— Rhine Wine Cup ———

(serves 6–8)

1 bottle chilled Rhine wine
1 oz (2 tbsp) brandy

(continued)

1 oz (2 tbsp) Triple Sec or curaçao
1 oz (2 tbsp) maraschino
8 oz chilled club soda
strips of cucumber peel
sprigs of fresh mint

Mix brandy, Triple Sec, and maraschino and put into a pitcher with ice cubes. Add wine and soda, stir, and garnish with cucumber peels and mint. Serve in chilled wineglasses.

Rhine Wine Punch

(serves 6–8)

2 qts chilled Rhine wine
1 qt chilled club soda
3 oz (6 tbsp) brandy
3 oz (6 tbsp) Cointreau or Triple Sec
1 cup strong tea
juice of 3 lemons
sliced fresh fruit
sprigs of fresh mint

Pour liquid ingredients into a punch bowl over a block of ice and stir gently. Garnish with fruit and mint.

Rickey

A tall drink consisting of liquor (traditionally gin but often rum, vodka, or sloe gin) and lime juice topped off with club soda. For a list of rickey drinks, see *Rickey* in **Index by Type of Drink.**

─────── **Rittenhouse Special** ───────

Named for Philadelphia's famous square.

1½ oz (3 tbsp) bourbon
1 oz (2 tbsp) heavy cream
1 oz (2 tbsp) brown crème de cacao

Place all ingredients in shaker with 4 or 5 ice cubes. Cover and shake vigorously several times. Strain into chilled cocktail glass.

─────── **Road Runner** ───────

1½ oz (3 tbsp) vodka
¾ oz (1½ tbsp) amaretto
¾ oz (1½ tbsp) coconut milk
nutmeg

Shake liquid ingredients with ice and strain into a chilled cocktail glass. Sprinkle with nutmeg.

Variations: Sugar-rim the glass by rubbing with a slice of orange and dipping into sugar. The drink can also be made in a blender with ⅓ cup crushed ice (medium speed for 15 seconds) and poured into a chilled champagne glass or wineglass.

─────── **Rob Roy** ───────

Similar to a manhattan but made with Scotch instead of rye, it is named after Rob Roy (Robert Macgregor), the Scottish Robin Hood.

2 oz (4 tbsp) Scotch
1 oz (2 tbsp) sweet vermouth
1 dash Angostura bitters
maraschino cherry

(continued)

Stir liquid ingredients with ice and strain into a chilled cocktail glass. Garnish with the cherry.

Variations: Substitute orange bitters for Angostura. Substitute a twist of orange peel for the cherry.

Dry Rob Roy: Substitute dry vermouth for the sweet and garnish with a lemon twist instead of a cherry.

Perfect Rob Roy: Use equal parts (1/2 oz [1 tbsp] each) of dry and sweet vermouth.

——— Rolls Royce ———

1 oz (2 tbsp) cognac
3/4 oz (1 1/2 tbsp) Cointreau or Triple Sec
1 oz (2 tbsp) orange juice

Shake ingredients with ice and strain into a chilled cocktail glass.

——— Roman Punch ———

2 oz (4 tbsp) Jamaican rum
2 oz (4 tbsp) brandy
1 oz (2 tbsp) raspberry syrup
juice of 1 lemon

Mix ingredients in a chilled highball glass. Fill with shaved or crushed ice and stir.

Variations: Add 2 dashes curaçao or float port wine on top.

——— Rose Cocktail ———

1 1/2 oz (3 tbsp) gin
3/4 oz (1 1/2 tbsp) cherry brandy

3/4 oz (1 1/2 tbsp) dry vermouth
twist of orange peel (optional)
maraschino cherry (optional)

Stir liquid ingredients with ice and strain into a chilled cocktail glass. Garnish with orange peel and cherry.

Variation: Substitute apricot brandy for cherry brandy and add 1/2 tsp lemon juice. Shake with ice and strain into a sugar-rimmed cocktail glass. Do not garnish.

--------- **Rose Hall** ---------

Named in honor of the Jamaican landmark.

1 1/2 oz (3 tbsp) golden or dark Jamaican rum
1/2 oz (1 tbsp) banana liqueur
1 oz (2 tbsp) orange juice
1 tsp lime juice
thin slice of lime (optional)

Place half a cup of cracked ice in shaker. Add liquors and juices, cover, and shake vigorously several times. Strain into a chilled cocktail glass. Garnish with lime slice, if desired.

--------- **Roselyn Cocktail** ---------

1 1/2 oz (3 tbsp) gin
3/4 oz (1 1/2 tbsp) dry vermouth
2 dashes grenadine
twist of lemon peel

Stir liquid ingredients with ice and strain into a chilled cocktail glass. Garnish with lemon peel.

———— Rosita ————

1½ oz (3 tbsp) tequila
1 oz (2 tbsp) Campari
½ oz (1 tbsp) dry vermouth
½ oz (1 tbsp) sweet vermouth
thin slice lemon

Fill a large old-fashioned glass two-thirds with cracked ice. Add liquors and stir gently. Float lemon slice on top of drink.

———— Rough Rider ————

2 oz (4 tbsp) whiskey
1 oz (2 tbsp) apple brandy
½ oz (1 tbsp) sloe gin
chilled club soda

Pour first 3 ingredients in a highball glass filled with cracked ice. Top with soda and stir.

———— Royal Clover Club Cocktail ————

2 oz (4 tbsp) gin
juice of ½ lemon or lime
½ oz (1 tbsp) grenadine

Shake ingredients vigorously with ice and strain into a chilled cocktail or champagne glass.

———— Royal Cocktail ————

1½ oz (3 tbsp) gin
juice of ½ lemon
½ tsp sugar

Shake ingredients vigorously with ice and strain into a chilled cocktail glass.

——— Royal Gin Fizz ———

2 oz (4 tbsp) gin
1 oz (2 tbsp) lemon juice
2 tsp sugar
chilled club soda
slice of lemon

Shake first 3 ingredients with ice. Strain into a chilled highball glass over ice cubes. Top with soda, stir, and garnish with lemon slice.

——— Royal Jamaican ———

1½ oz (3 tbsp) Tia Maria
½ oz (1 tbsp) heavy cream

Pour liqueur into a cordial glass. Carefully float cream on top.

——— Royal Smile Cocktail ———

1½ oz (3 tbsp) apple brandy
¾ oz (1½ tbsp) gin
2 dashes lemon juice
2 dashes grenadine

Stir ingredients with ice and strain into a chilled cocktail glass.

——— Rue de la Paix ———

1 oz (2 tbsp) brandy
1 oz (2 tbsp) dry vermouth
½ tsp Pernod or Ricard
½ tsp maraschino
½ tsp curaçao

(continued)

1–2 dashes orange bitters
long-stemmed cherry

Shake first 6 ingredients with cracked ice and strain into chilled cocktail glass. Garnish with cherry.

RUM

First manufactured in the West Indies in the early 17th century, rum is made from the distilled juice of sugarcane or, more commonly, from distilled molasses, a byproduct of sugar refining. Although rum is now manufactured in many parts of the world, the chief producers are still in the West Indies. There are two kinds of rum: light and dark. Light rum, which is light-bodied and usually dry, comes mainly from Puerto Rico, Cuba, and the Virgin Islands. Dark rum, which is heavier and full-bodied, is made in Jamaica, Barbados, and Guyana. Variations within the two basic types are the result of the quality of the ingredients and the methods of fermentation, distillation, and aging. All rum is colorless when first distilled, and those that are aged for only a year are often artificially colored with caramel. Even the better rums, which are aged in oak casks for up to 20 years (during which time they acquire some of their color), are sometimes subjected to artificial coloring.

——— Rum and Cola (Cuba Libre) ———

3 oz (6 tbsp) light rum
juice of ½ lime
6 oz chilled cola
slice of lime

Pour rum, lime juice, and cola into a chilled collins glass over ice cubes. Stir and garnish with lime slice.

———— **Rum Collins** ————

See *Tom Collins*.

———— **Rum Cow** ————

1½ oz (3 tbsp) light rum
2 or 3 drops vanilla extract
1 dash nutmeg
1 dash Angostura bitters
8 oz chilled milk
1½ tsp sugar

Shake ingredients with ice and pour into a chilled highball glass.

———— **Rum Daisy** ————

2 oz (4 tbsp) light rum
1½ tsp raspberry syrup
juice of ½ lemon
½ tsp sugar (optional)
fresh fruit for garnish

Shake ingredients, except fruit, with ice cubes or crushed ice and pour into an old-fashioned glass. Garnish with fruit and serve with a straw.

Variation: Substitute grenadine for raspberry syrup. Pour into a highball glass and top with chilled club soda.

———— **Rum Dubonnet** ————

1½ oz (3 tbsp) light rum
½ oz (1 tbsp) Dubonnet
1 tsp lime juice
twist of lime peel

(continued)

Shake liquid ingredients with ice and strain into a chilled cocktail glass. Garnish with lime peel.

——————— **Rum Fix** ———————

2 oz (4 tbsp) light rum
juice of ½ lemon
1 tsp sugar
1 dash curaçao (optional)
slice of lemon

Stir liquid ingredients in a chilled highball glass and fill with crushed ice. Garnish with lemon slice and serve with a straw.

——————— **Rum Manhattan** ———————

See *Manhattan.*

——————— **Rum Martini** ———————

See *Martini.*

——————— **Rum Old-Fashioned** ———————

See *Old-Fashioned.*

——————— **Rum Punch I** ———————

The mnemonic jingle for this is "one of sour, two of sweet, three of strong, and four of weak." The "parts," of course, can be tablespoons, cups, or whatever, and vary widely according to taste.

1 oz (2 tbsp) lime juice
4 tbsp brown sugar

3 oz (6 tbsp) dark rum
1/2 cup crushed ice and/or chilled water
(optional)
orange slice and/or maraschino cherry

Put first 4 ingredients in a blender and blend at medium speed for 10–15 seconds. Pour into a frosted collins glass and decorate with orange slice and/or maraschino cherry if desired.

——— **Rum Punch II** ———

(serves 25–30)

1 bottle Jamaican rum
4 oz (8 tbsp) brandy
2 qts seltzer water
1 pt lemon juice (approx. 16 lemons)
2 cups white wine
2 lemons thinly sliced
2 1/2 cups sugar
block of ice

Mix sugar with water and stir till completely dissolved. Add other liquid ingredients and combine thoroughly. Pour over block of ice in large punch bowl and float lemon slices. Ladle into punch cups.

——— **Rum Screwdriver** ———

See *Screwdriver.*

——— **Rum Sour** ———

See *Whiskey Sour.*

——— **Rum Swizzle** ———

See *Swizzle.*

——— **Rum Toddy, Hot** ———

See *Hot Toddy.*

——— **Russian Bear** ———

See *White Russian.*

——— **Russian Cocktail** ———

$^3/_4$ oz (1$^1/_2$ tbsp) vodka
$^3/_4$ oz (1$^1/_2$ tbsp) gin
$^3/_4$ oz (1$^1/_2$ tbsp) white crème de cacao

Stir or shake ingredients with ice and strain into a chilled cocktail glass.

——— **Rusty Nail** ———

1$^1/_2$ oz (3 tbsp) Scotch
1$^1/_2$ oz (3 tbsp) Drambuie
twist of lemon peel (optional)

Pour Scotch and Drambuie into a chilled old-fashioned glass over ice cubes. Stir gently and garnish with lemon peel.

Variations: Stir liquid ingredients with ice and strain into a chilled cocktail glass. Instead of stirring, float Drambuie on top of the Scotch. Amount of Drambuie can be reduced to $^3/_4$ oz (1$^1/_2$ tbsp).

RYE

Probably the first grain whiskey distilled in the United States, rye dates from the arrival of Scottish and Irish immigrants in Pennsylvania. It is distilled from a mash grain that contains at least 5 percent rye, filled out with barleys, corn, and oats. After fermentation the rectified (redistilled) spirit is barreled in charred white oak. Rye is almost always blended (combining the products of several distillations) for consistency of flavor and a wider appeal. However, there are a few brands of straight that have a devoted following. See *Whiskey.*

S

——— **Salty Dog** ———

2 oz (4 tbsp) gin
4 oz (8 tbsp) grapefruit juice

Salt-rim a chilled collins or highball glass. Pour ingredients over ice cubes and stir.

Variations: Use equal parts of gin and grapefruit juice.

Vodka Salty Dog: Substitute vodka for the gin.

——— **Sambuca Slide** ———

See **Shooters.**

——— Sambuca Straight ———

3 oz (6 tbsp) Sambuca
3 coffee beans

Pour Sambuca into a brandy snifter and drop in 3 coffee beans. It is considered bad luck to have any more or less than 3 coffee beans. The odd number of beans suggests that the guest is welcome in the home or establishment.

——— Sangaree ———

A forerunner of sangria. In Colonial days it was a mixture of red wine, fruit and fruit juice, sugar, and spices.

2 oz (4 tbsp) brandy
1/2 tsp sugar
1 tsp water
chilled club soda
1 tsp port
nutmeg

Dissolve sugar in water in a chilled old-fashioned glass. Add ice cubes and brandy. Top with soda and stir. Float port on top and sprinkle with nutmeg.

Variations: Substitute flavored brandy, sherry, gin, or whiskey for the brandy, and the sangaree is named after the liquor used (gin sangaree).

See also *Port Wine Sangaree.*

——— Sangria ———

(serves 4–6)

1 qt dry red wine
1–2 oz (4 tbsp) Spanish brandy (optional)

½ cup sugar
1 cup chilled water or club soda
juice of 1 orange
juice of 1 lemon
1 sliced orange
1 sliced lemon

Dissolve sugar in wine in a large pitcher. Add remaining ingredients and stir. Allow mixture to stand at room temperature for an hour before serving. Serve in large chilled wineglasses over ice cubes. Put pieces of lemon and orange in each glass.

See also *Santa Clara Sangría.*

——— **Sangria Mexicali** ———

(serves 12)

1 cup fresh orange juice
½ cup fresh lemon (or lime) juice
¼ cup superfine sugar
2 lemons (or limes) thinly sliced
2 oranges thinly sliced
1 bottle dry red (or white) wine
1 liter seltzer or club soda (chilled)
1½ oz (3 tbsp) brandy
thin lemon slices for garnish (optional)

In a large pitcher (or punch bowl) combine above ingredients, except garnish. Add 10–12 ice cubes. Pour or ladle into glasses or punch cups. Garnish each with lemon slice if desired. Makes approximately one dozen 6-oz servings.

---------   **Sangrita**   ---------

(serves 4)

Variation on the above. A shot of tequila is downed
and "chased" with the following:

$\frac{1}{2}$ cup tomato juice
$\frac{1}{2}$ cup fresh orange juice
$\frac{1}{4}$ cup fresh lemon juice
dash or two of Tabasco, to taste
$\frac{1}{2}$ tsp salt
freshly ground pepper
$\frac{1}{2}$ tsp sugar

In small pitcher combine the above and divide among
4 small glasses. This makes 4 servings but can easily be doubled and repeated as needed.

---------   **Sanibel Cooler**   ---------

2 oz (4 tbsp) gin
2 tsp fresh lime juice
1 tsp sugar syrup
1 tsp grenadine
chilled club soda

In collins glass filled with cracked ice add first 4 ingredients and stir. Top with soda and stir again before
serving with long straw.

---------   **San Juan**   ---------

1$\frac{1}{2}$ oz (3 tbsp) light rum
1 oz (2 tbsp) grapefruit juice
1 tsp coconut milk
2 tsp lime juice
$\frac{1}{3}$ cup crushed ice
2 tsp brandy

Put all ingredients, except brandy, into a blender and blend at low speed for 15 seconds. Pour into a chilled wineglass or champagne glass. Float brandy on top.

——— San Sebastian ———

1 oz (2 tbsp) gin
1/4 oz (1 1/2 tsp) light rum
1/4 oz (1 1/2 tsp) Triple Sec
1/2 oz (1 tbsp) grapefruit juice
1/2 oz (1 tbsp) lemon juice

Shake ingredients with ice and strain into a chilled cocktail glass.

——— Santa Clara Sangria ———

(serves 16–18)

1 gal California zinfandel
1 cup lemon juice (approx. 4 large lemons)
1/2 cup sugar
1/2 cup brandy
2 oz (4 tbsp) Strega
1 qt orange juice
1 qt club soda
thin slices of orange and lemon

Mix lemon juice and orange juice with sugar. Stir in brandy and Strega and pour over block of ice in a large punch bowl (2-gal capacity). Add the wine and soda just before serving, stir gently, and float the fruit slices.

Santiago Cocktail

1½ oz (3 tbsp) light rum
juice of 1 lime
2 dashes grenadine
½ tsp sugar

Shake ingredients with ice and strain into a chilled cocktail glass.

Variation: Substitute 2 dashes curaçao for the grenadine.

Saratoga Cocktail

2 oz (4 tbsp) brandy
2 dashes Angostura bitters
1 tsp pineapple juice
1 tsp lemon juice (optional)

Shake ingredients with ice and strain into a chilled cocktail glass.

Saturday Night Special

See *Mothers Milk.*

Saucy Sue Cocktail

2 oz (4 tbsp) apple brandy
1 dash apricot brandy
1 dash Pernod
twist of orange peel (optional)

Stir liquid ingredients with ice and strain into a chilled cocktail glass. Garnish with orange peel.

─────── **Sauternes Cup** ───────

(serves 6)

1 qt chilled sauternes wine
3 oz (6 tbsp) brandy
3 oz (6 tbsp) Cointreau or Triple Sec
3 tsp sugar
6 oz chilled club soda
1 cup sliced fresh fruit (oranges, lemons,
grapefruit, strawberries, cucumber peel, etc.)

Mix ingredients in a large pitcher or punch bowl with ice cubes or a block of ice. Serve in chilled wineglasses or punch cups.

Variation: Soak the fruit in the brandy and Cointreau for an hour before adding other ingredients.

─────── **Savoy Hotel** ───────

1/3 oz (2 tsp) brandy
1/3 oz (2 tsp) Benedictine
1/3 oz (2 tsp) crème de cacao

Pour ingredients, in order given, into a pousse-café glass, being careful that the layers do not mix.

─────── **Saxon Cocktail** ───────

2 oz (4 tbsp) light rum
2 dashes grenadine
juice of 1/2 lime
twist of orange peel

Shake liquid ingredients with ice and strain into a chilled cocktail glass. Garnish with orange peel.

Sazerac

2 oz (4 tbsp) rye whiskey
2 dashes Peychaud bitters
2 dashes Pernod
½ tsp sugar
twist of lemon peel

Dissolve sugar in whiskey in a chilled old-fashioned glass. Add ice cubes, Pernod, and bitters. Stir gently and garnish with lemon peel.

Scarlett O'Hara

2 oz (4 tbsp) Southern Comfort
1 oz (2 tbsp) cranberry juice
2 dashes lime juice

Shake ingredients with ice and strain into a chilled cocktail glass.

Scorpion

2 oz (4 tbsp) light rum
1 oz (2 tbsp) brandy
½ oz (1 tbsp) orgeat
1½ oz (3 tbsp) orange juice
1½ oz (3 tbsp) lemon juice
½ cup crushed ice
slice of orange
sprig of fresh mint

Put first 6 ingredients in a blender and blend at low speed for 15 seconds. Pour into a chilled old-fashioned glass over ice cubes. Garnish with orange slice and mint.

SCOTCH

Considered by many to be the finest whisky in the world, Scotch is produced only in Scotland. Distilled from fermented cereal grains, virtually all commercially available Scotches are *blends* of several types and distillations. A high proportion of grain whisky from a patent still is blended with a quantity of full-flavored malt whisky. Scotch malt whisky has a unique smoky quality due primarily to the peat that is used to dry the malted barley.

Scotch Cobbler

See *Whiskey Cobbler.*

Scotch Collins

See *Tom Collins.*

Scotch Cooler

2 oz (4 tbsp) Scotch
3 dashes white crème de menthe
chilled club soda

Pour Scotch and crème de menthe into a chilled collins or highball glass over ice cubes. Top with soda and stir gently.

Scotch Highball
(Scotch and soda)

2 oz (4 tbsp) Scotch
chilled club soda or ginger ale
twist of lemon

(continued)

Fill a highball glass with ice. Pour in Scotch and fill with ginger ale or soda. Top with a twist of lemon.

Scotch Holiday Sour

(serves 2)

3 oz (6 tbsp) Scotch
2 oz (4 tbsp) cherry brandy
1 oz (2 tbsp) sweet vermouth
2 oz (4 tbsp) lemon juice
1 egg white (optional)
2 slices of lemon

Shake first 5 ingredients with ice and strain into a chilled old-fashioned glass over ice cubes. Garnish with lemon slices.

Scotch Manhattan

See *Rob Roy.*

Scotch Mist

2 oz (4 tbsp) Scotch
twist of lemon peel

Pack a chilled old-fashioned glass with crushed ice. Add Scotch and lemon twist. Serve with a short straw.

Bourbon Mist: Substitute bourbon for Scotch.

Scotch Old-Fashioned

See *Old-Fashioned.*

——————   **Scotch Solace**   ——————

2½ oz Scotch
½ oz (1 tbsp) Triple Sec
½ oz (1 tbsp) honey
4 oz (8 tbsp) chilled milk
1 oz (2 tbsp) cream
pinch of grated orange rind

Put Scotch, Triple Sec, and honey into a chilled high-ball glass and stir until honey is dissolved. Add milk, cream, orange rind, and ice cubes. Stir well.

——————   **Scotch Sour**   ——————

See *Whiskey Sour.*

——————   **Scotch Stinger**   ——————

See *Stinger.*

——————   **Scotch Symphony**   ——————

2 oz (4 tbsp) Scotch
1 oz (2 tbsp) Drambuie
lemon zest

Place liquors in an old-fashioned glass with 3 or 4 ice cubes. Twist zest over drink to release oils and drop in.

——————   **Screwdriver**   ——————

The numerous theories as to the origin of this drink all revolve around its being first stirred with a screw-driver due to the lack of a proper stirring spoon. Who

(continued)

did the stirring and where it was done remain a mystery. The drink has been around for some time and continues to be one of the most popular vodka-based drinks in this country.

2 oz (4 tbsp) vodka
chilled orange juice to taste

Pour vodka into a chilled Old-Fashioned or collins glass over ice cubes. Fill with orange juice and stir.

Variations: Add 1 tsp lemon juice.

Rum Screwdriver: Substitute rum for vodka.

See also *Creamy Screwdriver,
Harvey Wallbanger.*

Seaboard

1 oz (2 tbsp) rye whiskey
1 oz (2 tbsp) gin
½ oz (1 tbsp) lemon juice
1 tsp sugar
2 sprigs of fresh mint

Shake first 4 ingredients with ice and strain into a chilled old-fashioned glass over ice cubes. Garnish with mint.

Sensation Cocktail

2 oz (4 tbsp) gin
juice of ¼ lemon
2–3 dashes maraschino
2 sprigs of fresh mint

Shake liquid ingredients with ice and strain into a chilled cocktail glass. Garnish with mint.

———— **September Morn Cocktail** ————

1½ oz (3 tbsp) light rum
juice of ½ lime
2–3 dashes grenadine
1 egg white

Shake ingredients vigorously with ice and strain into
a chilled cocktail glass.

———— **Seventh Heaven Cocktail** ————

1½ oz (3 tbsp) gin
½ oz (1 tbsp) maraschino
½ oz (1 tbsp) grapefruit juice
sprig of fresh mint

Shake liquid ingredients with ice and strain into a
chilled cocktail glass. Garnish with mint.

———— **Sevilla Cocktail** ————

1 oz (2 tbsp) light rum
1 oz (2 tbsp) port
½ tsp sugar

Shake ingredients with ice and strain into a chilled
cocktail or wine glass.

Variation: Substitute dark rum for light and sweet
vermouth for the port.

———— **Sex on the Beach I** ————

A name used for two different drinks. Try them both.

1 oz (2 tbsp) vodka
1 oz (2 tbsp) peach schnapps

(continued)

3 oz (6 tbsp) cranberry juice, chilled
3 oz (6 tbsp) pineapple juice, or, optionally,
orange or grapefruit juice

Combine all ingredients in shaker with ice and shake vigorously. Strain into a chilled collins glass over ice.

See also **Shooters.**

Sex on the Beach II

1 oz (2 tbsp) vodka
½ oz (1 tbsp) Midori or other melon liqueur
½ oz (1 tbsp) Chambord or
other raspberry liqueur
1 oz (2 tbsp) cranberry juice
2 oz (4 tbsp) pineapple juice

Combine all ingredients in shaker with ice and shake vigorously. Strain into a chilled collins glass over ice.

Shady Lady

1½ oz (3 tbsp) tequila
1 oz (2 tbsp) cranberry juice
½ oz (1 tbsp) apple brandy
1 tsp fresh lime juice

Place ingredients in shaker with ½ cup cracked ice. Cover and shake vigorously several times. Pour into a sour glass filled halfway with cracked ice. Serve with small straw.

Shamrock Cocktail

1 oz (2 tbsp) Irish whiskey
1 oz (2 tbsp) dry vermouth

3 dashes green crème de menthe
stuffed green olive

Stir liquid ingredients with ice and strain into a chilled cocktail glass. Garnish with the olive.

Variation: Add 3 dashes green Chartreuse.

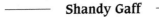 **Shandy Gaff**

4 oz (8 tbsp) beer or ale
4 oz (8 tbsp) ginger beer

Pour ingredients into a chilled collins or highball glass over ice cubes and stir gently.

Variation: Substitute ginger ale for ginger beer.

Shanghai Cocktail

1½ oz (3 tbsp) dark rum
½ oz (1 tbsp) Pernod
¾ oz (1½ tbsp) lemon juice
½–1 tsp grenadine

Shake ingredients with ice and strain into a chilled cocktail glass.

Shanghai Lady

1½ oz (3 tbsp) golden rum
½ oz (1 tbsp) Sambuca
2 tsp lemon juice
1–2 dashes bitters
orange zest

In shaker place liquors, juice, and bitters with 5 or 6 ice cubes. Cover and shake vigorously several times.

(continued)

Strain into a chilled cocktail glass. Run zest through the flame of a match 2 or 3 times and add to drink.

Shark's Tooth

1½ oz (3 tbsp) dark rum
¼ oz (1½ tsp) sloe gin
¼ oz (1½ tsp) sweet vermouth
¼ oz (1½ tsp) lemon juice
¼ oz (1½ tsp) passionfruit syrup
1 dash Angostura bitters
twist of orange peel
maraschino cherry

Shake liquid ingredients with ice and strain into a chilled cocktail glass. Garnish with orange peel and cherry.

Variations: Sugar-rim the glass by rubbing with lemon and dipping into sugar. Substitute light rum for dark. Add ¼ oz (½ tbsp) cherry brandy.

Sharky Punch

1½ oz (3 tbsp) calvados or other apple brandy
½ oz (1 tbsp) rye whiskey
1 tsp honey or sugar syrup
club soda

Place first three ingredients in shaker with ½ cup of cracked ice. Cover and shake vigorously several times. Strain into a large old-fashioned glass half-filled with cracked ice. Top off with club soda and serve.

Sherry Cobbler

2 oz (4 tbsp) sherry
2 oz (4 tbsp) chilled water or club soda

1 tsp sugar
slices of fresh fruit (lemon, orange,
pineapple, etc.)

Dissolve sugar in water in a stemmed goblet. Fill glass two-thirds full of crushed ice, add sherry, and stir. Garnish with fruit and serve with a straw.

Variation: Substitute ½ oz (1 tbsp) orange juice for the water and add 1 oz (2 tbsp) brandy.

——— **Sherry Eggnog** ———

2 oz (4 tbsp) sherry
½ oz (1 tbsp) brandy
1 tsp sugar
1 whole egg
chilled milk
nutmeg

Shake sherry, brandy, sugar, and egg vigorously with ice. Strain into a chilled collins glass and top with milk. Stir and sprinkle with nutmeg.

——— **Sherry Sangaree** ———

See *Sangaree.*

——— **Shriner Cocktail** ———

1½ oz (3 tbsp) sloe gin
1½ oz (3 tbsp) brandy
2 dashes sugar syrup
2 dashes Angostura or Peychaud bitters
twist of lemon peel

Stir liquid ingredients with ice and strain into a chilled cocktail glass. Garnish with lemon peel.

Sidecar

Once an extremely popular drink, it is thought to have originated in Paris during World War I. The sidecar makes an interesting after-dinner drink as well as a before-dinner cocktail. Go easy on the Cointreau or the drink will be sticky sweet.

2 oz (4 tbsp) brandy
1 oz (2 tbsp) Cointreau or Triple Sec
½ oz (1 tbsp) lemon juice
twist of lemon peel (optional)

Shake liquid ingredients with ice and strain into a chilled cocktail glass. Garnish with lemon peel.

Variations: Sugar-rim the glass by rubbing with lemon and dipping into sugar.

Boston Sidecar: Substitute lime juice for lemon and add ¾ oz (1½ tbsp) light rum.

Silk Stocking

1½ oz (3 tbsp) gin
½ oz (1 tbsp) apple brandy
1 oz (2 tbsp) orange juice

Place ingredients in shaker with 4 or 5 ice cubes. Cover and shake vigorously several times. Strain into a wineglass half filled with cracked ice and serve with a small straw.

Silver Arrow

2 oz (4 tbsp) vodka
½ oz (1 tbsp) crème de cassis
½ oz (1 tbsp) heavy cream

Place ingredients in shaker with ice cubes. Cover and shake vigorously several times. Strain into a chilled cocktail glass.

Silver Bullet

1 oz (2 tbsp) gin
1 oz (2 tbsp) kümmel
1/4 oz (1 1/2 tsp) lemon juice

Stir ingredients with ice and strain into a chilled cocktail glass.

Silver Cocktail

1 oz (2 tbsp) gin
1 oz (2 tbsp) dry vermouth
2 dashes orange bitters
1/2 tsp maraschino
twist of lemon peel

Stir liquid ingredients with ice and strain into a chilled cocktail glass. Garnish with lemon peel.

Silver Fizz

2 oz (4 tbsp) gin
1 oz (2 tbsp) lemon juice
1 tsp sugar
2 oz (4 tbsp) chilled club soda

Shake ingredients, except soda, with ice and strain into a chilled collins glass or wineglass over ice cubes. Top with soda.

——— **Silver Jubilee** ———

1½ oz (3 tbsp) gin
1½ oz (3 tbsp) banana liqueur
¾ oz (1½ tbsp) cream
2–3 slices banana (optional)
slice of orange (optional)

Shake liquid ingredients with ice and strain into a chilled cocktail glass. Garnish with banana and orange if desired.

——— **Silver King Cocktail** ———

1½ oz (3 tbsp) gin
juice of ½ lemon
½ tsp sugar
1 egg white
2 dashes orange bitters

Shake ingredients with ice and strain into a chilled cocktail glass.

——— **Silver Streak** ———

1½ oz (3 tbsp) gin
1½ oz (3 tbsp) kümmel

Stir ingredients with ice and strain into a chilled cocktail glass.

——— **Singapore Sling I** ———

1½ oz (3 tbsp) gin
½ oz (1 tbsp) lemon juice
1 tsp grenadine
½ oz (1 tbsp) cherry brandy
chilled club soda

slice of lemon or lime
maraschino cherry

Mix gin, lemon juice, and grenadine in a chilled high-ball or collins glass. Add crushed ice, top with soda, and stir. Float brandy on top, garnish with fruit, and serve with a straw.

——— Singapore Sling II ———

1 1/2 oz (3 tbsp) gin
1/2 oz (1 tbsp) lemon juice
1/2 oz (1 tbsp) lime juice
1 tsp grenadine
1/4 oz (1 1/2 tsp) sloe gin
1/2 oz (1 tbsp) crème de cassis
chilled club soda
1/2 oz (1 tbsp) cherry brandy
slice of lemon or lime
maraschino cherry

Mix first 6 ingredients in a chilled highball glass. Add crushed ice, top with soda, and stir. Float brandy on top. Garnish with fruit and serve with a straw.

Variation: Substitute 1/4 oz (1 1/2 tsp) Benedictine and 1/4 oz (1 1/2 tsp) brandy for the cherry brandy.

——— Sling ———

A drink of liquor, sweetened and flavored with cherry brandy, grenadine, sloe gin, etc., with both lemon or lime juice and peel, and often stretched with club soda. For a list of sling drinks, see *Sling* in the **Index by Type Drink**.

2 oz (4 tbsp) gin
1 oz (2 tbsp) cherry brandy

(continued)

juice of ½ lemon
1 tsp sugar
1 tsp water
twist of lemon peel

Shake liquid ingredients with ice and strain into a chilled old-fashioned glass over ice cubes. Garnish with lemon peel.

Variations: Strain into a chilled highball or collins glass over ice cubes and top with chilled water or club soda. Various liquors and brandies can be substituted for the gin and cherry brandy, and the sling is then named after the liquor used (gin sling, rum sling, etc.).

See also *Singapore Sling I and II.*

——— **Sloe Gin Cocktail** ———

2 oz (4 tbsp) sloe gin
¼–½ oz (½–1 tbsp) dry vermouth
1 dash orange bitters

Stir ingredients with ice and strain into a chilled cocktail glass.

Variation: Use ¼ oz (1½ tsp) dry vermouth and add ½ oz (1 tbsp) sweet vermouth.

——— **Sloe Gin Fizz** ———

See *Gin Fizz.*

——— **Sloe Gin Rickey** ———

See *Gin Rickey.*

Sloe Tequila

1 oz (2 tbsp) tequila
1/2 oz (1 tbsp) sloe gin
1/2 oz (1 tbsp) lime juice
1/2 cup crushed ice
cucumber peel

Put first 4 ingredients into a blender and blend at low speed for 15 seconds. Pour into a chilled old-fashioned glass over ice cubes and garnish with cucumber peel.

Sloe Vermouth

1 oz (2 tbsp) sloe gin
1 oz (2 tbsp) dry vermouth
1/2 oz (1 tbsp) lemon juice

Shake ingredients with ice and strain into a chilled cocktail glass.

Smash

See *Brandy Smash.*

Snowball Cocktail

1 1/2 oz (3 tbsp) gin
1/2 oz (1 tbsp) anisette
1/2 oz (1 tbsp) cream

Shake ingredients with ice and strain into a chilled cocktail glass.

Variation: Add 1/2 oz (1 tbsp) white crème de menthe.

——— Snowball Fizz ———

2 oz (4 tbsp) grapefruit juice
1 oz (2 tbsp) orange juice
1 tsp sugar
3 oz (6 tbsp) gin
2 oz (4 tbsp) club soda

In shaker combine juices, sugar, and gin and stir till sugar is completely dissolved. Add club soda and several ice cubes. Cover and shake vigorously several times. Strain into a chilled cocktail glass or wineglass.

——— Snowbird ———

2 oz (4 tbsp) vodka
½ oz (1 tbsp) crème Yvette
1 oz (2 tbsp) heavy cream

Place ingredients in blender with 4 or 5 ice cubes. Cover and blend at high speed 15 or 20 seconds or until ice cubes are just puréed. Pour into a chilled wineglass.

——— Snowflake ———

2 oz (4 tbsp) gin
½ oz (1 tbsp) fresh lemon juice
1 tsp sugar syrup
1 tsp grenadine
½ oz (1 tbsp) heavy cream
club soda

Place all ingredients except soda in shaker with 6 or 8 ice cubes. Cover and shake vigorously. Strain into a chilled highball glass and top with soda. Stir before serving.

Sombrero

1½ oz (3 tbsp) coffee brandy
1 oz (2 tbsp) cream

Shake ingredients with ice and strain into a chilled cocktail glass or into an old-fashioned glass over ice cubes.

Variation: Pour brandy into an old-fashioned glass over ice cubes and float the cream on top.

Sophia

4 oz (8 tbsp) dry white wine
1 oz (2 tbsp) Strega
1 tsp fresh lime juice
thin slice lime

Add first three ingredients to wineglass filled halfway with cracked ice. Stir gently, float lime slice, and serve with small straw.

Sorrento

2 oz (4 tbsp) gin
1 oz (2 tbsp) Galliano
½ oz (1 tbsp) fresh lemon juice
1 tsp orgeat or sugar syrup

Place ingredients in shaker with ½ cup cracked ice. Cover and shake vigorously several times. Strain into a chilled cocktail glass.

SOUR

A classic mixed drink combining liquor, fruit juice, and sugar. For a list of sour drinks, see *Sour* in the **Index by Type of Drink**.

——— **Southern Belle** ———

2 oz (4 tbsp) Southern Comfort
½ oz (1 tbsp) crème de banane
1 tsp crème de cassis
½ oz (1 tbsp) heavy cream

Place all ingredients in shaker with 5 or 6 ice cubes. Cover and shake vigorously. Strain into a chilled wineglass half-filled with cracked ice.

——— **Southern Bride** ———

1½ oz (3 tbsp) gin
¾ oz (1½ tbsp) grapefruit juice
2 dashes maraschino

Shake ingredients with ice and strain into a chilled cocktail glass.

——— **Southern Gin Cocktail** ———

2 oz (4 tbsp) gin
2 dashes orange bitters
2 dashes Triple Sec
twist of lemon peel

Stir liquid ingredients with ice and strain into a chilled cocktail glass. Garnish with lemon peel.

———— Southern Peach ————

1 oz (2 tbsp) Southern Comfort
1 oz (2 tbsp) peach schnapps
1 oz (2 tbsp) orange juice
1 oz (2 tbsp) sours mix
1 dash Angostura bitters (optional)
slice of fresh peach

Shake liquid ingredients with ice and strain into a chilled old-fashioned glass over ice cubes. Garnish with peach slice.

———— South-Side Cocktail ————

2 oz (4 tbsp) gin
juice of $\frac{1}{2}$ lemon
1 tsp sugar
2 sprigs of fresh mint

Shake first 3 ingredients with ice and strain into a chilled cocktail glass. Garnish with mint.

———— Soviet ————

$1\frac{1}{2}$ oz (3 tbsp) vodka
$\frac{1}{2}$ oz (1 tbsp) dry vermouth
$\frac{1}{2}$ oz (1 tbsp) amontillado sherry
twist of lemon peel

Shake or stir liquid ingredients with ice and strain into a chilled old-fashioned glass over ice cubes. Garnish with lemon peel.

Spanish Town Cocktail

2 oz (4 tbsp) light rum
2 dashes Triple Sec
nutmeg (optional)

Stir liquid ingredients with ice and strain into a chilled
cocktail glass. Sprinkle with nutmeg.

Special Rough Cocktail

1½ oz (3 tbsp) apple brandy
1½ oz (3 tbsp) brandy
1 dash Pernod

Stir ingredients with ice and strain into a chilled cocktail glass.

Spritzer Highball

3–4 oz (6–8 tbsp) chilled dry white wine
peel of 1 lemon cut in a continuous spiral
chilled club soda

Put lemon peel into a large chilled wine or collins
glass. Add ice cubes and wine. Top with soda.

Star Cocktail

1½ oz (3 tbsp) apple brandy
1½ oz (3 tbsp) sweet vermouth
1 dash Angostura or orange bitters
twist of lemon peel (optional)

Stir liquid ingredients with ice and strain into a chilled
cocktail glass. Garnish with lemon peel.

--------- **Star Daisy** ---------

1½ oz (3 tbsp) gin
1½ oz (3 tbsp) apple brandy
2 tsp crème de framboise
½ oz (1 tbsp) lemon juice
1 tsp sugar syrup

Shake all ingredients with 4 or 5 ice cubes and strain into a large old-fashioned glass filled with cracked ice.

--------- **Stars & Stripes** ---------

⅓ oz (2 tsp) maraschino or grenadine
⅓ oz (2 tsp) cream
⅓ oz (2 tsp) blue curaçao

Pour, in order given, into a cordial glass.

See also *Pousse-Café.*

--------- **Stinger** ---------

2¼ oz (4½ tbsp) brandy
¾ oz (1½ tbsp) white crème de menthe

Shake ingredients with ice and strain into a chilled cocktail glass or into an old-fashioned glass over ice cubes or crushed ice.

Variations: Although the classic stinger is always made with brandy, various liquors can be substituted, and the stinger is then named after the liquor used (Scotch stinger, etc.)

See also *White Spider.*

Stirrup Cup

1 oz (2 tbsp) brandy
1 oz (2 tbsp) cherry brandy
juice of ½ lemon
½ tsp sugar

Shake ingredients with ice and strain into a chilled
old-fashioned glass over ice cubes.

Stone Fence

2 oz (4 tbsp) Scotch
1–2 dashes Angostura bitters
chilled club soda or cider

Pour Scotch and bitters into a highball or collins glass
over ice cubes. Top with soda or cider and stir.

Variation: Substitute apple brandy for Scotch.

Strawberry Cream Cooler

1½ oz (3 tbsp) gin
¼ cup frozen strawberries (thawed)
¾ oz (1½ tbsp) lemon juice
1 oz (2 tbsp) cream
1 tsp sugar
chilled club soda
1 fresh strawberry for garnish

Put first 5 ingredients into a blender and blend at
high speed for 10 seconds. Pour into a chilled wine
or highball glass. Add a splash of soda and ice cubes
and stir. Garnish with the strawberry.

———— **Strawberry Daiquiri** ————

See *Daiquiri.*

———— **Strawberry Fizz** ————

2 oz (4 tbsp) gin
6 strawberries
½ tsp sugar
juice of ½ lemon
chilled club soda

Crush 5 strawberries with the sugar and lemon juice in a chilled collins or highball glass. Add ice cubes and gin and top with soda. Stir gently and garnish with the remaining strawberry.

———— **Suissesse Cocktail** ————

2 oz (4 tbsp) anisette
1 oz (2 tbsp) Pernod

Shake ingredients vigorously with ice and strain into a chilled cocktail glass.

Variations: Add a dash of lemon juice or heavy cream. Strain into a larger glass and add a splash of chilled club soda.

See also *Absinthe Suissesse.*

———— **Sunburst Cocktail** ————

1½ oz (3 tbsp) apple brandy
½ oz (1 tbsp) orange-flavored brandy
1–2 dashes orange bitters
cold champagne

(continued)

In a chilled wineglass add brandies and bitters. Top with champagne and stir briefly. Serve with a short straw.

Sunflower Cocktail

1½ oz (3 tbsp) light rum
½ oz (1 tbsp) orange juice
1 tsp fresh lemon juice
½ oz (1 tbsp) Triple Sec
2–3 dashes orange bitters
maraschino cherry

Place first 5 ingredients in shaker with 4 or 5 ice cubes. Cover and shake vigorously. Strain into a chilled cocktail glass and garnish with the cherry.

Sure Shot

2 oz (4 tbsp) Scotch whisky
2 tsp fresh lime juice
dash bitters
club soda chilled

Fill highball glass with ice cubes and add first 3 ingredients. Top off with soda and stir several times before serving.

Sutton Place Cocktail

1 oz (2 tbsp) apricot brandy
1 oz (2 tbsp) white crème de menthe
1 oz (2 tbsp) Cointreau

Shake all ingredients with cracked ice and strain into chilled cocktail glass.

——— **Sweet Martini** ———

See *Martini.*

——— **Sweet Patootie Cocktail** ———

1 oz (2 tbsp) gin
½ oz (1 tbsp) Cointreau or Triple Sec
½ oz (1 tbsp) orange juice

Shake ingredients with ice and strain into a chilled cocktail glass.

——— **Swizzle** ———

Originally a drink of the West Indies, where it was stirred with a twig called a "swizzle stick."

2 oz (4 tbsp) gin
juice of 1 lime
1 tsp sugar
1–2 dashes Angostura bitters
chilled club soda

Mix sugar, lime juice, and a small amount of soda in a chilled collins glass. Fill two-thirds full of crushed or shaved ice and stir. Add gin and bitters and top with soda. Stir again and serve with a swizzle stick.

Variations: Various liquors can be substituted for the gin, and the swizzle is then named after the liquor used (Scotch swizzle, etc.).

———— Syllabub ————

(serves 6)

A festive favorite for well over 400 years.

2 cups dry white wine
1/2 cup powdered sugar
1/4 cup fresh lemon juice
2 cups light cream
freshly grated nutmeg

Place wine, sugar, lemon juice, and cream in mixing bowl and whisk until frothy. Spoon into 6-oz glasses and sprinkle with nutmeg before serving.

———— Sylvie ————

1 1/2 oz (3 tbsp) golden rum
1/2 oz (1 tbsp) dry vermouth
2 oz (4 tbsp) orange juice
1 tsp lemon juice
1/2 tsp orgeat

Place ingredients in shaker with 1/2 cup cracked ice. Cover and shake vigorously. Strain into a chilled wineglass.

T

———— Tahiti Club ————

2 oz (4 tbsp) light rum
1/2 oz (1 tbsp) lime juice
1/2 oz (1 tbsp) lemon juice
1/2 oz (1 tbsp) pineapple juice
2 dashes maraschino
slice of lemon

Shake liquid ingredients with ice and strain into a chilled old-fashioned glass over ice cubes. Garnish with lemon slice.

―――――― **Tailspin** ――――――

1 oz (2 tbsp) gin
1 oz (2 tbsp) sweet vermouth
1 oz (2 tbsp) green Chartreuse
1–2 dashes orange bitters
twist of lemon (optional)

Shake together first 4 ingredients with 4 or 5 ice cubes. Strain into a wineglass half-filled with cracked ice. Add twisted lemon peel if desired.

―――――― **Tango Cocktail** ――――――

1½ oz (3 tbsp) gin
¾ oz (1½ tbsp) dry vermouth
¾ oz (1½ tbsp) sweet vermouth
2 dashes curaçao
½ oz (1 tbsp) orange juice

Shake ingredients with ice and strain into a chilled cocktail glass.

Variation: Use equal parts of gin and sweet and dry vermouth (1 oz [2 tbsp] of each).

―――――― **Tarantella** ――――――

2 oz (4 tbsp) white rum
1 oz (2 tbsp) Strega
lemon zest

(continued)

Shake liquors with cracked ice and strain into a chilled cocktail glass after rubbing rim with peel. Twist peel over glass to release oils and drop into drink.

Tea Punch

(serves 16–18)

1 qt cold strong black tea
1 fifth light rum
1 pt orange juice
1 pt lemon juice
sugar to taste
orange and lemon slices

Pour ingredients, except orange and lemon slices, into a punch bowl over a block of ice. Garnish with the fruit and serve in chilled punch cups.

Temptation Cocktail

1½ oz (3 tbsp) rye or bourbon
½ tsp Triple Sec
½ tsp Pernod
½ tsp Dubonnet
twist of lemon or orange peel

Shake liquid ingredients with ice and strain into a chilled cocktail glass. Garnish with lemon or orange peel.

Tempter Cocktail

1½ oz (3 tbsp) ruby port wine
1½ oz (3 tbsp) apricot brandy

Stir ingredients with ice and strain into a chilled cocktail glass.

TEQUILA

The national alcoholic beverage of Mexico, tequila is a clear spirit distilled from the fermented mash of some species of the agave plant, usually maguey. A strong liquor, it is often drunk straight preceded by a taste of salt and followed by a taste of lemon or lime. See *Shooters* for a detailed explanation of how to properly drink a shot of tequila.

Tequila Acapulco

See *Acapulco.*

Tequila Collins

3 oz (6 tbsp) tequila
1 tsp sugar
1½ oz (3 tbsp) fresh lime juice
chilled seltzer or club soda
sprig of fresh mint (optional)

In a highball glass place several ice cubes and add tequila, sugar, and lime juice. Top with seltzer and stir gently. Garnish with mint.

Tequila Cooler

2 oz (4 tbsp) tequila
juice of ½ lime
chilled tonic water

Pour tequila and lime juice into a highball glass with 4 or 5 ice cubes. Top with tonic water and stir before serving.

Tequila Old-Fashioned

See *Old-Fashioned.*

Tequila Punch

(serves 25–30)

1 qt tequila
6 bottles chilled dry white wine
½ cup sugar or to taste
6 cups sliced fresh fruit

Mix ingredients and let stand for an hour. Before serving pour into a large chilled punch bowl over a block of ice and stir. Serve in chilled punch cups or wineglasses.

Variation: Add 1 fifth chilled champagne just before serving.

Tequila Sour

See *Whiskey Sour.*

Tequila Sunrise

2 oz (4 tbsp) tequila
4 oz (8 tbsp) chilled orange juice
½–¾ oz (1–1½ tbsp) grenadine

Pour tequila and then orange juice into a chilled collins or highball glass over ice cubes and stir gently. Add grenadine slowly.

Variation: Stir tequila and orange juice with ice. Strain into a large chilled cocktail glass and add grenadine.

─────── **Tequila Sunset** ───────

Said to be a morning-after antidote to the preceding drinks.

1½ oz (3 tbsp) orange juice
1½ oz (3 tbsp) pineapple juice
1 oz (2 tbsp) tequila
granulated sugar
lime peel

In a blender put 4–6 ice cubes and the liquids. Blend at high speed until ice cubes are just puréed. Serve in a chilled wineglass. Sugaring the rim first is entirely optional. Rub the rim with lime peel to make sugar adhere.

─────── **Tequini** ───────

See *Martini.*

─────── **Thanksgiving Special Cocktail** ───────

1 oz (2 tbsp) gin
1 oz (2 tbsp) apricot brandy
1 oz (2 tbsp) dry vermouth
1 dash lemon juice
maraschino cherry

Shake liquid ingredients with ice and strain into a chilled cocktail glass. Garnish with the cherry.

─────── **Third Degree Cocktail** ───────

1½ oz (3 tbsp) gin
¾ oz (1½ tbsp) dry vermouth
3–4 dashes Pernod

(continued)

Stir ingredients with ice and strain into a chilled cock-tail glass.

Third Rail Cocktail

1 oz (2 tbsp) light rum
1 oz (2 tbsp) brandy
1 oz (2 tbsp) apple brandy
1–2 dashes Pernod

Shake ingredients with ice and strain into a chilled cocktail glass.

Thistle Cocktail

1½ oz (3 tbsp) Scotch
1½ oz (3 tbsp) sweet vermouth
2–3 dashes bitters

In mixing glass combine ingredients with several ice cubes. Stir well and strain into an old-fashioned glass half-filled with cracked ice.

Three Miller Cocktail

1½ oz (3 tbsp) brandy
¾ oz (1½ tbsp) light rum
1 dash lemon juice
1 tsp grenadine

Shake ingredients with ice and strain into a chilled cocktail glass.

Three Rum Punch

½ oz (1 tbsp) white rum
½ oz (1 tbsp) golden rum

½ oz (1 tbsp) dark rum
1 oz (2 tbsp) pineapple juice
1 tsp fresh lime juice
½ oz (1 tbsp) apricot brandy
club soda
orange slice (optional)

Place liquors and juices in shaker with several ice cubes. Cover and shake vigorously several times. Strain into a highball glass half-filled with cracked ice and top off with club soda. Stir gently before serving. Garnish, if desired, with half an orange slice.

Variation: Blend liquors and juices with ½ cup cracked ice. Pour into chilled highball glass and top off, if necessary, with a little soda. Stir before serving.

——— **Three Stripes Cocktail** ———

1½ oz (3 tbsp) gin
¾ oz (1½ tbsp) dry vermouth
¾ oz (1½ tbsp) orange juice

Shake ingredients with ice and strain into a chilled cocktail glass.

——— **Thunder Cocktail** ———

2 oz (4 tbsp) brandy
1 tsp sugar
1 pinch cayenne pepper
splash of club soda

Shake ingredients with ice and strain into a chilled cocktail glass.

Tiger's Milk

(serves 15–20)

Perhaps so-named because of its deceptively attractive appearance.

1 qt pineapple juice
1 qt grapefruit juice
1 qt gin or vodka

Pour ingredients over a block of ice in a punch bowl. Stir briefly and ladle into punch cups.

Tiger Tail

2 oz (4 tbsp) Pernod
8 oz chilled orange juice
slice of lime

Pour liquid ingredients into a chilled highball glass over ice cubes. Garnish with lime slice.

Tipperary Cocktail

³/₄ oz (1¹/₂ tbsp) Irish whiskey
³/₄ oz (1¹/₂ tbsp) green Chartreuse
³/₄ oz (1¹/₂ tbsp) sweet vermouth

Stir ingredients with ice and strain into a chilled cocktail glass.

T.N.T. Cocktail

1¹/₂ oz (3 tbsp) rye whiskey
1¹/₂ oz (3 tbsp) Pernod

Shake ingredients with ice and strain into a chilled cocktail glass.

―――――― **Tobago** ――――――

1 oz (2 tbsp) light rum
1 oz (2 tbsp) gin
1/2 oz (1 tbsp) lime juice
1 tsp guava syrup
1/2 cup crushed ice
twist of lemon peel

Put first 5 ingredients into a blender and blend at low speed for 15 seconds. Pour into a chilled old-fashioned glass over ice cubes and garnish with lemon peel.

TODDY

A favorite bedtime drink or cold remedy, it consists primarily of a jigger or two of liquor (whiskey, rum, brandy, etc.) in a glass of hot water, sweetened, and often spiced with nutmeg or cinnamon or flavored with lemon peel. For a list of toddy drinks, see *Toddy* in the **Index by Type of Drink.**

―――――― **Tom-and-Jerry** ――――――

1/3 cup milk
1/2 oz (1 tbsp) butter
1 egg (separated)
1 tsp sugar
1 dash vanilla extract (optional)
1 1/2 oz (3 tbsp) dark rum
3/4 oz (1 1/2 tbsp) brandy
nutmeg

Heat milk and butter together until hot. Beat egg yolk and egg white separately until frothy. Add the egg

(continued)

white to the yolk and beat in the sugar and vanilla. Put into a heated mug, add milk and rum, and stir. Top with the brandy and sprinkle with nutmeg.

Variations: Substitute hot water for milk. Add ¼ tsp allspice. Substitute bourbon for brandy.

––––––– **Tomate** –––––––

2 oz (4 tbsp) Pernod
1 tsp grenadine
2–3 oz (6 tbsp) chilled water

Pour ingredients into a chilled wineglass over ice cubes and stir.

––––––– **Tom Collins** –––––––

The Tom Collins, the most popular collins drink, originated in England in the late 19th century and was first made with sweetened Old Tom gin. A less popular collins, the John Collins, was made with Dutch gin. A John Collins, headwaiter at a London bar, is referred to in a rhyme published in 1892 and may be the source of the word *collins.* Today a John Collins is made with whiskey and a Tom Collins is made with gin. They are among the most popular of "long, refreshing drinks."

2 oz (4 tbsp) gin
juice of ½ lemon
1 tsp sugar
chilled club soda
slice of lemon or orange
maraschino cherry

Mix lemon juice and sugar in a chilled collins glass. Add ice cubes and gin. Top with soda and stir. Garnish with lemon or orange slice and cherry.

Variations: Rum, vodka, Scotch, bourbon, rye, brandy, or applejack can be substituted for the gin, and the collins is then named after the liquor used (rum collins, etc.), except that it is called a John Collins if made with rye or bourbon.

─────── **Toreador** ───────

1½ oz (3 tbsp) tequila
½ oz (1 tbsp) crème de cacao
½ oz (1 tbsp) cream
whipped cream
cocoa

Shake tequila, crème de cacao, and cream with ice and strain into a chilled cocktail glass. Top with a spoonful of whipped cream and sprinkle with cocoa.

─────── **Torridora Cocktail** ───────

1½ oz (3 tbsp) light rum
½ oz (1 tbsp) coffee brandy
¼ oz (½ tbsp) cream
1 tsp 151-proof rum

Shake first 3 ingredients with ice and strain into a chilled cocktail glass. Float 151-proof rum on top.

─────── **Tovarich Cocktail** ───────

1½ oz (3 tbsp) vodka
1 oz (2 tbsp) kümmel
juice of ½ lime

(continued)

Shake ingredients with ice and strain into a chilled cocktail glass.

Trade Winds

2 oz (4 tbsp) rum
1/2 oz (1 tbsp) lime juice
1/2 oz (1 tbsp) sloe gin
1 tsp sugar
1/3 cup crushed ice
black cherry

Put first 5 ingredients into a blender and blend at low speed for 15 seconds. Pour into a large chilled cocktail glass and garnish with the cherry.

Variation: Substitute plum brandy for the sloe gin.

Trilby Cocktail

2 oz (4 tbsp) bourbon
1 oz (2 tbsp) sweet vermouth
2 dashes orange bitters

Stir ingredients with ice and strain into a chilled cocktail glass.

Variation: Add 1–2 dashes Pernod and/or parfait d'amour.

Trois Rivières

1 1/2 oz (3 tbsp) Canadian whisky
1/2 oz (1 tbsp) Dubonnet
1/4 oz (1 1/2 tsp) Cointreau or Triple Sec
twist of orange peel

Shake liquid ingredients with ice and strain into a chilled cocktail glass or into an old-fashioned glass over ice cubes. Garnish with orange peel.

——— Tulip Cocktail ———

1 oz (2 tbsp) apple brandy
1 oz (2 tbsp) sweet vermouth
½ oz (1 tbsp) apricot brandy
½ oz (1 tbsp) fresh lemon juice

Shake ingredients with cracked ice and strain into a chilled cocktail glass.

——— Turf Cocktail ———

1 oz (2 tbsp) gin
1 oz (2 tbsp) dry vermouth
2 dashes Pernod
¼ oz (1½ tsp) lemon juice (optional)
2 dashes Angostura bitters (optional)

Shake ingredients with ice and strain into a chilled cocktail glass or into an old-fashioned glass over ice cubes.

——— Tuxedo Cocktail ———

1½ oz (3 tbsp) gin
1½ oz (3 tbsp) dry vermouth
2 dashes Pernod
2 dashes maraschino liqueur
2 dashes orange bitters
maraschino cherry

Stir liquid ingredients with ice and strain into a chilled cocktail glass. Garnish with the cherry.

—— Twin Hills ——

2 oz (4 tbsp) rye or bourbon
2 tsp Benedictine
1 1/2 tsp lemon juice
1 1/2 tsp lime juice
1 tsp sugar
slice of lime and lemon

Shake first 5 ingredients with ice and strain into a chilled sour glass. Garnish with slices of lemon and lime.

—— Twin Six Cocktail ——

1 1/2 oz (3 tbsp) gin
3/4 oz (1 1/2 tbsp) sweet vermouth
1/2 oz (1 tbsp) orange juice
1 dash grenadine
splash club soda

Shake first 4 ingredients vigorously with ice and strain into a chilled cocktail glass. Finish with a splash of club soda.

—— Twister ——

2 oz (4 tbsp) vodka
juice of 1/2 lime
7-Up, chilled
thin slice lime

In a highball glass half-filled with cracked ice pour vodka and lime juice. Top with 7-Up and stir. Float lime slice before serving.

Variation: Substitute club soda for 7-Up.

U

Ulanda Cocktail

2 oz (4 tbsp) gin
1 oz (2 tbsp) Cointreau or Triple Sec
1 dash Pernod

Stir ingredients with ice and strain into a chilled cocktail glass.

Union Jack Cocktail

1½ oz (3 tbsp) gin
½ oz (1 tbsp) crème Yvette

Stir or shake ingredients with ice and strain into a chilled cocktail glass.

V

Valencia

2 oz (4 tbsp) apricot brandy
1 oz (2 tbsp) orange juice
4 dashes orange bitters

Shake ingredients with ice and strain into a chilled cocktail glass.

Variation: Stir ingredients with ice, strain into a chilled wineglass, and top with chilled champagne or sparkling wine.

——————— **Vanderbilt Cocktail** ———————

2 oz (4 tbsp) brandy
1 oz (2 tbsp) cherry brandy
2 dashes Angostura bitters
2 dashes sugar syrup

Stir ingredients with ice and strain into a chilled cocktail glass.

Variation: Use equal parts of brandy and cherry brandy.

——————— **Velvet Hammer** ———————

1½ oz (3 tbsp) vodka
1 oz (2 tbsp) crème de cacao
½ oz (1 tbsp) cream

Shake ingredients with ice and strain into a chilled cocktail glass.

Variations: Substitute Strega for vodka. Substitute 1 oz (2 tbsp) brandy for vodka and add 1 oz (2 tbsp) Cointreau or Triple Sec.

——————— **Verboten** ———————

1½ oz (3 tbsp) gin
½ oz (1 tbsp) Forbidden Fruit
½ oz (1 tbsp) lemon juice
½ oz (1 tbsp) orange juice
brandied cherry

Shake liquid ingredients with ice and strain into a chilled cocktail glass. Garnish with the cherry.

Vermouth Cassis

2 oz (4 tbsp) dry vermouth
1 oz (2 tbsp) crème de cassis
chilled club soda
twist of lemon peel (optional)

Stir vermouth and crème de cassis with ice cubes in a chilled highball glass or large wineglass. Top with soda and stir gently. Garnish with lemon peel.

Vermouth Cocktail

1½ oz (3 tbsp) dry vermouth
1½ oz (3 tbsp) sweet vermouth
2 dashes Angostura or orange bitters
maraschino cherry

Stir liquid ingredients with ice and strain into a chilled cocktail glass. Garnish with the cherry.

Variation: Use only dry or sweet vermouth instead of both.

Via Veneto

(serves 2)

3½ oz (7 tbsp) brandy
1 oz (2 tbsp) Sambuca
4 tsp lemon juice
2 tsp sugar syrup

Shake ingredients vigorously with ice and strain into chilled cocktail glasses or into old-fashioned glasses over ice cubes.

─────── **Victor** ───────

1½ oz (3 tbsp) gin
1 oz (2 tbsp) brandy
½ oz (1 tbsp) sweet vermouth

Shake ingredients with ice and strain into a chilled cocktail glass.

─────── **Vin Chaud** ───────

See *Hot Spiced Wine*.

─────── **Virgin Cocktail** ───────

1 oz (2 tbsp) gin
1 oz (2 tbsp) white crème de menthe
1 oz (2 tbsp) Forbidden Fruit

Shake ingredients with ice and strain into a chilled cocktail glass.

─────── **Virgin's Kiss** ───────

1½ oz (3 tbsp) peach brandy
½ oz (1 tbsp) amaretto
1–2 dashes orange bitters
½ oz (1 tbsp) heavy cream

Place all ingredients in shaker with 5 or 6 ice cubes. Cover and shake vigorously. Strain into a chilled cocktail glass.

VODKA

The traditional alcoholic beverage of Russia, Poland, and the Baltic States, vodka is distilled from a variety of agricultural products (most often rye, corn, barley, wheat, potatoes, and, less frequently, sugar beets). The base from which vodka is made is not especially important because it is first distilled at or above 190 proof, which is almost pure alcohol. This liquid is reduced to a marketable strength by the addition of distilled water. The most neutral of spirits, vodka does not have a distinctive aroma or a taste other than fiery hot. It is consequently popular as an ingredient in mixed drinks because it does not change the taste of the other ingredients (orange juice, tomato juice, etc.). Vodka is sold in variety of popular flavors, including citrus, orange, berries, pepper, and vanilla. Flavored vodkas can be used to create a variety of cocktails, many of which are listed below.

When making vodka (or flavored vodka) on the rocks, chill vodka with ice in a shaker and strain over ice into an old-fashioned glass.

Vodka & Tonic

See *Gin & Tonic.*

Vodka Collins

See *Tom Collins.*

Vodka Cooler

2 oz (4 tbsp) vodka
½ tsp sugar
chilled club soda
peel of 1 lemon cut in a continuous spiral

Dissolve sugar in a little soda in a chilled collins or highball glass. Add crushed ice and vodka and top with club soda. Garnish with the lemon peel.

——— **Vodka Cranberry** ———

2½ oz (5 tbsp) vodka
5 oz (10 tbsp) cranberry juice
lime wedge

Shake liquid ingredients with ice to chill; strain into a highball glass over ice. Garnish with lime.

——— **Vodka Daisy** ———

2 oz (4 tbsp) vodka
½ oz (1 tbsp) fresh lemon juice
1 tsp sugar syrup
1 tsp grenadine
garnish of orange or lemon slice

Shake first 4 ingredients together with cracked ice and strain into a collins glass filled with ice cubes. Garnish with fruit slice.

——— **Vodka Gimlet** ———

See *Gimlet.*

——— **Vodka Martini** ———

See *Martini.*

——— **Vodka Sling** ———

See *Sling.*

——— **Vodka Stinger** ———

See *Stinger.*

BERRY (KURANT)-FLAVORED VODKA

——— Fruitini (Kurant Martini) ———
See *Martini*.

——— Kurant and Cranberry ———

2½ oz (5 tbsp) currant-flavored vodka
6 oz (10 tbsp) cranberry juice
lime wedge

Shake liquid ingredients with ice to chill; strain into highball glass over ice. Garnish with lime.

——— Kurant and Soda ———

2½ oz (5 tbsp) currant-flavored vodka
2 oz (4 tbsp) club soda
lime wedge

Pour vodka into a chilled highball or old-fashioned glass filled with ice. Pour in club soda and garnish with lime wedge.

——— Kurant Cooler ———

2½ oz (5 tbsp) currant-vodka
½ oz (1 tbsp) Rose's lime juice
2 oz (4 tbsp) cranberry juice
splash of club soda
lime wedge

Shake first 3 ingredients with ice, until chilled. Pour over ice into a highball glass. Add soda and garnish with lime wedge.

———— Kurant on the Rocks ————

3 oz (6 tbsp) chilled currant-flavored vodka
ice
wedge of lime

Stir vodka with ice and strain into an ice-filled, old-fashioned glass or wineglass, the rim of which has been rubbed with the cut edge of the lime. Garnish with lime.

LEMON (CITRON)-FLAVORED VODKA

———— Citron and Soda ————

2½ oz (5 tbsp) citrus-flavored vodka
2 oz (4 tbsp) club soda
lemon wedge

Pour vodka into a chilled highball or old-fashioned glass filled with ice. Pour in club soda and garnish with lemon wedge.

———— Citron on the Rocks ————

3 oz (6 tbsp) chilled citrus vodka
ice
twist of lemon peel

Stir vodka with ice and strain into an ice-filled old-fashioned glass or wineglass, the rim of which has been rubbed with the cut edge of the lemon peel. Garnish with lemon peel.

———— Frozen Citron ————

2 oz (4 tbsp) citron vodka
1 oz (2 tbsp) melon liqueur or schnapps

1 oz (2 tbsp) sours mix
1/2 oz (1 tbsp) Rose's Lime Juice
1/2 cup crushed ice
lime wedge

Blend all liquid ingredients on low speed for 20–30 seconds. Pour into a chilled wineglass. Garnish with lime.

Lemon Pepper Martini

See *Martinis.*

ORANGE-FLAVORED VODKA

Orange and Campari

2 oz (4 tbsp) orange-flavored vodka
1 oz (2 tbsp) Campari
1–2 splashes club soda
twist of orange peel

Stir vodka and Campari with ice; strain into an ice-filled old-fashioned glass, the rim of which has been rubbed with the cut edge of the orange twist. Top with club soda; stir and garnish with orange zest.

Orange Negroni

1 1/2 oz (3 tbsp) orange vodka
1 1/2 oz (3 tbsp) Campari
1 1/2 oz (3 tbsp) sweet vermouth
orange slice

Stir liquid ingredients with ice and strain into a chilled martini glass. Garnish with orange slice.

Orange Squared

2½ (5 tbsp) orange vodka
2 oz (4 tbsp) orange juice
slice of orange

Shake liquid ingredients with ice to chill; strain into an old-fashioned glass filled with ice. Garnish with orange slice.

Orange Vodka and Soda

2½ oz (5 tbsp) orange-flavored vodka
2 oz (4 tbsp) club soda
orange slice

Pour vodka into a chilled highball or old-fashioned glass filled with ice. Pour in club soda and garnish with orange slice.

Orange Vodka on the Rocks

3 oz (6 tbsp) chilled orange-flavored vodka
ice
twist of orange peel

Stir vodka with ice and strain into an ice-filled old-fashioned glass or wineglass, the rim of which has been rubbed with the cut edge of the orange twist. Garnish with orange twist.

PEPPER (PEPPAR)-FLAVORED VODKA

Peppertini

See *Martini.*

—————— **Pepper Vodka and Soda** ——————

2½ oz (5 tbsp) pepper-flavored vodka
2 oz (4 tbsp) club soda
caperberry

Pour vodka into a chilled highball or old-fashioned glass filled with ice. Pour in club soda and garnish with caperberry.

—————— **Pepper Vodka on the Rocks** ——————

3 oz (6 tbsp) chilled pepper-flavored vodka
ice
caperberry

Stir liquid ingredients with ice and strain into an ice-filled old-fashioned glass or wineglass. Garnish with a caperberry.

RASPBERRY-FLAVORED VODKA

—————— **Berritini** ——————
(Raspberry Vodka Martini)

See *Martini.*

—————— **Raspberry Cooler** ——————

2½ oz (5 tbsp) raspberry-flavored vodka
1 oz (2 tbsp) Rose's lime juice
2 splashes chilled club soda
2 raspberries

Shake liquid ingredients, except soda, with ice. Strain into a highball glass over ice. Top with soda and garnish with raspberries.

——————   **Raspberry Vodka and Soda**   ——————

2½ oz (5 tbsp) raspberry-flavored vodka
2 oz (4 tbsp) club soda
2 raspberries

Pour vodka into a chilled highball or old-fashioned glass filled with ice. Pour in club soda and garnish with raspberries.

——————   **Raspberry Vodka on the Rocks**   ——————

3 oz (6 tbsp) chilled raspberry-flavored vodka
ice
2 raspberries

Stir liquid ingredients with ice and strain into an ice-filled old-fashioned glass or wineglass. Garnish with raspberries.

VANILLA-FLAVORED VODKA

——————   **Creamsoda**   ——————

2½ oz (5 tbsp) vanilla-flavored vodka
2 oz (4 tbsp) 7-Up or Sprite

Shake ingredients together; pour into a chilled highball glass filled with ice.

——————   **Vanilla Vodka and Soda**   ——————

2½ oz (5 tbsp) vanilla-flavored vodka
2 oz (4 tbsp) club soda
strawberry (cut lengthwise across the bottom)

Pour vodka into a chilled highball or old-fashioned glass filled with ice. Pour in club soda and garnish with a strawberry.

—— Vanilla Vodka on the Rocks ——

3 oz (6 tbsp) chilled vanilla-flavored vodka
ice
strawberry (cut lengthwise across the bottom)

Stir vodka with ice and strain into an ice-filled old-fashioned glass or wineglass. Garnish with a strawberry.

W

—— Wallaby ——

1 oz (2 tbsp) peach brandy
1 oz (2 tbsp) Dubonnet
1 tsp lime juice
1/2 tsp red maraschino liqueur

Place ingredients in shaker with several ice cubes. Shake well and strain into a chilled cocktail glass.

—— Wallis Blue Cocktail ——

1 oz (2 tbsp) gin
1 oz (2 tbsp) blue curaçao
juice of 1 lime

Sugar-rim a chilled old-fashioned glass by rubbing with lime and dipping into sugar. Shake ingredients with ice and pour into the glass over ice cubes.

——— Wall Streeter ———

2 oz (4 tbsp) gin
½ oz (1 tbsp) white crème de menthe
2 tsp lemon juice
cold champagne

Shake first 3 ingredients with cracked ice and strain into a chilled wine or champagne glass. Top with champagne.

——— Ward Eight ———

2 oz (4 tbsp) rye whiskey
juice of ½ lemon
1 tsp sugar
½–1 tsp grenadine
slices of fresh fruit

Shake first 4 ingredients with ice and strain into a large chilled wineglass over cracked ice. Garnish with fruit and serve with a straw.

——— Warsaw Cocktail ———

1½ oz (3 tbsp) vodka
½ oz (1 tbsp) blackberry vodka
½ oz (1 tbsp) dry vermouth
1 dash lemon juice
twist of lemon peel

Shake liquid ingredients with ice and strain into a chilled cocktail glass. Garnish with lemon peel.

——— Washington Cocktail ———

1½ oz (3 tbsp) dry vermouth
¾ oz (1½ tbsp) brandy

2 dashes Angostura bitters
2 dashes sugar syrup

Stir ingredients with ice and strain into a chilled cocktail glass.

——————— **Wassail Bowl** ———————

(serves 8–10)

6 12-oz bottles of beer
1 cup sweet sherry
1/4 lb sugar
1 1/2 tsp nutmeg
1 dash ginger
slices of lemon

Heat the sherry and 1 bottle of beer but do not boil. Add sugar and spices and stir until dissolved. Add remaining beer and stir again. Let mixture stand at room temperature for 2–3 hours. Pour into a punch bowl, garnish with lemon slices, and serve in punch cups.

Variation: Garnish with several apples that have been baked with sugar and spices.

——————— **Waterbury Cocktail** ———————

1 1/2 oz (3 tbsp) brandy
juice of 1/2 lime
1/2 tsp grenadine
1/2 tsp sugar
1 egg white

Shake ingredients vigorously with ice and strain into a chilled cocktail glass.

Variation: Sugar-rim the glass by rubbing with lime and dipping into sugar.

--------   ### Watermelon Cooler   --------

½ cup diced watermelon (seeds removed)
2 oz (4 tbsp) vodka
2–3 dashes grenadine
½ cup crushed ice
slice of lime or sprig of fresh mint

Put first 4 ingredients into a blender and blend at low speed until smooth. Pour into a chilled collins glass and garnish with lime or mint.

Variations: Add ½ oz (1 tbsp) lime juice and 1 tsp sugar. Substitute light rum for the vodka.

--------   ### Watermelon Punch   --------

(serves 28)

1 large watermelon
2 qts lemonade
1 qt vodka
2 cups melon balls
large container of crushed ice

Slice top third off the watermelon. Scoop out 2 cups of balls and set aside. Scoop out remaining meat and reserve. Refrigerate shell and balls. Press reserved watermelon meat through a colander or cheesecloth to obtain 2 cups juice. Combine juice, lemonade, and vodka and chill several hours. To serve, place watermelon shell in bed of crushed ice. Add vodka mixture and melon balls. Fill punch cups half-full of crushed ice and ladle in punch. Makes about 28 4-oz servings.

Webster Cocktail

1½ oz (3 tbsp) gin
¾ oz (1½ tbsp) dry vermouth
½ oz (1 tbsp) apricot brandy
juice of ½ lime

Shake ingredients with ice and strain into a chilled cocktail glass.

Wedding Belle Cocktail

1 oz (2 tbsp) gin
1 oz (2 tbsp) Dubonnet
½ oz (1 tbsp) cherry brandy
½ oz (1 tbsp) orange juice

Shake ingredients with ice and strain into a chilled cocktail glass.

Wembly Cocktail

1½ oz (3 tbsp) gin
¾ oz (1½ tbsp) dry vermouth
2 dashes apple brandy

Stir ingredients with ice and strain into a chilled cocktail glass.

Variation: Add a dash of apricot brandy.

Western Rose

1 oz (2 tbsp) gin
½ oz (1 tbsp) apricot brandy
½ oz (1 tbsp) dry vermouth
1 dash lemon juice

(continued)

Shake ingredients with ice and strain into a chilled cocktail glass.

─────── **Whip Cocktail** ───────

$3/4$ oz ($1\,1/2$ tbsp) brandy
$3/4$ oz ($1\,1/2$ tbsp) Pernod
$3/4$ oz ($1\,1/2$ tbsp) dry vermouth
$3/4$ oz ($1\,1/2$ tbsp) Triple Sec or orange curaçao
twist of orange peel

Stir or shake liquid ingredients with ice and strain into a chilled cocktail glass. Garnish with orange peel.

WHISKEY

The distilled spirits of rye, corn, or other grain, usually containing about 40 percent alcohol (80 proof). In general, when a customer asks merely for "whiskey," the bartender will understand it to mean rye whiskey (blended type). *Whiskey* is the preferred spelling of the product distilled in the United States and Ireland. *Whisky* is the preferred spelling of the product distilled in Scotland and Canada.

Canadian whisky is made only from cereal grains, usually with large amounts of corn and some barley and rye. Canadian whisky is similar to American but lighter in body. The Hiram Walker Company and Seagram are two of the largest Canadian distilleries.

Scotches are blends of grain whisky with full-flavored malt whisky. The unique smoky quality of Scotch malt whisky is due to the peat used to dry the malted barley. Irish whiskey is usually blended with any number of whiskeys from other distillations to ensure smoothness and consistency of taste. Irish whiskey is distilled from a grain mixture that is low in malted barley. It is cured over charcoal to avoid the heavy flavor found in Scotch whisky.

Whiskey Cobbler

2 oz (4 tbsp) bourbon
½ tsp sugar syrup
½ oz (1 tbsp) orange juice
chilled club soda

Mix together syrup and juice and pour into a high-ball glass filled with cracked ice. Add bourbon and top with soda. Stir gently and serve with a pair of straws.

Whiskey Cocktail

2 oz (4 tbsp) rye or bourbon
1–2 dashes Angostura bitters
1 tsp sugar syrup
maraschino cherry

Stir liquid ingredients with ice and strain into a chilled cocktail glass. Garnish with the cherry.

Variation: Substitute Scotch for the rye, eliminate the sugar syrup, and add ½ oz (1 tbsp) orange curaçao.

Whiskey Collins

See *Tom Collins.*

Whiskey Flip

2 oz (4 tbsp) rye or bourbon
2 tsp cream

(continued)

1 tsp sugar
nutmeg

Shake first 3 ingredients vigorously with ice and strain into a chilled cocktail glass. Sprinkle with nutmeg.

———— **Whiskey Frost** ————

1½ oz (3 tbsp) whiskey
1½ oz (3 tbsp) medium sherry
1½ oz (3 tbsp) port
½ tsp sugar syrup
lemon slice

In mixing glass stir liquors and syrup with several ice cubes. Strain into a large old-fashioned glass filled with cracked ice. Garnish rim with lemon slice.

———— **Whiskey Highball** ————

Though this type of drink has been a longtime favorite, the term *highball* didn't become popular until the 1890s, when it referred to a mixture of Scotch and soda. *Ball* was a slang term for glass, and a *highball* was a tall glass.

2 oz (4 tbsp) rye, Scotch, bourbon, or brandy
chilled ginger ale or club soda
twist of lemon peel (optional)

Pour whiskey into a chilled highball glass over ice cubes. Fill with ginger ale or soda and stir gently. Garnish with lemon peel.

Presbyterian: Use bourbon whiskey and equal parts of ginger ale and club soda.

——— **Whiskey Sangaree** ———

See *Sangaree.*

——— **Whiskey Sling** ———

See *Sling.*

——— **Whiskey Smash** ———

See *Smash.*

——— **Whiskey Sour** ———

The whiskey sour, one of the first of the sours, has gained such popularity that a specially shaped glass has been named for it. It is one of the most basic of the classic drinks, containing only whiskey, lemon, and sugar. It can be served with or without ice but is most popular "up" (no ice). The garnishes are also optional. Sours first became popular in the 1860s, when they were made with brandy. The whiskey sour was introduced in 1891.

2 oz (4 tbsp) rye whiskey
$1/2$–$3/4$ oz (1–$1^1/2$ tbsp) lemon juice
1 tsp sugar
maraschino cherry
slice of lemon or orange

Shake first 3 ingredients with ice and strain into a chilled sour glass. Garnish with the fruit.

Variations: Various liquors can be substituted for the rye (rum, Scotch, bourbon, tequila, gin, or flavored brandies), and the sour is named for the liquor used (Rum Sour, Amaretto Sour, etc.).

─────── **Whiskey Toddy, Hot** ───────

See *Hot Toddy*.

─────── **White Cloud** ───────

1½ oz (3 tbsp) Sambuca
club soda
lime slice or wedge (optional)

Put 2 or 3 ice cubes in a highball glass. Pour in Sambuca and fill with soda. Stir and garnish with lime.

─────── **White Lady Cocktail** ───────

2 oz (4 tbsp) gin
¾ oz (1½ tbsp) Cointreau
¾ oz (1½ tbsp) lemon juice

Shake ingredients with ice and strain into a chilled cocktail glass.

─────── **White Lily** ───────

1 oz (2 tbsp) gin
1 oz (2 tbsp) rum
1 oz (2 tbsp) Triple Sec
½ tsp anisette

Shake with cracked ice and strain into a chilled cocktail or champagne glass.

─────── **White Lion Cocktail** ───────

1½ oz (3 tbsp) light rum
juice of ½ lemon
1 tsp sugar

2 dashes Angostura bitters
2 dashes grenadine

Shake ingredients with ice and strain into a chilled cocktail glass.

Variation: Substitute dark rum for the light. Substitute raspberry syrup for the grenadine.

—— White Rose Cocktail ——

1 oz (2 tbsp) gin
1/2 oz (1 tbsp) orange juice
1/2 oz (1 tbsp) lime juice
1 tsp sugar
1 egg white

Shake ingredients vigorously with ice and strain into a chilled cocktail glass.

—— White Russian (Russian Bear) ——

2 oz (4 tbsp) vodka
1 oz (2 tbsp) white crème de cacao
2 tsp cream

Shake ingredients with ice and strain into a chilled cocktail glass.

—— White Spider ——

2 oz (4 tbsp) vodka
1 oz (2 tbsp) white crème de menthe

Stir ingredients with ice and strain into a chilled cocktail glass.

——— **White Velvet** ———

1½ oz (3 tbsp) vodka
1 oz (2 tbsp) white crème de menthe
½ oz (1 tbsp) heavy cream
1–2 dashes orange bitters

Shake all ingredients briskly with several ice cubes and strain into a chilled cocktail glass.

——— **Why Not?** ———

1 oz (2 tbsp) gin
¾ oz (1½ tbsp) apricot brandy
¾ oz (1½ tbsp) dry vermouth
1 dash lemon juice

Shake ingredients with ice and strain into a chilled cocktail glass.

——— **Widow's Kiss Cocktail** ———

1½ oz (3 tbsp) calvados or other apple brandy
½ oz (1 tbsp) yellow Chartreuse
½ oz (1 tbsp) Benedictine
dash of bitters

Place all ingredients in shaker with 4 or 5 ice cubes. Cover and shake vigorously. Strain into a chilled cocktail glass.

——— **Wild Irish Rose** ———

2 oz (4 tbsp) Irish whiskey
½ oz (1 tbsp) grenadine
juice of ½ lime
chilled club soda

Shake whiskey, grenadine, and lime juice with ice. Strain into a chilled highball glass over ice cubes and top with soda.

———— Will Rogers ————

1½ oz (3 tbsp) gin
¾ oz (1½ tbsp) dry vermouth
¾ oz (1½ tbsp) orange juice
2 dashes Triple Sec

Shake ingredients with ice and strain into a chilled cocktail glass.

———— Wine Spritzer ————

6 oz chilled white wine
2 splashes of club soda
twist of lemon peel

Pour white wine into a chilled wineglass, the rim of which has been rubbed with the cut edge of the lemon. Add two splashes of club soda. Garnish with a twist.

———— Woodstock ————

1½ oz (3 tbsp) gin
1 oz (2 tbsp) lemon juice
2 tsp maple syrup
1 dash orange bitters

Shake ingredients vigorously with ice and strain into a chilled cocktail glass.

X

Xanthia Cocktail

1 oz (2 tbsp) gin
1 oz (2 tbsp) cherry brandy
1 oz (2 tbsp) yellow Chartreuse

Stir ingredients with ice and strain into a chilled cocktail glass.

Xeres Cocktail

The name probably derives from the ancient name of Jerez, Spain, a city noted for its fine sherry.

2 oz (4 tbsp) dry sherry
2 dashes orange bitters
2 dashes peach bitters

Stir ingredients with ice and strain into a chilled cocktail glass.

XYZ Cocktail

1½ oz (3 tbsp) dark rum
¾ oz (1½ tbsp) Triple Sec
¾ oz (1½ tbsp) lemon juice

Shake ingredients with ice and strain into a chilled cocktail glass.

Y

———— Yacht Club Punch ————

2 oz (4 tbsp) light rum
3 dashes Pernod
1 oz (2 tbsp) lemon juice
½ oz (1 tbsp) grenadine
chilled club soda
slices of fresh fruit

Shake rum, Pernod, lemon juice, and grenadine with ice and strain into a chilled collins or highball glass over shaved ice. Top with soda and garnish with fruit.

———— Yale Cocktail ————

1½ oz (3 tbsp) gin
½ oz (1 tbsp) dry vermouth
2 dashes orange bitters
2 dashes blue curaçao

Stir ingredients with ice and strain into a chilled cocktail glass.

Variation: Substitute a dash of sugar syrup and a dash of maraschino for the curaçao.

———— Yankee Clipper ————

(serves 16–18)

2 qts rye whiskey
1 pt dark rum
½ cup sugar
4 qts water
1 lemon thinly sliced

(continued)

Dissolve sugar in rum. Pour all ingredients over block of ice in a large punch bowl and stir gently. Garnish with lemon slices.

Variation: Substitute pineapple juice and/or soda water for 1 or 2 qts of the water.

Yellow Bird

2 oz (4 tbsp) golden rum
½ oz (1 tbsp) Cointreau
½ oz (1 tbsp) Galliano
2 tsp lime juice

Place ingredients in blender with ½ cup cracked ice and blend at high speed 10–15 seconds, or just till ice is puréed. Pour into a chilled sour glass and serve at once.

Yellow Fingers

1 oz (2 tbsp) gin
1 oz (2 tbsp) blackberry brandy
½ oz (1 tbsp) banana liqueur
½ oz (1 tbsp) cream

Shake ingredients with ice and strain into a chilled cocktail glass.

Yellow Parrot Cocktail

1 oz (2 tbsp) yellow Chartreuse
1 oz (2 tbsp) apricot brandy
1 oz (2 tbsp) Pernod

Shake ingredients with ice and strain into a chilled cocktail glass.

Z

Zaza Cocktail

1½ oz (3 tbsp) Dubonnet
¾ oz (1½ tbsp) gin
1 dash orange bitters (optional)
twist of orange peel

Stir liquid ingredients with ice and strain into a chilled cocktail glass.

Variation: Use 1½ oz (3 tbsp) gin and ¾ oz (1½ tbsp) Dubonnet.

Zombie

2 oz (4 tbsp) light rum
1 oz (2 tbsp) dark rum
½ oz (1 tbsp) apricot brandy
juice of 1 lime
1 oz (2 tbsp) pineapple juice
1 oz (2 tbsp) passionfruit juice
1 tsp sugar
½ cup crushed ice
½ oz (1 tbsp) 151-proof rum
slice of fresh pineapple and orange
maraschino cherry

Put first 8 ingredients into a blender and blend at low speed until smooth. Pour into a chilled highball glass and float 151-proof rum on top. Garnish with fruit.

Variation: Add a dash of Pernod or grenadine.

SHOOTERS

Not quite a cocktail and more than a shot, shooters usually involve mixing one or more liquors with juice, soda, or milk in a shaker and pouring the resulting concoction into a shot glass or even an old-fashioned glass. The shooter is often consumed all at once but can also be sipped if the drinker so desires. Serving a round of shooters at a party can be a great ice-breaker.

Around the World

1 oz (2 tbsp) gin
1 oz (2 tbsp) crème de menthe
1 oz (2 tbsp) pineapple juice

Shake ingredients with ice until well chilled. Strain into a shot glass.

B-52

1 oz (2 tbsp) Kahlúa
1 oz (2 tbsp) Irish cream
1 oz (2 tbsp) Chambord

Slowly pour ingredients into a shot glass over a demi-tasse spoon, in order listed above, to create layers.

Black Licorice

1 oz (2 tbsp) Sambuca
1 oz (2 tbsp) Kahlúa

Slowly pour ingredients into shot glass over a demi-tasse spoon, in order listed above, to create layers.

——— Chocolate-Covered Banana ———

½ oz (1 tbsp) chocolate liqueur
½ oz (1 tbsp) banana liqueur
½ oz (1 tbsp) amaretto

Shake ingredients with ice until well chilled. Strain into a shot glass.

Variation: Substitute Kahlúa for chocolate liqueur.

——— Chocolate-Covered Cherry ———

½ oz (1 tbsp) Kahlúa
½ oz (1 tbsp) amaretto
½ oz (1 tbsp) white crème de cacao
drop of grenadine

Shake ingredients with ice until well chilled. Strain into a shot glass; add a drop of grenadine.

Variation: Substitute chocolate liqueur for Kahlùa

——— Chocolate-Covered Strawberry ———

½ oz (1 tbsp) strawberry schnapps
½ oz (1 tbsp) chocolate liqueur
½ oz (1 tbsp) white crème de cacoa

Shake ingredients with ice until well chilled. Strain into a shot glass.

——— Creamsicle ———

1 oz (2 tbsp) Triple Sec
1 oz (2 tbsp) amaretto
½ oz (1 tbsp) orange juice
½ oz (1 tbsp) milk or cream

Shake ingredients with ice until well chilled. Strain into a shot glass.

Grape Crush

1 oz (2 tbsp) vodka
1 oz (2 tbsp) Chambord
1/2 oz (1 tbsp) cranberry juice
1/2 oz (1 tbsp) 7-up or Sprite

Shake ingredients with ice until well chilled. Strain into a shot glass.

Jolly Rancher

1 oz (2 tbsp) melon liqueur
1 oz (2 tbsp) dark rum
1 oz (2 tbsp) pineapple juice

Shake ingredients with ice until well chilled. Strain into a shot glass.

Kamikaze

1 oz (2 tbsp) vodka
1 oz (2 tbsp) Triple Sec
1 oz (2 tbsp) Rose's lime juice

Shake ingredients with ice until well chilled. Strain into a shot glass.

Lemon Drop

2 1/2 oz (5 tbsp) vodka
1 tsp lemon juice
wedge of lemon
sugar

(continued)

Shake ingredients with ice until well chilled. Strain into a shot glass. Serve with a slice of sugared lemon on the side. After drinking the shooter, suck on the sugared lemon for a few seconds.

Mudslide

1 oz (2 tbsp) vodka
1 oz (2 tbsp) Kahlúa
1 oz (2 tbsp) Irish cream

Shake ingredients with ice until well chilled. Strain into a shot glass.

Variation: It can also be poured over ice as a drink.

Nuts and Berries

1 oz (2 tbsp) vodka
1 oz (2 tbsp) Chambord
1 oz (2 tbsp) Frangelico
½ oz (1 tbsp) cream or milk

Shake ingredients with ice until well chilled. Strain into a shot glass.

Nutty Professor

1 oz (2 tbsp) Grand Marnier
1 oz (2 tbsp) Irish cream
1 oz (2 tbsp) Frangelico

Shake ingredients with ice until well chilled. Strain into a shot glass.

Peppermint Patty

1 oz (2 tbsp) crème de cacao (white)
1 oz (2 tbsp) crème de menthe (green)
1 oz (2 tbsp) chocolate liqueur

Slowly pour ingredients into shot glass over a demitasse spoon, in order listed above, to create layers.

Purple Haze

1 oz (2 tbsp) vodka
1 oz (2 tbsp) Chambord
1 oz (2 tbsp) cranberry juice

Shake ingredients with ice until well chilled. Strain into a shot glass.

Purple Hooter

1 oz (2 tbsp) vodka
1 oz (2 tbsp) Triple Sec
1 oz (2 tbsp) blackberry brandy

Shake ingredients with ice until well chilled. Strain into a shot glass.

Rattlesnake

1 oz (2 tbsp) Kahlúa
1 oz (2 tbsp) crème de cacao
1 oz (2 tbsp) Irish cream

Shake ingredients with ice until well chilled. Strain into a shot glass.

——— Sambuca Slide ———

1 oz (2 tbsp) Sambuca
1 oz (2 tbsp) vodka
$1/2$ oz (1 tbsp) cream or milk

Shake ingredients with ice until well chilled. Strain into a shot glass.

——— Sex on the Beach ———

1 oz (2 tbsp) vodka
1 oz (2 tbsp) peach schnapps
$1/2$ oz (1 tbsp) cranberry juice
$1/2$ oz (1 tbsp) pineapple juice

Shake ingredients with ice until well chilled. Strain into a shot glass.

——— Slippery Nipple ———

2 oz (4 tbsp) Sambuca
1 oz (2 tbsp) Kahlúa
drop of grenadine

Shake ingredients with ice until well chilled. Strain into a shot glass; add drop of grenadine.

——— Sour Apple ———

1 oz (2 tbsp) vodka
1 oz (2 tbsp) green apple schnapps
1 oz (2 tbsp) sours mix

Shake ingredients with ice until well chilled. Strain into a shot glass.

———— **Tequila Shot** ————

The traditional way of drinking tequila, that is, "neat," involves a carefully prescribed ritual that should be followed using these ingredients:

1½ oz (3 tbsp) shot of tequila
salt
lemon wedge

When ingredients are assembled, moisten the area between your left thumb and index finger with your tongue. Then sprinkle the area with salt. Take a bite of the lemon wedge, lick the salt, and down the shot of tequila in one gulp. A second bite of lemon is permissible. A chaser of cold beer is also sanctioned.

Variation: Add a dash or two of Tabasco to the shot of tequila. If carefully done, a delicate rose is said to form in the glass. Proceed as above. This version is sometimes called a Desert Rose.

———— **Terminator** ————

½ oz (1 tbsp) Kahlúa
½ oz (1 tbsp) Irish cream
½ oz (1 tbsp) Sambuca
½ oz (1 tbsp) vodka
½ oz (1 tbsp) Grand Marnier

Shake ingredients with ice until well chilled. Strain into a shot glass.

———— **Toasted Almond** ————

1 oz (2 tbsp) Kahlúa
1 oz (2 tbsp) amaretto
1 oz (2 tbsp) cream or milk

(continued)

Shake ingredients with ice until well chilled. Strain into a shot glass.

———————   **Woo Woo**   ———————

1 oz (2 tbsp) peach schnapps
1 oz (2 tbsp) vodka
1 oz (2 tbsp) cranberry juice

Shake ingredients with ice until well chilled. Strain into a shot glass.

NONALCOHOLIC BEVERAGES

Recipes for some popular nonalcoholic "drinks" are given below. In addition, remember that most of the collinses, coolers, fizzes, eggnogs, etc., in the body of the book can be made without liquor.

——— Appleade ———

2 large apples, diced
2 cups boiling water
1 tsp sugar
slices of apple

Pour water over the apple pieces and add sugar. Strain and allow to cool. Pour into a highball glass over ice cubes and garnish with apple slices.

——— Berry Frost ———

1/4 cup raspberries, in syrup
1 cup prepared lemonade
1/2 cup milk
1/2 cup crushed ice

Blend first 3 ingredients for 20–30 seconds. Add crushed ice and blend until smooth.

——— Bloody Shame (Virgin Mary) ———

6 oz tomato juice
1/2 oz (1 tbsp) lemon juice
2 dashes Worcestershire sauce
2–3 drops Tabasco sauce
dash of celery salt

(continued)

¹/₂ tsp sugar (optional)
salt and pepper to taste
stalk of celery

Shake first 4 ingredients with ice and strain into a large chilled wineglass. Sprinkle with salt, celery salt, and pepper. Garnish with celery stalk.

Variations: Serve with ice cubes or at room temperature. Substitute Clamato juice for tomato.

Cherry Zest

1 cup orange juice
1 or 2 tsp maraschino cherry juice
¹/₂ orange slice
maraschino cherry

Pour liquids over ice cubes in chilled glass and stir. Garnish with orange slice and cherry.

Cinderella

1 oz (2 tbsp) lemon juice
1 oz (2 tbsp) pineapple juice
1 oz (2 tbsp) orange juice
1 dash grenadine
chilled club soda
slice of fresh pineapple

Shake juices with ice and pour into a chilled collins or highball glass. Top with soda, add grenadine, and garnish with pineapple.

Cranberry Cocktail

3 oz (6 tbsp) cranberry juice
3 oz (6 tbsp) pineapple juice

2 oz (4 tbsp) 7-Up or Sprite
lime wedge

Shake all liquid ingredients with ice. Pour into a high-ball glass. Garnish with lime wedge.

—————— Cranberry Cooler ——————

4 oz (8 tbsp) cranberry juice
2 oz (4 tbsp) Rose's lime juice
3 oz (6 tbsp) club soda
lime wedge

Shake all liquid ingredients with ice. Pour into a high-ball glass. Garnish with lime wedge.

—————— Creamsicle ——————

3 oz (6 tbsp) orange juice
3 oz (6 tbsp) pineapple juice
2 oz (4 tbsp) cream or milk
orange slice

Shake all liquid ingredients with ice. Pour into a high-ball glass. Garnish with orange slice.

—————— Egg Cream ——————

2 tbsp chocolate syrup
6 oz cold milk
6 oz seltzer

Mix chocolate syrup and milk in a highball glass. Top with seltzer and stir.

————— **Fruit Spritzer** —————

2 oz (4 tbsp) cranberry juice
2 oz (4 tbsp) grapefruit juice
2 oz (4 tbsp) pineapple juice
2 oz (4 tbsp) Rose's lime juice
splash of seltzer or club soda
lime wedge

Shake first 4 ingredients with ice. Pour into a high-ball glass. Add seltzer and garnish with lime wedge.

————— **Himbeersaft** —————

1 1/2 oz (3 tbsp) raspberry syrup
chilled club soda
sprig of fresh mint

Pour raspberry syrup over crushed ice in a chilled highball glass. Fill with soda and stir. Garnish with mint and serve with a straw.

————— **Honeydew** —————

1/3 cup diced honeydew melon
3/4 oz (1 1/2 tbsp) lemon juice
1/2 tsp sugar (optional)
1/2 oz (1 tbsp) cream
1/2 cup crushed ice
chilled club soda

Put all ingredients, except soda, into a blender and blend at low speed for 20 seconds. Pour into a large chilled stemmed glass or highball glass over ice cubes. Top with soda.

Johnny Julep

1½ oz (3 tbsp) lemon juice
1 tsp sugar syrup
1–2 dashes Angostura bitters
ginger ale
maraschino cherry

Combine lemon juice, syrup, and bitters with cracked ice in a chilled highball glass. Fill with ginger ale and garnish with maraschino cherry.

Lemonade

juice of 1 lemon
2 tsp sugar
chilled water
slice of lemon
maraschino cherry

Mix lemon juice and sugar in a chilled collins glass. Add ice cubes and water and stir. Garnish with lemon slice and cherry.

Limeade

juice of 3 limes
3–4 tsp sugar
chilled water
wedge of lime
maraschino cherry

Mix lime juice and sugar in a chilled collins glass. Add ice cubes and water and stir. Garnish with lime wedge and cherry.

——— Lime Cooler ———

2 oz (4 tbsp) Rose's lime juice
3 oz (6 tbsp) seltzer water or club soda
1 oz (2 tbsp) cranberry juice
lime wedge

Shake all liquid ingredients with ice. Pour into a highball glass. Garnish with lime wedge.

——— Orange Whip ———

4 oz (8 tbsp) orange juice
2 oz (4 tbsp) cream or milk
1/2 cup crushed ice

Blend all ingredients on low for 20–30 seconds. Pour into a chilled collins glass.

——— Pussyfoot ———

1 oz (2 tbsp) lemon juice
1 oz (2 tbsp) orange juice
1 oz (2 tbsp) lime juice (optional)
2 dashes grenadine
1 egg yolk
maraschino cherry

Shake first 5 ingredients with cracked ice and pour into a chilled wineglass. Garnish with the cherry.

——— Shirley Temple (Roy Rogers) ———

Primarily a children's drink, though some adults might like one, too. What you call it depends on whether it's being served to a girl or a boy.

chilled ginger ale
2 dashes grenadine

maraschino cherry
slice of orange

Put ice cubes into a chilled collins glass. Fill with ginger ale and add grenadine. Garnish with orange slice and cherry.

Variation: Substitute 7-Up or Sprite for ginger ale.

Spiced Cider

(serves 6–8)

1 qt cider
2 oz (4 tbsp) brown sugar
4 whole cloves
cinnamon sticks (optional) or
powdered cinnamon

In a large saucepan, combine cider, sugar, and cloves and bring to a boil. Cool and refrigerate overnight or for several hours. Reheat before serving. Pour into coffee mugs and garnish each with a cinnamon stick or add a dash of powdered cinnamon.

Sunday School Punch

(serves 40)

A sprightly taste and enough for everybody.

juice of 12 lemons and 6 oranges
1 qt water
46-oz can pineapple juice
4 qts grape juice
sugar syrup to taste
3 qts ginger ale
crushed ice

(continued)

In a 3- or 4-gallon container combine juices, water, and sugar syrup. When ready to serve, add ginger ale and stir. Ladle into glasses containing crushed ice. Makes about 40 8-oz servings.

——— **Texas Sunshine** ———

(serves 12–24)

A variation on old-fashioned lemonade.

> 1½ cups sugar
> 2½ cups water
> juice of 6 lemons
> juice of 2 oranges
> juice of 2 limes
> 1 cup fresh mint leaves
> 2–3 qts club soda or water

Combine sugar and water in saucepan and bring to a boil. Remove from heat and cool. Combine fruit juices and mint leaves and pour sugar syrup over the mixture. Let stand 1 or 2 hours, then strain and refrigerate. To serve, combine concentrate with 2 quarts water or club soda in punch bowl containing block of ice. Ladle into punch cups or water glasses.

——— **Virgin Manhattan** ———

Virgin as a prefix for any drink indicates that it contains no liquor.

> ¼ cup cranberry juice
> ¼ cup orange juice
> ½ tsp maraschino cherry juice
> ¼ tsp lemon juice
> 1–2 dashes orange bitters
> maraschino cherry

Shake liquid ingredients with ice, strain, and serve in a chilled cocktail glass. Or serve on the rocks in an old-fashioned glass. Garnish with a maraschino cherry.

——— **Virgin Mary** ———

See *Bloody Shame.*

COFFEE RECIPES

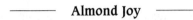

Almond Joy

1 oz (2 tbsp) chocolate liqueur
1 oz (2 tbsp) coconut liqueur
1 oz (2 tbsp) cream or milk
1 cup hot coffee

Add first 3 ingredients to Irish coffee glass; pour in coffee.

Variation: Substitute 1 cup of hot chocolate for coffee.

Amaretto Café

1 cup hot black coffee
1 oz (2 tbsp) amaretto
whipped cream (optional)

Add amaretto to coffee and top with whipped cream.

Variation: Decrease amaretto to ½ oz (1 tbsp) and add ½ oz (1 tbsp) Kahlúa or Tia Maria.

Black Maria

2 oz (4 tbsp) coffee brandy
2 oz (4 tbsp) light rum
2 tsp sugar
4 oz (8 tbsp) cold strong coffee

Stir ingredients in a large brandy snifter and add cracked ice.

——— **Black Rose** ———

1½ oz (3 tbsp) rum
1 tsp sugar
cold black coffee

Mix rum and sugar in a chilled collins glass. Add ice cubes, fill with coffee, and stir.

——— **Café Brûlot** ———

(serves 8)

1–2 sticks cinnamon
12 whole cloves
peel of 2 oranges and 2 lemons cut
into thin strips
4 lumps sugar
8 oz brandy or cognac
2 oz (4 tbsp) curaçao (optional)
1 qt hot strong black coffee

In a chafing dish or a large bowl, mash together the cinnamon, cloves, fruit peels, and sugar. Stir in the brandy and curaçao. Ignite carefully and gradually add black coffee, stirring until the flames go out. Serve in heated cups or goblets.

——— **Café Chocolat** ———

1 oz (2 tbsp) chocolate liqueur
1 oz (2 tbsp) Kahlúa
1 cup hot coffee
whipped cream (optional)

Add first 2 ingredients to Irish coffee glass; pour in coffee. Top with whipped cream.

Café Kirsch

1½ oz (3 tbsp) kirsch
1 tsp sugar
1½ oz (3 tbsp) cold black coffee

Shake ingredients with ice and strain into a chilled cocktail glass.

Café Royale

2 oz (4 tbsp) cognac
1 lump sugar
1 cup hot black coffee
cream (optional)

Pour steaming hot coffee into a cup or mug. Rest a teaspoon on top of the cup and place the sugar lump in it. Soak the lump with cognac and after the spoon heats up ignite the lump and slide it into the coffee. Float cream on top.

Variation: Pour cognac directly into the coffee without flaming.

Café Tiki

1 oz (2 tbsp) Kahlúa
1 oz (2 tbsp) brandy
1 cup hot coffee

Add first 2 ingredients to Irish coffee glass; pour in coffee.

Caramel Cafe

1 oz (2 tbsp) Grand Marnier
1 oz (2 tbsp) B & B

(continued)

1 oz (2 tbsp) cream or milk
1 cup hot coffee
whipped cream (optional)

Add first 3 ingredients to Irish coffee glass; pour in coffee. Top with whipped cream.

Chocolate Almond Café

1 oz (2 tbsp) amaretto
1 oz (2 tbsp) chocolate liqueur
1 cup hot coffee
½ oz (1 tbsp) cream (optional)

Add first 3 ingrdients to the coffee cup; pour in coffee. If using cream, pour in before coffee.

Espresso Royal

(serves 6)

Coffee, dessert, and after-dinner drink all in one.

1 cup sugar
2 cups water
1 cup brewed espresso (strong)
Kahlúa, Tia Maria, or other
coffee-flavored liqueur
whipped cream

In a saucepan dissolve sugar in water over low heat. Add espresso and stir to combine thoroughly. Remove from heat and cool. Freeze 3–4 hours until slushy. Spoon into chilled wineglasses and top with a tablespoon or two of liqueur and a dollop of whipped cream.

——— **Frangelico Café** ———

2½ oz (5 tbsp) Frangelico
1 cup hot coffee
whipped cream (optional)

Add Frangelico to Irish coffee glass; pour in coffee.
Top with whipped cream.

——— **Frappuccino** ———

(serves 4)

4 oz (8 tbsp) coffee or espresso
4 oz (8 tbsp) cream or milk
1 oz (2 tbsp) vanilla syrup
1½ cups ice
chocolate powder
foam from steamed milk

Foam milk first. Blend first 4 ingredients on low for
20–30 seconds. Pour into a highball glass. Top with
1 tbsp foam; sprinkle with chocolate powder.

——— **Grand Marnier Café** ———

2½ oz (5 tbsp) Grand Mariner
1 cup hot coffee

Add Grand Marnier to Irish coffee glass; pour in coffee.

——— **Greek Coffee** ———

Not exactly the real thing, but a perfectly acceptable
substitute.

6 oz hot coffee
1 oz (2 tbsp) Metaxa brandy

(continued)

¹/₂ oz (1 tbsp) Kahlúa, Tia Maria, or
other coffee liqueur
1–2 oz (2–4 tbsp) cream (optional)

In a heavy glass mug pour in Kahlúa, followed by the Metaxa. Fill to desired level with the coffee. Top with cream, if desired.

——— Irish Coffee ———

1¹/₂ oz (3 tbsp) whiskey
1 tsp sugar (optional)
5 oz strong hot black coffee
whipped cream

Put sugar into a heated cup or stemmed goblet. Add whiskey and coffee and stir. Top with a dollop of whipped cream.

Variation: Float heavy cream on top instead of whipped cream.

——— Mama Maria ———

1 oz (2 tbsp) Tia Maria
1 oz (2 tbsp) brandy
1 cup hot coffee
whipped cream (optional)

Add first 2 ingredients to Irish coffee glass; pour in coffee. Top with whipped cream.

——— Nutter Butter ———

¹/₂ oz (1 tbsp) Frangelico
¹/₂ oz (1 tbsp) amaretto
¹/₂ oz (1 tbsp) butterscotch schnapps
1 cup hot coffee

Add first 3 ingredients to Irish coffee glass; pour in coffee.

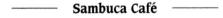

Sambuca Café

1 oz (2 tbsp) Sambuca
single espresso

Add Sambuca to the espresso cup; brew espresso and pour in cup.

Sambuca Machiato

1 oz (2 tbsp) Sambuca
single espresso
foam from steamed milk

Foam milk first. Add Sambuca to espresso cup; brew espresso. Spoon on 2 tsp foam.

Tennessee Mud

1 oz (2 tbsp) chocolate liqueur
1 oz (2 tbsp) Tennessee whiskey
½ oz (1 tbsp) amaretto
1 cup hot coffee

Add first 3 ingredients to Irish coffee glass; pour in coffee.

Variation: Substitute 1 cup of hot chocolate for coffee.

BEFORE-DINNER DRINKS

Generally speaking, an apéritif can be any drink taken before a meal to stimulate the appetite. In the United States the most common form of before-dinner drink is the cocktail, for which the reader will find hundreds of recipes in the preceeding pages. Sometimes, however, a guest may prefer simply beer (see page 369), a glass of wine (see page 365), or a drink containing no alcohol (see page 339) before a meal. As another alternative, there are a number of ready-to-serve apéritif wines that have become increasingly popular. These are of relatively low alcoholic content (usually below 20 percent) and may be served "straight up" (the dry sherries in particular) or "on the rocks," often with a twist of peel or slice of orange, lemon, etc., as a garnish.

Among the most popular apéritifs are the sherries. A white wine fortified with brandy, sherry comes from Spain and is categorized roughly, according to sweetness, as dry, medium, or rich. The dry and very dry sherries (manzanilla, fino, amontillado, etc.) are best served well chilled without ice. The medium drys (some olorosos, such as the popular Dry Sack) may be chilled slightly or served at room temperature. Increasingly, however, these medium-dry sherries are served on the rocks with a twist of lemon peel. The rich sherries (other olorosos, amoroso, Harvey's Bristol Cream, etc.) are full-bodied and are generally not chilled. For this reason most people prefer them as an after-dinner drink as a substitute for port or a liqueur.

France produces a number of very popular apéritif wines and liqueurs. Among those readily available are:

- Byrrh—reddish color with an aromatic flavor, made from a red-wine base. It is dry and has a slight quinine and orange flavor.

- Dubonnet—an aromatic French apéritif that is a blend of sweet red wine and quinine. There is also a dry blond version of Dubonnet manufactured in the United States.

- Lillet—a light, medium-dry, vermouth-type apéritif with a slight orange flavor, produced in France. The most common type is white, but there is also a sweeter red variety.

- Pernod or Ricard—anise-flavored liqueurs, similar to absinthe, a drink that is now banned because of the toxic wormwood used in its manufacture.

- St. Raphael—red, quinine-flavored, often served on the rocks.

Other suggested apéritifs are *Campari,* a bitter red wine from Italy, often served with soda; *Cynar,* also Italian, made from artichokes; *ouzo,* a strong anise-flavored liqueur from Greece, usually served on the rocks in the United States; *raki* (or *arrack*), from the Middle East, similar to ouzo; *sake,* a Japanese rice wine, usually served warm; *aquavit,* a potent, sometimes caraway-flavored drink of Scandinavia; *Fernet-Branca,* a very bitter herbal Italian apéritif and *vermouth,* either sweet or dry, served on the rocks with a slice of lemon or bit of orange peel.

AFTER-DINNER DRINKS

Chief among after-dinner drinks are brandies, ports, and liqueurs, the latter available in almost any conceivable flavor. Another favorite is one of the full-bodied sherries, such as an oloroso or Harvey's Bristol Cream. All of these are usually served at room temperature. After a particularly rich or heavy meal, the after-dinner drink may take the place of dessert. Some experienced diners would be quite content with a snifter of fine brandy, a glass of vintage port, or a well-chilled glass of dessert wine, such as sauternes. And don't forget the exotic coffees, made with brandy, rum, or liqueurs (café brûlot, café royale, etc.).

Brandy is a distillation of the fermented juice of grapes or other fruits. Although made all over the world, the chief producers are France and the United States. When a fruit other than grapes is used, the type of fruit is used in the name of the brandy (apple brandy, cherry brandy, etc.). The best-known types of brandy are Cognac and Armagnac, both named after the districts in western France where they are produced. Cognac is generally more subtle than Armagnac and is more popular. Among the most popular brands of cognac are Courvoisier, Hennessy, Bisquit, Rémy Martin, and Martell. Cognac labels carry initials: *V.S.*—Very Special (aged about five years); *V.S.O.P.*—Very Superior Old Pale (aged 10–15 years); *V.O.*—Very Old (aged slightly longer than *V.S.O.P.*, it has a soft, woody flavor); *X.O.*—Extra Old; and *X.X.O.*—Extra Extra Old, which are very expensive and rare, having been aged as long as 50 years. The word *Napoleon* on the label means only that the cognac has been aged at least five years and is considered a premium blend.

Unlike cognac, which is double-distilled, Armagnac is distilled only once and gains much of its flavor through aging. Both need time to mature and are seldom drinkable under five years of age. calvados, made in Normandy, is said to be the world's best apple brandy. In any case, it is a considerably more refined drink than its American cousin, applejack. There are many other types of fruit-flavored brandy, with peach, apricot, and blackberry being among the most popular.

Port is a ruby-red, fortified Portuguese wine that is now also manufactured elsewhere in the world. There are a number of brands and types, including a white port. Brandy is added to the wine during the fermentation process, and the wine is then aged in casks or bottles. If aged less than 12 years, it is called ruby port; after 12 years of aging, the wine is considered tawny port; after 15 to 20 years, it is considered vintage port.

There is a vast variety of liqueurs, and their flavorings are almost endless. Among the favorites are the following:

■ Advocaat—Dutch liqueur similar to brandy eggnog.

■ Amaretto—almond-flavored liqueur of Italy made from apricots.

■ Anisette—anise-flavored liqueur of France made from anise seed.

■ Apry—apricot liqueur made by the Marie Brizard company.

■ Benedictine—herb-flavored liqueur of France, often mixed with brandy and known as "B & B."

■ Chambord—black-raspberry-flavored liqueur of France.

■ Chartreuse—herbed liqueur, in green or yellow, created by the Carthusian monks of France.

■ Cointreau—orange-flavored liqueur of France, a brand of curaçao.

■ Crème de Cacao—brandy-based liqueur flavored with cacao beans.

■ Crème de Cassis—French liqueur flavored with black currants.

■ Crème de Fraise—a strawberry-flavored liqueur.

■ Crème de Framboise—a raspberry-flavored liqueur.

■ Crème de Noyaux (nwä yō´)—almond-flavored liqueur sometimes made with peach or apricot pits.

■ Crème de Menthe—mint-flavored liqueur in green or white

■ Crème de Violette—lavender-colored liqueur flavored with violets.

■ Crème Yvette—American liqueur with strong taste of violets.

■ Curaçao—originally a Dutch liqueur made of West Indian oranges. It comes in a variety of colors including white, blue, green, and dark orange.

■ Drambuie— a Scotch-based herbal liqueur made from Highland malt whisky, heather honey, and herbs.

■ Galliano—Italian liqueur flavored with herbs and spices.

■ Godiva—chocolate-flavored liqueur.

■ Goldwasser—liqueur of France and Germany flavored with herbs and spices (especially caraway in the German version) and flecked with bits of gold leaf.

■ Grand Marnier—liqueur of champagne and curaçao.

- Irish Mint—liqueur combining Irish whiskey with cream.

- Kahlúa—coffee-flavored liqueur from Mexico.

- Kümmel—caraway-flavored liqueur of Germany.

- Mandarine Napoléon—tangerine-flavored liqueur with a brandy base, made in Belgium.

- Midori—melon-flavored liqueur from Japan.

- Ouzo—anise-flavored liqueur of Greece, usually served on the rocks.

- Parfait d'Amour—a sweet, citrus liqueur flavored with essence of violets. It is usually purple in color.

- Peter Heering—cherry-flavored liqueur of Denmark.

- Prunelle—plum-flavored liqueur of France.

- Sabra—Israeli liqueur flavored with orange and chocolate.

- Sambuca—An Italian liqueur flavored with anise. It is often served flamed with three coffee beans floating on the top.

- Schnapps flavored liqueurs (included peppermint, peach, apple)—similar to crème de menthe, but lighter and less sweet.

- Sloe Gin—not a gin, but a gin-based fruit liqueur flavored with sloes, the berries of the blackthorn.

- Southern Comfort—American bourbon-based liqueur with peach flavor.

- Strega—Italian liqueur flavored with orange peel and spices.

■ Tia Maria—Jamaican liqueur made from fermented sugarcane and flavored with coffee. A little lighter and drier than Kahlúa, it has a slight hint of chocolate.

■ Triple Sec—orange-flavored liqueur, a type of curaçao.

WINE AND CHAMPAGNE

Wine, in general, falls into the categories of *fortified wines* (sherry, port, Madeira, etc., with an alcohol content of 17–21 percent) and *table wines* (wines with 14 percent or less alcohol content). Table wines are further divided into the categories of red, white, and rosé, and are either dry, sweet, or semisweet. A home bar should stock at least several bottles of dry white, one full-bodied red, one semisweet rosé (such as white zinfandel), and one fortified wine.

When serving wine as an accompaniment to meals, it is traditional that red wine is served with red meat and white wine is served with white meat (veal or pork), poultry, and fish. This tradition has relaxed somewhat in recent years, and many people now believe that the choice of red or white wine should be dictated by personal preference. A good rule to follow is that the richer the food, the richer and more full-bodied the wine should be. The preparation, then, becomes the important factor: chicken sautéed with white wine and cream should be served with a white wine, but if it is roasted and served with a mushroom sauce, a red wine is called for. Even the stronger fish can be served with a red: grilled salmon or tuna go especially well with red wine. Use your judgment, and the possibilities are endless.

Wine bottles should be stored on their sides so the corks are kept moist, thereby maintaining a watertight seal on the bottle. An ideal storage area is well ventilated and has a fairly constant temperature of 50–60°F. White and rosé wines should be served chilled—either 2 hours of storage in the refrigerator or 20 minutes in a bucket of ice water. Red wines should be served a bit cooler than room temperature; twenty minutes in the refrigerator should do the trick. Stronger red wines can benefit from *breathing* for an hour or so before being poured in order to develop the bouquet and soften any tannic astringency. A wine will breathe by simply being uncorked, or it can be decanted into a decanter, carafe, pitcher, etc.

Removing the cork from a wine bottle can be accomplished easily with a bit of practice. With a knife (some openers are equipped with a small blade) remove the paper or foil covering the cork and the top of the bottle. Then insert the corkscrew so it penetrates straight down into the cork. When the corkscrew is firmly inserted, pull upward and the cork should slide out of the bottle with a pleasant popping sound. Then let the wine breathe, decant it, or serve it immediately, as appropriate.

The leading wine producers for the American market are France, Italy, Germany, Spain, and the state of California. The most popular French wines are named after the regions in which they are produced: Bordeaux (the dry reds of St. Emilion, Médoc, etc.), Burgundy (the reds of Côte de Beaune and Beaujolais, for instance, and the whites of Chablis and Montrachet), Rhône (the robust reds of Châteauneuf-du-Pape), and Loire (Sancerre, Muscadert, Vouvray). From Italy there are the red wines of Chianti, Barolo, Barbaresco, Valpolicella, Bardolino, and Lambrusco, and the dry white wines of Soave and Frascati. German wines are underrated, but go very well with food; the elegant white wines from the Moselle or Rhine Valley range from crisp and dry to sweet. Among the better-known California wines are the highly regarded reds Cabernet Sauvignon and Pinot Noir and the whites Chardonnay and Sauvignon Blanc.

The term *vintage* simply refers to the year in which the grapes for the wine were harvested. Good recent vintage years in Bordeaux, for example, include 1988, 1989, 1990, 1995, 1996, 1998, and 1999; for Burgundy, 1992, 1994, 1997 (red), 19948, 1996, (white). Since good vintages are clearly the exception rather than the rule, wines of these years are much sought-after and are relatively higher in price.

There are many good, pleasing wines selling for moderate prices, however. You can easily find the wines that best suit your taste and budget by trial and error or through the recommendations of a knowledgeable friend or wine dealer. Most wines are meant to be drunk soon after they are made, so vintages are less important for less expensive wines.

Unused wine that is left over should be recorked as soon as possible, because air will turn wine sour after a while. After being recorked, wines should be refrigerated, with reds allowed to warm up before serving. It is best not to buy wine in half-gallon or larger bottles unless it is to be consumed on one occasion.

Champagne. Most champagne sold in the United States is labeled either *brut* (extremely dry) or *extra dry* (meaning that it has no more than 2 percent added sugar), though sweeter varieties are available. The only French wines allowed to be labeled *Champagne* are those produced in the Champagne district of northeast France under strict government controls. However, champagne-type wines are produced in other countries, including Spain, Italy, Germany, and the United States, where California and New York State produce popular brands.

Champagne should always be served well-chilled. This is most easily done by refrigerating it for an hour or two prior to serving. Once removed from the refrigerator, the bottle can be nestled down into an ice bucket filled with cracked ice and water. To open, first remove the foil covering the head of the bottle, cover the cork with a dishtowel to prevent accidents, and then untwist the wires of the cage that secures the cork. When this is removed, hold the cork firmly with one hand on top of the dishtowel while rotating the bottle clockwise until the cork jumps out of the bottle with a gentle popping sound. Point the bottle away from you and your guests when opening it as the cork, and even some of the champagne, may erupt rather forcefully and dangerously. Pour and serve the champagne as soon as it is opened, then keep the opened bottle in the ice bucket.

Champagne is best served in either a well-chilled flute or tulip goblet. The traditional saucer-shaped goblet, sometimes hollow-stemmed, is attractive but spills easily, and its wide-open mouth tends to dissipate the wine's effervescence in a very short time.

BEER, ALE, AND CIDER

Most of the beer consumed in the United States—the world's largest beer producer—is *lager,* a light, dry, pale, heavily carbonated beer with an alcohol content of between 3 and 4.5 percent. *Pilsner beer,* a type of lager originally developed in Czechoslovakia, is a term now loosely applied to many dry, gold-colored beers with an alcohol content of 4 to 5 percent. *Dry beer* is a type of lager brewed to be less bitter, and the newer *ice beer* has a high alcohol content. *Light beer* is lower in calories and alcohol content (2.3 to 4 percent) and is typically served well-chilled.

Ale is an English style of beer with a heavier flavor and a copper color. Ales are made with a different type of yeast and fermented at different temperatures than lager. There are many varieties of ale. *Bitter ale,* favored in England, has a heavy hop flavor. *Pale ale,* also known as *India pale ale,* is slightly acidic and has a strong hop flavor. *Porter* is heavy, dark brown ale. *Brown ale,* becoming popular in America, is medium dark and richly (but not excessively) flavored. Ales should be served cool, not cold (but never at "room temperature," which would be too warm).

Bock beer, a German product now made also in the United States, is dark brown in color and has an alcohol content of around 6 percent. Formerly, it was available only during the Lenten season and was prized as the heavy, rich, sediment-filled beer that was first drawn off when the vats were tapped in early spring.

Stout, especially the Irish version called *bitter stout,* is the darkest and strongest of the beers, with an alcohol content between 4 and 7 percent. (It is no higher in calories than other beers, however.) Traditionally the national drink of Ireland, it is generally served at a cool temperature.

Cider is the pressed juice of apples. Hard cider is fermented and sometimes carbonated. Sweet cider is unfermented. Cider is very popular in England and Ireland.

SINGLE-MALT SCOTCH

There are two major varieties of Scotch: single malts, which are made solely from malted barley in a single distillery, and blends, which consist of many single malts mixed with neutral grain alcohol. While all the major brands of Scotch are blends, single malts are becoming increasingly popular due to their individuality.

The character of a Scotch varies greatly with its region. The Lowland malts are typically mild and soft with a light body; two examples are Auchentoshan and Glenkinchie. The Highlands is the largest and best-known region, and its whiskies are elegant and well-balanced. The Speyside area in the Highlands includes the light-bodied Glenfiddich, Glenlivet, and Knockando; heavier Scotches are Macallan and Glenfarclas. The other important region is the Islands, which generally produce very smoky, powerful whiskies. Some examples are Laphroaig and Lagarulin from the island of Islay, and the seaweedy Talisker from the island of Skye. Single-malt Scotch should be drunk neat and at room temperature; ice, lemon, or soda obscure the taste and should be used only with cheaper blends. A small amount of water can help bring out the flavor in the stronger Scotches.

EXOTIC LIQUORS

Absinthe
Illegal in the United States since 1912 because it was found to cause permanent brain damage, it may still be consumed legally in some countries, including Spain. In addition to wormwood, absinthe is made from star anise, licorice, and other aromatics. Too potent to be drunk straight, it is usually diluted with water, which changes its yellowish green color to milky white. Absinthe substitutes include anisette and Pernod.

Amer Picon
A French brand of bitters that derives much of its flavor from gentian root and oranges. It is often served with water or club soda and ice.

Aquavit
Popular in the Scandinavian countries, it is similar to vodka. It is a high-proof neutral spirit made from grain or potatoes. Usually served chilled in small glasses, it is produced either unflavored or flavored with caraway, dill, or coriander.

Bitters
Bitters are neutral spirits flavored with roots, herbs, and fruits, particularly gentian and orange. The most popular brand is Angostura, which is made in Trinidad from a rum-spirit base and has a bright-red color. Bitters are closely related to liqueurs, and a dash or two are often added to a cocktail for zest.

Calisay
A mixture of herbs and quinine, this liqueur is a specialty of Catalonia, Spain. The recipe is said to have originated in Bohemia.

Calvados
An apple brandy made in the Normandy region of France. Considered the world's finest apple distillate, it is aged in oak for 3 to 10 years before being blended and bottled.

Glogg (glo͞og)
A Swedish hot punch. See *Glogg* in **Classic Cocktails**.

Grappa
The Italian name for a strong, pungent brandy that is distilled from the pulp that remains after grapes have been pressed and the juice drained off. Grappa that has not been aged is extremely fiery; it mellows slightly with age.

Kirsch (Kirschwasser)
A clear, cherry-flavored brandy made in the border region of France, West Germany, and Switzerland.

Madeira
A wine fortified with brandy (added during the fermentation process) that is made on the island of Madeira off the northwestern coast of Africa. It is relatively sweet and is usually drunk as an apéritif or dessert wine.

Metaxa
A strong, aromatic Greek brandy.

Punt e Mes
A reddish-brown, vermouth-type Italian apéritif with a sweet orange flavor.

Sake
Commonly referred to as "rice wine," this traditional alcoholic beverage of Japan is not a true wine be-

cause a raw material other than grapes is used. Sake is fermented from a mixture of rice and malted barley, and because the fermented beverage is colorless or amber-colored and slightly sweet, it resembles a wine in both taste and appearance.

Slivovitz
A rich, spicy, plum brandy made in Yugoslavia.

Strega
A sweet, spicy Italian liqueur similar to yellow Chartreuse and containing over 70 herbs.

Swedish Punch
A rum-based, spicy liqueur that is a traditional Swedish drink. It is sometimes mixed with hot water and drunk as a punch. Others prefer to drink it straight as a liqueur.

BLOOD ALCOHOL CHART

The total of amount of alcohol in one's bloodstream is measured in Blood Alcohol Concentration (BAC) percentages. For example, a BAC% of .2 means that there are two parts alcohol for every 1,000 parts blood in a person's bloodstream. Alcohol level or BAC% is affected by age, gender, physical condition, amount of food in one's system, so the chart below is intended only as a guide, not a guarantee, of your BAC%.

Use the chart below to estimate your BAC% by subtracting .015% from the total BAC% for every hour that has passed since you began drinking. For example, if you weigh 160 pounds and have consumed four drinks in three hours, your BAC% would be .09 minus .045 (.015 x 3 hours) or .045.

While driving impairment begins with your first drink, most states define driving with a BAC% of .08% or above as a crime.

No. of Drinks*	Body Weight							
	100	120	140	160	180	200	220	240
1	.04	.03	.03	.02	.02	.02	.02	.02
2	.08	.06	.05	.05	.04	.04	.03	.03
3	.11	.09	.08	.07	.06	.06	.05	.05
4	.15	.12	.11	.09	.08	.08	.07	.06
5	.19	.16	.13	.12	.11	.09	.09	.08
6	.23	.19	.16	.14	.13	.11	.10	.09
7	.26	.22	.19	.16	.15	.13	.12	.11
8	.30	.25	.21	.19	.17	.15	.14	.13
9	.34	.28	.24	.21	.19	.17	.15	.14
10	.38	.31	.27	.23	.21	.19	.17	.16

* One drink equals one 1.25 oz shot of 80 proof (40% alcohol) liquor or one 5 oz glass of 20 proof (10% alcohol) table wine or one 12 oz beer.

INDEX BY TYPE OF DRINK

SLINGS

RICKEYS

SHOOTERS

SOURS

SWIZZLES

TODDIES

INDEX BY MAIN INGREDIENT

BOURBON

BRANDY

CAMPARI

CANADIAN WHISKY

CHAMBORD

CHAMPAGNE AND SPARKLING WINE

CHERRY BRANDY/LIQUEUR

DUBONNET

CURACAO

GIN

GRAND MARNIER

IRISH WHISKEY

SCOTCH

SAMBUCA

VODKA

TEQUILA

VODKA (FLAVORED)

WHISKEY (RYE)

INDEX BY NAME OF DRINK

C

H

I

J

M

Q

R

S